Reforming the State

Fiscal and Welfare Reform in Post-Socialist Countries

Edited by

JÁNOS KORNAI
Harvard University and Collegium Budapest

STEPHAN HAGGARD
University of California, San Diego

ROBERT R. KAUFMAN
Rutgers University

Contributors
Vladimir Gimpelson
Béla Greskovits
Stephan Haggard
Jerzy Hausner
Robert R. Kaufman
János Kornai
Assar Lindbeck
Joan M. Nelson
Matthew S. Shugart
Vito Tanzi

 CAMBRIDGE UNIVERSITY

D1382213

PUBLISHED BY THE PRESS SYNDICATE OF THE UNIVERSITY OF CAMBRIDGE
The Pitt Building, Trumpington Street, Cambridge, United Kingdom

CAMBRIDGE UNIVERSITY PRESS
The Edinburgh Building, Cambridge CB2 2RU, UK
40 West 20th Street, New York, NY 10011-4211, USA
10 Stamford Road, Oakleigh, VIC 3166, Australia
Ruiz de Alarcón 13, 28014 Madrid, Spain
Dock House, The Waterfront, Cape Town 8001, South Africa

http://www.cambridge.org

First published 2001

Printed in the United States of America

Typeface Times New Roman 10/12 pt.   *System* QuarkXPress [BTS]

A catalog record for this book is available from the British Library.

Library of Congress Cataloging in Publication data

Reforming the state: fiscal and welfare reform in post-socialist countries / edited by
János Kornai, Stephan Haggard, Robert R. Kaufman.
      p.   cm.
   Includes bibliographical references (p.).
   ISBN 0-521-77301-6 (hard) – ISBN 0-521-77488-8 (pbk.)
   1. Europe, Eastern – Social policy.   2. Russia (Federation) – Social policy.   3.
Hungary – Social policy.   I. Kornai, János.   II. Haggard, Stephan.   III. Kaufman,
Robert R.
HN380.7.A8 R45 2000
361.6'1'0947–dc21

                                                                    00-036286

ISBN 0 521 77301 6   hardback
ISBN 0 521 77488 8   paperback

Contents

v

Tables and Figures

Tables

Figures

Contributors

Vladimir Gimpelson
Senior Research Economist, Russian Academy of Sciences, Institute of World Economy and International Relations, Moscow

Béla Greskovits
Associate Professor, Political Science Department, Central European University, Budapest

Stephan Haggard
Professor, Graduate School of International Relations and Pacific Studies, University of California, San Diego

Jerzy Hausner
Professor of Economics, Cracow University of Economics

Robert R. Kaufman
Professor of Political Science, Rutgers State University of New Jersey

János Kornai
Professor of Economics, Harvard University, and Permanent Fellow, Collegium Budapest

Assar Lindbeck
Professor of International Economics, Stockholm University

Joan M. Nelson
Senior Associate, Overseas Development Council, Washington, D.C.

Matthew S. Shugart
Associate Professor, Graduate School of International Relations and
Pacific Studies, University of California, San Diego

Vito Tanzi
Director of the Fiscal Affairs Department, International Monetary
Fund, Washington, D.C.

Preface

JÁNOS KORNAI

Collegium Budapest, the first institute for advanced study in Eastern Europe, plays host to one or several "focus groups" every academic year. These special collaborative research formations offer the chance for a group of researchers in various disciplines to concentrate their attention on a common subject of their choice. The result is lively interdisciplinary collaboration. Members of the group spend shorter or longer periods at the Collegium. While there, they discuss their ideas at seminars with each other and interested members of the Hungarian academic community. The results of their research are made public at conferences organized by the Collegium for a wider professional public.

The research topic of the focus group for the 1997–98 academic year concerned the interaction between politics and economic policy in the period of the post-socialist transition. I had proposed that this subject be placed on the agenda and then acted, on behalf of Collegium Budapest, as the convenor for the focus group. So I think it is appropriate for me to give a brief and, to some extent, personal account of the events leading up to the group's formation.

I am not just an observer and analyst of the post-socialist transformation in Eastern Europe but an active participant in it. On several occasions, in books, studies, and lectures, I have taken a position on issues of short- and long-term economic policy during the transition. On each occasion I contributed as a social scientist: I have not tied myself with any political party and remain unaffiliated. Although I have addressed some of my remarks and recommendations to Parliament and the government of the day, and I have often spoken personally to politicians, government members, and senior public officials on current issues, I did not undertake the public position of an official government advisor.

Amid all this activity, I have had to realize, time after time, that the question of whether some proposal of mine gains acceptance is decided in the political arena. Of course, it is important what rational arguments I advance to support my opinion, but the key question is not the force of the arguments, but the openness of the currently authorized political decision makers to the idea concerned. It would only be a slight exaggeration to say that they will accept the expert opinion of an economist so long as that is what they would have done in any case, without the advice. The expert opinion will at most confirm them in their existing view, or perhaps provide them with further ammunition to support it and bring the details of the idea into focus.

The king in the fairy story or the "benevolent dictator" of economic models listens to various advisors and then adopts the opinion he finds most convincing. In my experience the process is quite different in real life. The political sphere that makes the ultimate decision follows a certain logic of its own. The experts selected in the first place are ones who say the kind of things the decision makers want to hear.

However, there are exceptional situations: the circumstances of a serious crisis (or those leading up to one) when otherwise confident politicians may be at a loss and look to the experts for aid.

Let me mention another personal experience of mine. I have taken part in several international polemics. To give examples, they have included those on shock therapy versus gradualism; privatization through the free issue of coupons versus the sale of state assets; pension reform; and, most recently, health-care reform. It is worth considering why country A chose position I while country B chose position II, although rational arguments for and against were heard on both sides. Furthermore, why should policy within the same country have switched to course beta, having followed course alpha up to 1992? I do not accept as an explanation the actual, "objective" difference between the two countries or periods. International comparisons have convinced me that the resultant of the differences has to be sought in the political sphere. It depends on the attitude of leading political forces; the trend in political power relations; the system of political institutions; and, to some extent, the personal views, values, and characters of top leaders.

These impressions prompted me to assemble a group that would examine the interaction between political and economic reform. Interdisciplinary work was required, with cooperation among economists, political scientists, and sociologists. But what should the group's aspirations be in setting about this assignment? It was tempting to apply a strict methodology, to frame exact hypotheses whose validity could be tested statistically. With twenty-five post-socialist countries involved, one approach might be to do regression and other statistical analyses with the data. However, I felt the situation was not yet ripe for that. The period was too short, the sample too small, and the changes too rapid for a stricter, quantitative analysis of that kind. It would be better to admit honestly to a high degree of ignorance, to acknowledge that we were only at an initial stage in the cognitive process of exploring an extremely difficult problem.

So the group's work has not produced a set of strictly argued theoretical propositions. It would be more accurate to call the material before the reader a set of carefully expressed conjectures. These are observations whose truth is quite strongly supported by evidence in certain countries, but stricter verification and a greater degree of generalization will require further research. We have at least tried to take the first and perhaps the most important step toward scientific cognition: we have gazed in wonder at what we saw.

The methodology chosen also affected the form of cooperation among members of the group. It was a much closer relationship than simply having the researchers interested in the subject gather for a two- or three-day conference. For weeks and even months, the members worked in the same building, had coffee or lunch together, and frequently discussed their research topics with each other. They held repeated debates in seminars as the first drafts developed into their final form. Findings were presented by each group member in public lectures before a Budapest audience, thus building a bridge between the international research team and the Eastern European intelligentsia. These lectures and other meetings with experts in Hungary gave all the researchers a great deal of assistance.

Although the exchange of ideas and intellectual interaction took many forms, the focus group's activity cannot be called "teamwork" in a stricter sense. It was not a case of preparing a joint study based on common hypotheses. Members based their work on their own hypotheses, individually, or possibly as a research pair, guided by their own inspiration. So each author is responsible for his or her findings.

Another feature of the cooperation is worth emphasizing. The members of the focus group included several researchers who are citizens of the post-socialist region (Hungarian, Russian, Polish, and Romanian researchers), which means they have experienced the changes "from inside." Working beside them were those who studied the change of system "from outside": American, German, Swedish, and Italian researchers. Some members had been specializing in this area for a long time. But it also proved extremely useful that one or two of them were meeting the post-socialist transition for the first time, with fresh eyes, bringing to bear on it experience gained elsewhere in the world.

In the event, twelve studies were completed. These were debated at a public conference, with the inclusion of invited discussants: university professors, researchers, and experts, all outstanding representatives of their fields. They had come from several countries: Nicholas Barr from the United Kingdom; Fabrizio Coricelli from Italy; Guy Ellena, Joel Hellman, George Kopits, John McHale, and Michal Rutkowski from the United States; Wolfgang Glatzer from Germany; and Klára Mészáros, János Köllő, Tamás Réti, and György Szapáry from Hungary. Their views on the papers, suggestions to the authors, and contribution to the general debate were highly appreciated by the members of the group and were made good use of in finalizing the papers.

The three editors have selected from the set of studies the writings that appear in this volume. The main selection criterion was to maximize the extent to which the studies in the volume form a coherent whole. Those included deal with fiscal reform, revision of the role of the state, and transformation of the welfare sector. Additionally, publication separate from the volume was recommended to group members whose studies, however excellent, fell outside this subject area. So the volume in the reader's hands represents a further narrowing of the focus, within the subject area on which the group originally focused: the interaction between politics and economic reform.

The members of the group are aware of several limitations in their work. Many topics within this diverse overall subject were omitted from the examinations. There was no analysis of how division and differentiation on the political scene over the national question affect the economic changes: the reception of foreign capital, sale of domestic resources to foreign owners, relations with the globalizing financial world, or the dismantling of customs barriers. There has been a reestimation of the role of the churches in the post-socialist region, which also exerts an influence on some aspects of economic policy (family benefits, reform of the welfare state, and so on), but this important influence could not be analyzed either. The reform of fiscal policy and institutions is augmented by reform of the banking sector and other financial institutions; the group mainly examined the former and did not manage to analyze the latter. The resulting volume certainly cannot be considered a comprehensive examination covering all the essential questions. It is more of an attempt to identify certain puzzles and to try to find solutions to them. If we have succeeded, that is something to be proud of.

Finally, there is one more point to stress: post-socialist transformation is a process; whatever aspect of it is taken as the subject of thorough analysis, the time factor plays an important part in formulating conclusions. This volume contains chapters that were finalized in 1998. However, most authors have made use of the fact that the book goes into press in 2000 and have reconsidered their views and conclusions in the light of recent economic and political developments. Thus, they have reinforced their arguments and put their findings in a wider context, encompassing that process commonly known as post-socialist transition. As a result, the volume we now hand over is largely, in the best sense of the word, an updated version of work done earlier.

The work of the focus group has ended. Readers can estimate the results of it from this volume and other publications. It can already be said, however, that the period spent in Budapest provided every participant with a fruitful, inspiring environment. A great deal of intellectual enjoyment was gained from this cooperation.

Members of the group would like to take this opportunity to express their gratitude to Collegium Budapest, which hosted their research work in the true sense of the word, and to the Swedish and Hungarian sponsors: the Bank of Sweden Tercentenary Foundation and Magyar Hitel Bank Rt. for their generous financial support.

Each chapter and the volume as a whole have gained greatly from the devotion that Julianna Parti brought to the tasks of coordination, linguistic control, and technical editing. She contributed a notable perfectionism, professionalism, and precision, as well as a willingness to take active initiatives and to assist all the authors. I would like to express our thanks to her, in the name of the editors and all the authors.

We are grateful to Scott Parris of Cambridge University Press for his help and enthusiasm and also to Brian R. MacDonald for a most attentive job of copyediting and supervising the book's production.

Introduction

STEPHAN HAGGARD AND
ROBERT R. KAUFMAN

Countries of the former Soviet Union and Eastern Europe are now entering the second decade of political transformation and economic reform. The first decade was marked by the dramatic disintegration of the Soviet empire, severe macroeconomic problems, and, in many countries, hyperinflation. At the same time, countries in the region undertook transitions to democratic rule. This combination of economic crisis and "extraordinary politics" by no means led to uniform outcomes, but it did create opportunities for reformers to initiate fundamental economic transformations.[1]

The transition from command to market economies has unfolded through a series of overlapping policy and institutional reforms. Attempts to adjust fiscal, monetary, and exchange-rate policies constituted one feature of the initial phase of reform, as governments wrestled with severe fiscal and balance-of-payments disequilibria. At the same time, many governments also began a complex set of microeconomic reforms that have been at the center of the literature on the transition to the market. Some of these reforms, such as the adjustment of relative prices through decontrol and liberalization of trade, took place relatively quickly. The reform of property rights through privatization and the rehabilitation of state-owned enterprises has necessarily been more prolonged and is very far from complete.

These challenges are still relevant as we enter the next decade of transition; as the economic crisis of 1998 in Russia demonstrated clearly, some countries are still grappling with macroeconomic stabilization and dismantling of the state sector. For other countries, however, the period

---

[1] For a broad assessment of the progress of reforms, see Murrell 1996. On the role of "extraordinary politics" in the early transition, see Balcerowicz 1996.

1

of acute crisis has passed and the policy and political agenda have expanded to encompass a new generation of policy issues.

At the most basic level, this new policy agenda centers on the nature of the social contract between citizens and their governments. Early reforms rejected the command economy and sought a corresponding reduction of the state's role on a number of dimensions (Kornai 1990; Aslund 1992; Havlik 1991; Klaus 1992; Murrell 1992). However, in some areas, including the provision of social welfare, the transition was less radical and governments sustained extensive commitments – for example, in the areas of pensions and health care. The current reform agenda centers on reexamining these initial choices. Was liberalization precipitous? Are the social commitments made under the old regime sustainable, and if not, what should take their place? What is the appropriate boundary between the obligations of the public sector and the responsibilities of the individual citizen? What range of public goods should the government supply? Who benefits from, and who pays for, their provision?

The chapters in this volume focus on two interrelated issues that are central to these crucial social choices: the making of fiscal policy and the provision of citizens' welfare, particularly with respect to pensions and health care. Debates over alternative models of democratic capitalism, of course, go well beyond these two policy areas. Nevertheless, economic and political choices with respect to fiscal policy and welfare reform do much to define the size and boundaries of the state, both in the narrow sense of its claim on total resources and in the more expansive sense of the delimitation of its sphere of competence and obligation.[2]

This volume, the outgrowth of a collaborative project among economists, political scientists, and sociologists, explores the political economy of these policy issues by posing two basic questions. First, what are the welfare effects of contending proposals for fiscal reform and the restructuring of pension and health programs? Second, what are the political processes through which such choices are made, and what consequences do those processes have for policy outcomes?

As the wide diversity among advanced capitalist democracies suggests, there is no single model of a market economy (Berger and Dore 1996; Garrett 1998). Even within the European Union, which a number of Central European countries aspire to join, countries vary widely with respect to the size of government, the extent and nature of welfare commitments, the flexibility of labor markets, the organization of financial markets, and a number of other key political and market institutions. The

---

[2] For contrasting views of these issues, see Kornai 1996; Elster, Offe, and Preuss 1998.

deepening of the European Union and the possibility of membership have produced strong pressures for convergence around Western European norms in a number of policy areas, particularly in Central Europe. But it is unlikely that national differences will be fully erased. Thus, despite claims about a transition to "the" market, countries in transition in fact have a variety of economic and social models to choose from, and these choices will certainly be at the center of political debate over the next decade.

The Welfare Effects of Policy Choice: Fiscal Policy and Social-Sector Reform

Reforming Fiscal Institutions

The dismantling of the command economy and the emergence of a private sector have fundamentally transformed the nature of public finances.[3] On the revenue side, the line between taxation and profit was always nebulous in the command economy. "Centralized net income" flowed into the state coffers, but the state set prices, wages, and turnover taxes. The transition to the market eliminates the easy option of collecting taxes from a few thousand large, state-owned enterprises by simply ordering a monopoly, state-owned bank to deduct the sums due from each enterprise's account. Instead, the government must decide the kind and level of taxes appropriate to a market economy.

However, increasing revenues is not simply a function of setting the appropriate tax rate, or even of widening the tax base through the introduction of new types of taxes, such as taxes on real estate or copayments for social services. Rather, the government must install the administrative mechanisms to collect those taxes from hundreds of thousands of firms, millions of households, and even larger numbers of market transactions.

On the expenditure side, the state no longer has to finance the vast bureaucratic apparatus required by a command economy; many, if not most, of the functions of that apparatus have been taken over by the market. Nor need it support loss-making firms or even whole industries; as a result, the system of subsidies can be dramatically reduced, if not altogether eliminated.

The inevitable shrinking of the state associated with the transition to a market economy, however, does not necessarily mean that a small government will emerge. In the early stages of the transition, and currently

---

[3] The following draws on Kornai 1998. See also Kornai 1992; Tanzi 1992.

in a number of the republics of the former Soviet Union, the collapse in output and unprecedented social dislocations have placed strong pressure on governments to maintain subsidies and expand individual welfare entitlements. These pressures have arisen just as traditional sources of revenue in the state-owned enterprise sector collapsed.

Even where immediate problems of the transition and macroeconomic stabilization appear to be overcome, societies face significant fiscal choices: how to manage macroeconomic policy across the business cycle, the amount and character of public goods to be provided, and the extent to which the government should act through tax and spending decisions to redistribute income. Such decisions not only influence short-run economic performance but have implications for long-run growth as well. For example, there is considerable evidence that human capital, and thus investment in education, is an important determinant of long-run growth (see, e.g., Barro 1991). The history of the welfare state in Western Europe, and even the United States, suggests that public programs that cushion individuals against the dislocation of the market have contributed to the political and social stability necessary for a capitalist economy to function effectively (see, e.g., Garrett 1998). At the same time, as Assar Lindbeck argues forcefully in his analysis of Sweden in this volume, there are clearly thresholds beyond which the size of government imposes serious limits on growth.

As on the revenue side, expenditure choices relate not only to the short run, but to longer-term institutional questions, including privatization, the administrative reorganization and streamlining of the government, and the permanent reduction of the number of public employees. Total spending on wages by the state sector will be reduced only temporarily by restraining the rise in the nominal wages of public employees; it will be reduced permanently if the state performs fewer functions, the state-owned share of total output falls, and overstaffing is reduced.

Institutional reforms also extend to the policy-making process. The nature of Communist rule made budget processes opaque. The transition to democratic rule, and the demands for transparency associated with it, require a fundamental change in the entire budget process, from the drafting of the budget within the government to the organization of its passage through the legislature and to the monitoring and auditing of its implementation.

For all of the post-socialist countries, fiscal policy involves both distributive issues and problems of coordination. The distributive questions center on the extent to which interest groups and citizens draw a clear link between the collective and private benefits they enjoy from government expenditure, their tax contribution, and their after-tax incomes.

Because of the paternalism of the Communist state, post-socialist publics suffer from tax illusion to an even greater extent than they do in the West; citizens insist on the provision of services without realizing the extent to which these reduce net earnings.

Yet even were such fiscal illusion altogether absent, conflicts would necessarily arise over the way benefits and costs are allocated across income classes, interest groups, and political jurisdictions. A common problem, to be discussed in more detail, is that at the time of the transition a wide range of recipients were entitled to free or almost free provision of social services. The result, however, is that resources are often inadequate for those who truly require public assistance. Of course, decreasing expenditures and increasing taxes is always difficult, but fiscal adjustments that involve dramatic changes in the beneficiaries from government spending or the incidence of taxation will clearly be more difficult than those that do not.

The coordination issues surrounding fiscal policy relate directly to institutions and the political process as well. If we view fiscal politics as a commons problem (Tornell 1995), the decision-making process on the budget must be rationalized to avoid the tendency to "overgraze" – the untenable situation in which each politician, interest group, or citizen seeks a net transfer from the fisc. These problems have their correlates within the government itself. On the spending side, governments must design institutions that permit centralized control over the budget and limit "leakage" of spending for unauthorized purposes. On the taxing side, a coherent revenue service requires a similar degree of coordination, including the elimination of corruption and other political influences that allow significant portions of income and wealth to escape taxation.

The chapters in the first part of the volume examine these issues from a number of perspectives. Vladimir Gimpelson focuses on the situation – still characteristic of many post-Soviet republics – in which macroeconomic stabilization remains problematic. He argues that wage arrears in the Russian Federation have evolved as a mechanism for softening the social and political impact of cuts in state subsidies and the public wage bill. Setting unrealistic wage targets may appear irrational, but it facilitates budgetary agreements between the government and legislature and allows both public and private employers to shift the burden of real wage cuts onto relatively weak sectors of the work force, which prefer wage arrears to open unemployment.

Whatever their political rationale, Gimpelson emphasizes that such mechanisms introduce allocative rigidities that affect both public finances and the development of labor markets over the long run.

Gimpelson suggests, moreover, that, despite perceptions to the contrary, it is far from clear that arrears reduce the risks of a political backlash against reform. Regions with high arrears are less likely to vote for reformist incumbents than those with high unemployment. He speculates that this occurs because arrears affect a relatively large segment of the work force, compared with the burdens of reform-induced unemployment, but do not open up new opportunities for prospective "winners" in the reform process.

The chapter by Vito Tanzi also deals with two countries – Russia and Georgia – in which macroeconomic stabilization remains at issue, but focuses on the institutional and political problems of rationalizing tax administration. Both countries have been plagued by administrative particularism. Particularism and outright corruption occur not only during the policy stage through exemptions in the tax codes but even more importantly through negotiations between authorities and large payers when taxes are actually collected.

Whereas Russia's tax system remains riddled with exceptionalism – Tanzi likens it to a Swiss cheese – the government in Georgia has made some progress in closing loopholes. Tanzi attributes this progress to the establishment of a more centralized and autonomous tax administration. But his chapter has a political as well as administrative point. Russian tax policy has been hampered by multiple veto points, both within the central government and emanating from the strong influence of provincial and local governments in the country's emerging federal structure. Georgia's tax reforms came only after important constitutional reforms that enhanced the powers of the presidency, a landslide electoral victory for reformers, and the weakening of important interest groups that had effectively held tax policy hostage.

The chapters on fiscal policy in Hungary, along with those on pension and health reform in the second part of the volume, deal with Central European countries that have moved beyond the acute macroeconomic crisis and profound political uncertainty that continue to plague the former Soviet republics. These countries have undertaken substantial fiscal adjustments, and now confront the question of how to sustain them while also recrafting the socialist welfare state. These reform efforts depend quite substantially on the interplay between executives on the one hand and legislators and interest groups on the other; this interplay is emphasized by Béla Greskovits and Stephan Haggard, Robert Kaufman, and Matthew Shugart in the first part of the volume, as well as by Jerzy Hausner and Joan Nelson in the second.

Greskovits's contribution focuses on the relationship between prime ministers and finance ministers in shaping Hungarian fiscal policy.

Greskovits argues that the timing and nature of fiscal-policy choices depended heavily on the extent to which prime ministers perceived finance ministers as political rivals or allies; political rivalry made reform more difficult. His account thus emphasizes the way policy choices are driven by personal political strategies. Haggard, Kaufman, and Shugart also focus on fiscal reform in Hungary but place greater emphasis on how constitutional and electoral institutions shape the incentives and capabilities of the political leadership. Like Greskovits, they contrast the inability of the first post-transition government under Antall to undertake needed fiscal adjustments with the more decisive efforts by Horn's Socialist government to restrain expenditures, centralize government spending institutions, and control welfare spending. They argue that decisive action was possible not only because of the resolution of personal rivalries at the top, but because of the establishment of a more disciplined and stable legislative coalition under the new government. Attempts to reform fiscal institutions – in particular, pension and welfare systems – met with greater constraints than fiscal policy adjustment, however. These incomplete reforms can be traced to institutional and legal arrangements that augmented the organizational resources of opposing interest groups, particularly corporatist bodies that granted labor unions direct influence over health and welfare spending.

Differences between the two contributions on fiscal reform in Hungary are partly matters of emphasis. Greskovits agrees with Haggard, Kaufman, and Shugart that the discretionary authority of the prime minister declined and the importance of parliamentary politics increased after the initial transition period. Nevertheless, there are also fruitful points of disagreement. Haggard, Kaufman, and Shugart suggest that both institutional arrangements and coalitional dynamics constitute important constraints on fiscal-policy choice, although coalitions can shift in directions more favorable to reform over time. Greskovits, by contrast, focuses to a greater extent on the executive branch and bureaucratic dynamics, which he portrays as more fluid and amenable to tactical manipulation; we return to these issues in greater detail in discussing the politics of reform.

Adjusting Welfare Entitlements

One aspect of the debate over welfare spending centers on the macroeconomic and fiscal policy issues just discussed. In the early transition, governments maintained and in some cases even expanded their social commitments; this fact may help explain why the transition was less politically explosive, at least in Eastern Europe, than many had anticipated

(Kapstein and Mandelbaum 1997). Nonetheless, there are important questions about whether these social commitments are sustainable and, even for social democrats, whether they are appropriately designed.

Assar Lindbeck's analysis of the Swedish case provides a cautionary tale for Central European countries in which welfare expenditures have reached "Scandinavian" proportions despite much lower national incomes. From the 1970s to the 1990s, Sweden's welfare state expanded rapidly: public spending leapt from roughly 40 percent of GDP to between 60 and 70 percent. During the same period, however, economic growth lagged well behind that of other OECD countries. Lindbeck presents a variety of arguments linking these two phenomena, showing how rigidities in labor markets as well as disincentives to work and investment served to undermine the dynamism of the Swedish economy. Because the "Swedish model" is an important point of reference in debates over the long-term evolution of welfare-state capitalism in the transition economies, Lindbeck provides an important, if controversial, bridge to the other articles in this part.

The debate on the welfare state is not simply about the size of government and its macroeconomic consequences; it is also about how to redeploy public resources effectively, efficiently, and fairly and about what obligations should rightly be left in the hands of private citizens. Pension reform, and particularly the reform of pay-as-you-go (PAYG) systems, raises crucial issues of intergenerational equity. Health-care reform raises painful moral dilemmas of how to undertake the necessary rationing required to avoid bloated and bankrupt systems. These questions lie at the core of new efforts to redesign the social contract and are addressed in chapters on the reform of the health-care and pension systems in Hungary and Poland by Kornai, Hausner, and Nelson.

János Kornai begins his chapter on health-care reform by asking how citizens should balance the tension between the principles of individual responsibility and social solidarity, and how the costs associated with government provision of collective and private goods should be allocated. Kornai identifies the problem of health-care provision as the central problem of the dismal science more generally; people always want more health care than society can reasonably afford. There must therefore be a way of rationing such care fairly and efficiently. Kornai argues for the merits of a basic guarantee financed by the state, complemented by a market-oriented means of both financing and provision that provides individuals the opportunity to buy the additional health care they want. Kornai places great faith in the transparency of the policy-making process: by making fiscal decisions with respect to aggregate health-care spending clear, citizens can make the links between the

8

taxes they pay and the services they receive. He is modest in his political expectations, however; he admits that increased transparency does not, in and of itself, give rise to pressures for reform.

Similar issues are raised in the contributions by Hausner and Nelson, which examine the question of pension reform as well as health care. The rapid expansion of the pension system in the post-transition period was driven not only by the aging of the population but also by the use of disability and early retirement provisions to cover the dislocations of the transition to the market. As a consequence, the number of pensioners has risen rapidly relative to the tax-paying contributors to the system, and the average age of retirement has fallen sharply. By the mid-1980s it had become increasingly clear that existing PAYG pension systems were not only financially unsustainable but highly inequitable. In particular, PAYG pension systems distributed benefits and burdens highly unequally across generations, transferring resources from the current generation of workers to their elders and leaving "time bombs" for the next generation.

To stave off budgetary pressures, officials in both Poland and Hungary have manipulated the indexation of payments, a practice that has severely reduced the transparency of the system. In both countries, the PAYG system has also been marbled through with special exemptions and benefits for politically powerful groups – miners, farmers, military, and police – at the expense of the general tax-paying public and other pensioners.

Hausner and Nelson both observe that public opinion had become increasingly skeptical about the long-term viability of these systems and increasingly receptive to changing them. Nevertheless, serious disagreements initially existed over the direction those changes should take. Much of the debate over the relative role of PAYG and the introduction of "private pillars" centered precisely on the trade-off between individual responsibility and collective solidarity that animates Kornai's contribution. To what extent should benefits be linked to actual contributions? To what extent do the government and current taxpayers bear social responsibility for fellow citizens who are disabled or retired? Similar questions were implicit in controversies over reforming inequities within the PAYG pillar, financing the transition to multipillar systems, and establishing procedures to regulate private pension funds.

It is important to underline an important difference between debates on macroeconomic policy and pension and health reform. Even if there are disagreements about the optimal size of the state, widespread consensus exists on the adverse consequences of macroeconomic instability and the need to restore fiscal equilibrium. Much less consensus exists on the design of pension and health systems. Nelson argues that the absence of a "blueprint" in these areas has implications for the politics of reform, issues to which we now turn.

The Politics of Economic Reform

Debates about fiscal and welfare policies are not simply matters of aggregate growth and efficiency; they are inherently matters of politics as well. The way these issues are resolved therefore depends heavily on the policy-making process. For societies that have moved beyond the immediate challenges of macroecomic crisis, both the urgency and resultant freedom of maneuver that early governments enjoyed have now passed. We have moved from extraordinary to normal politics, in which public opinion, interest groups, and routine legislative processes influence decision making to a much more substantial degree.

Two political issues arise in all of the chapters in the volume. The first concerns the nature of the conflicts surrounding the reform process. Who are the interested parties, and to what extent are they divided by distributional conflicts and the imposition of losses as opposed to collective action or coordination problems? To what extent do these conflicts vary according to the type of reform in question? Second, what are the political and institutional mechanisms for resolving these conflicts? Does the resolution of such conflicts require centralized leadership or can they be resolved by more consensual forms of consultation and bargaining? Does increased political competition help or hinder the reform process?

The answers to these questions are crucial for the sustainability of both economic and political reform. The transition to a market economy opens extraordinary opportunities for enhancing growth and improving efficiency in the allocation of resources. At the same time, it is a traumatic process accompanied by substantial social dislocation, an increase in both upward and downward mobility, and often wrenching individual adjustments. The political issues generated by this process and the way governments respond to them constitute important tests for new, and in some cases quite fragile, democracies.

Distributive Conflicts and Problems of Coordination

The literature on economic reform typically draws a distinction between a "first round" of stabilization and structural adjustment measures and a "second round" of reforms that include not only the social sector and fiscal initiatives discussed in this volume, but other changes such as the restructuring of the civil service, the creation of regulatory agencies, and the establishment of a more effective legal system. This second round is presumed to pose different and more difficult types of political challenges than the first (Naim 1995; Haggard and Kaufman 1995a).

These distinctions are useful, but can also lead to some confusion about the nature of the political problems reformers face. For example, some first-round reforms, such as exchange-rate adjustments, could indeed be accomplished through executive fiat. But others, such as privatization or the establishment of independent central banks, involved complex and politically difficult administrative reorganization. The chapters in this volume also indicate that there are substantial differences in the politics of different second-round reforms. The pension reforms analyzed by Nelson and Hausner are not necessarily more administratively complex than first-round reforms, such as privatization, and can be designed in ways that minimize distributive conflicts. Health-care reform, by contrast, generates sharper distributive issues – among both clients and health-care providers – over financing, coverage, and services. Given that health care is currently provided by the government, reforming the system also involves complex administrative reorganization, some of which is likely to be highly controversial, such as the closing of hospitals.

Given the differences within, as well as between, first- and second-round reforms, it *is* useful to distinguish the political challenges posed by reform in a more general way. Three characteristics of the reforms themselves and the setting in which they are introduced can provide the basis for some more discrete hypotheses about the politics of reform: the sense of crisis associated with the reform; the extent to which it involves an alteration of the behavior and routines of complex administrative organizations; and the extent to which the reforms imply the imposition of losses and distributive conflicts between "winners" and "losers."

The Role of Crisis

Incentives to reform are clearly affected by the costs political actors attach to maintaining the status quo (Heller, Keefer, and McCubbins 1998). Such incentives would appear to be quite strong during severe economic crises, such as sharply accelerating inflation or a collapse of demand that affects large portions of the population. Under these circumstances, distributive conflicts may actually be muted. Both legislators and publics will be more inclined to delegate authority to executives, granting them the latitude to "do something." Deteriorating economic circumstances contributed to the dramatic macroeconomic stabilization in Poland as well as the tax reforms Tanzi describes in Georgia.

Such incentives are weaker in the case of the institutional and welfare reforms discussed in this volume. Efforts to rationalize fiscal decision making, discussed by Haggard, Kaufman, and Shugart, involve problems that are not usually salient to the electorate at large. Even in the case of health and pension reform, publics that are unhappy with the existing system may nonetheless prefer the status quo to changes that put particular benefits at risk. Indeed, the nature of past welfare commitments may itself constitute a barrier to reform precisely because it has served to shield publics from at least some of the adjustment costs of the transition. Among the Central European countries, this declining sense of urgency, more than anything else, distinguishes second-generation reforms from those adopted during the initial era of crisis and extraordinary politics.

Although crisis circumstances provide opportunities for reform, they also pose important political challenges in their own right. First, even when crises reduce the incentives and capacity for competing groups to press their claims, reformers nonetheless face significant coordination problems. Tanzi's discussion of tax collection in Russia and Georgia provides a perfect example of a policy area in which such dilemmas are common, as were efforts to reduce inertial inflation in Latin America and the former Soviet republics.

Reforms undertaken during crisis periods also face problems of sustainability when crises pass. Haggard, Kaufman, and Shugart show how reformers were able to make difficult fiscal adjustments during the crisis of 1995, but were unable to press ahead with a comprehensive reform of fiscal institutions.

In some instances, finally, the costs of the crisis are not fully visible to publics; indeed, "crisis" circumstances may appear benign or even highly positive in the short run. The classic example is a boom that results in unsustainable current-account deficits and real appreciation. Although threatening over the medium run, such conditions may not be a spur to reform; indeed, they deter it.

Policy versus Institutional Change

Reforms can also be distinguished in terms of the extent to which they require fundamental institutional and organizational changes. A good proxy for this is the extent to which the reform in question is intensive in the use of administrative resources. In the early transition period, as noted, key macroeconomic decisions – for instance, on exchange rates or monetary policy – could be made by finance ministers and other top officials acting on their own.

By contrast, other reforms imply fundamental changes in organizational routines or the creation of altogether new institutions, such as regulatory agencies, new bureaus, and tax-collection agencies. Such reforms confront the weight of organizational inertia; they necessarily raise issues of organizational design, principal–agent problems, and the restructuring of incentives. Although not all of the reforms of interest to us here are administratively intense, some, such as the reform of health systems and basic fiscal institutions, are.

Imposing Losses

Finally, the most important question is the extent to which reforms imply losses for groups with significant political power and the capacity to block their passage. The conflict between "winners" and "losers" has been central to the literature on the politics of reform, although much of the discussion has been quite casual with surprisingly little information on how winners and losers behave politically or even who they are.[4] Moreover, the relative weight and even identity of "winners" and "losers" is not easily measured. In an influential article, Joel Hellman (1998) has pointed out that the main interest group resistant to reform in the transition economies is not the "losers," as traditionally conceived, but the "winners," who arise out of partial and incomplete reforms, such as the owners of recently privatized assets.

Even if we could clearly identify winners and losers and assess their influence in the policy process, such analyses would also have to consider the role that compensatory strategies and tactics play in the political fate of a particular reform effort. Such strategies are especially important when potential "losers" in the reform process are threatened with a loss of income. Kramer (1997) has argued, for example, that continuities in the social safety net in Eastern Europe have in fact been quite substantial. He uses this to explain why the transition was not more politically traumatic, but also why social reforms are difficult to undertake.

But even if incomes are shielded to some extent, reforms might also entail more fundamental losses of political power or organizational capability. In both Hungary and Poland, pension reform faced threats not from pensioners, who were weakly organized, but from unions, which saw government plans as undercutting an important source of labor's political power.

More generally, the relative organizational capabilities of groups are more important than the interests of the parties concerned; as has long been noted, there are substantial organizational asymmetries between the concentrated beneficiaries of the status quo (e.g., the medical profession) and the potential, but diffused, beneficiaries of reform (consumers of health care). Reform is clearly more difficult if its opponents

---

[4] For a critical review of this literature, see Haggard 1998.

are well organized, and a successful reform strategy has to consider ways in which the organizational advantages of those in favor of the status quo may be neutralized – for example, through the organization of those who have a stake in the reform.

It is an important finding of this volume that distributive conflicts are dependent on the design of the reform itself; tactics matter. Jerzy Hausner suggests that there are ways to design the introduction of pension reform that can mute the fears of those affected by it without necessarily undermining the integrity of the reform effort. Nelson comes to similar conclusions as Hausner, although both emphasize that these efforts can be costly in the short run; political compromises required large injections of resources at the initial phase, obtained in part through privatization. Kornai's proposal for reform of the Hungarian health-care system begins with the premise that the current level of public provision of health care initially be retained, so that in the short-run there are no losers at all.

Their examples provide evidence for the proposition that if a reform is Pareto-superior to the status quo, losers can in principle be compensated through transfers or, in some cases, through nonmaterial rewards. The lesson is a more generalizable one. As an earlier literature on corporatism pointed out, and a growing literature on globalization is reiterating, compensatory strategies are an integral aspect of a market economy (Rodrik 1997). Much depends, however, on the credibility of the promises for compensation and the related degree of uncertainty about the reform's effects (Fernandez and Rodrik 1991). If such promises lack credibility, and if benefits are uncertain, groups threatened by reform will be more inclined to mobilize to block it. How does democratic rule affect the ability to reach and sustain such social bargains?

Institutions of Decision Making and Implementation

Democracies and Dictatorships

A central theme of this book is how political institutions and decision-making processes influence policy outcomes. In this section, we consider the effects of institutions in two steps: first, differences in the type of political regime; second, differences in the institutional design of democracies.

The broadest institutional distinction across polities is between authoritarian and democratic regimes, the latter defined in terms of the guarantee of political and civil liberties and competitive elections. Although the debate about the relative performance of democratic and authoritarian regimes continues, most political scientists have reached the conclusion that any generalizations at this level are hiding substantial variation within each group (Haggard and Kaufman 1995b: chap. 5).

Among the former socialist countries, however, differences in the extent and thoroughness of democratic transitions do appear to have affected the extent of economic reform. Barbara Geddes was among the first to observe that changes in government are crucial to reform. For a sample of middle-income developing countries, she found that reforms were typically initiated "by executives who, for one reason or another are not beholden to the party, faction or group that has previously benefited from state intervention" (1995: 70). The implications for socialist systems are clear; policy reform requires a sharp political break with the ancien regime.

Steven Fish (1998) shows that one of the most important determinants of subsequent reform efforts among post-Communist countries was the outcome of the first post-transition election, including whether it was competitive and open. Joel Hellman (1998) demonstrates that governments that have remained in the hands of post-Communist strongmen or parties appear more vulnerable to be captured by nomenclature capitalists and newly rich oligarchs than those more systematically exposed to electoral challenges and partisan opposition.

The case studies presented in this volume point in similar directions. In the Hungarian case discussed by Haggard, Kaufman, and Shugart, the democratic transition played an important role in accelerating the breakdown of the command economy. Conversely, the particularistic Russian tax and wage bargains analyzed by Tanzi and Gimpelson would be more difficult to sustain in a system characterized by more open and accountable democratic processes.

Institutional Variation in Democratic Systems
In the cases that form the core comparisons of this volume, particularly Hungary and Poland, constitutional government had become firmly entrenched and early fears of populist upheavals or democratic collapse have proved misguided (Greskovits 1998). In the early transition period, government decision making in the new democracies was ad hoc and crisis-driven. Basic political and policy-making institutions were weak and residual planning bureaucracies inappropriate for a market economy. But as democratic governance has become consolidated over time, the organizational structure of the government, parliament, and party politics has come to look more and more like those in other advanced and middle-income democracies.

Across these polities, differences in the degree of democracy are less salient than differences in constitutional design and other political institutions that affect economic decision making. Democratic regimes differ in the extent to which the design of representative institutions centralizes decision making. This in turn is directly related to the number of "veto gates": institutions with the power to influence or block policy initiatives.[5] In Westminster parliamentary systems, the number of veto gates is effectively one: the cabinet. Depending on constitutional design, other veto gates might include the legislature, the government's coalition partners, the Constitutional or Supreme Court, or corporatist bargaining arrangements. As the number of veto gates rises, the government must accommodate a wider array of interests, and this process of accommodation may encourage compromises that broaden political support for reform. But it can also lead to the dilution of reform, delay, or even stalemate.

The party system also affects the degree of centralization within democratic regimes. An executive in control of a disciplined majority party is likely to have more authority than one who must accommodate a diverse legislative coalition. In coalition governments, conflicts among ministries can have a powerful influence on policy making. Intraparty discipline also appears as an important variable, emphasized in the case study of Hungary by Haggard, Kaufman, and Shugart. Here a government made up of parties subject to factional infighting compounded the problem of diversity of parties within the coalition.

The ongoing debate over the costs and advantages of centralized decision making within democratic systems has particular salience in a region just emerging from an egregious form of party dictatorship and political overcentralization. On the one hand, there is evidence that "strong" executives are an advantage for undertaking reform because of their ability to set the reform agenda, coordinate diverse interests, and implement policy swiftly and efficiently. Strong executives are also more likely to delegate authority to technocratic teams motivated by calculations of aggregate social welfare rather than particular interests. Somewhat counterintuitively, it may also be easier for electorates to hold executives in relatively centralized democratic systems responsible than in those where lines of authority are more decentralized and diffuse; centralization does not necessarily imply lack of accountability. This pole in the debate is represented in this volume by the chapter on Hungary by Haggard, Kaufman, and Shugart and by Tanzi's comparison of Russia and Georgia.

The advantages of decisive leadership must be weighed against the fact that the voices of contending groups of citizens will be fainter and have

---

[5] For an introduction to the role of veto gates in policy making, see Tsebelis 1995.

less influence in the decision-making process. This fact may have delete-rious consequences not only for the quality of democratic governance but also for the prospects of economic reform. Centralized decision making reduces the scope of policy advice the government receives and reduces the incentives for consensus building, consultation, and feed-back, which may be essential to the sustainability (if not the initiation) of the reform effort (see particularly Przeworski 1991). A more diffuse and consultative decision-making process slows policy making and nec-essarily expands the scope of interests to be accommodated, but precisely for that reason it makes any decision more stable (Tsebelis 1995).

This perspective is advanced most strongly in Jerzy Hausner's account of the Polish pension reform. Hausner emphasizes that consultation was a critical element of the reform process; persuasion allowed the govern-ment to dampen the fears of those concerned that they would lose under the new system, facilitated changes in the design of the reform that min-imized the losses of each group, and helped to legitimate and consoli-date the outcome.

One route to reconciling these apparent differences is to return to the political properties of the reform issue with which we began this dis-cussion: the extent to which it addresses a severe crisis, the extent of administrative coordination it requires, and the degree and nature of distributive conflicts. Different institutional arrangements may be more or less well suited for different types of reforms; this argument is summarized in Table I.1.

Centralized political institutions and decision-making processes are probably most important when reforms are necessary to *preempt* crises, such as those arising from increasing balance-of-payments and fiscal deficits, that do not initially generate widespread public concern. This argument is advanced in Haggard, Kaufman, and Shugart's discussion of Hungary's fiscal-policy adjustment in 1995. Strong executives can also set the agenda and establish guidelines for debate about implementation where there is broad dissatisfaction with the status quo but limited agree-ment on the way to change it. In Hausner's study, for example, reform-ers were able to lead and restructure the debate on pension reform by establishing a plenipotentiary who operated outside the normal routines of cabinet politics and reported directly to the prime minister.

The advantages of the institutional concentration of authority may be less important when crises have a direct and visible effect on voters and interest groups. In such circumstances, elected officials and citizens in democratic systems with a wide variety of constitutional arrangements may be inclined to delegate authority to executives. However, this result can by no means be taken for granted in systems characterized by

Table I.1. *The Politics of Reform*

	Crisis Circumstances	Complex Institutional and Organizational Change	Loss-Imposing Reforms
Political conflicts	Reduces salience of distributional conflicts but creates coordination problems Strengthens incentives to delegate	Organizational inertia Principal–agent and monitoring problems	Provide incentives for groups to mobilize to block reform
Advantages/disadvantages of concentrated decision-making process	Concentrated authority useful in preempting crises and solving coordination problems Allows for coherent policy when "crisis" is not politically salient	"Top down" reform possible when reforms do not require complex institutional and organizational change (e.g., exchange rate and monetary policy) Can set agenda and break bureaucratic logjams	Can set agenda and break political logjams Centralized decision-making processes useful for solving pure coordination problems, but may generate resistance when used to allocate losses
Advantages/ disadvantages of consultation and "checks and balances"	During crises, consultation and fragmented decision making can lead to indecisiveness and delay Can "lock in" reforms already initiated	Consultation necessary to induce compliance and manage principal–agent problems	Consultation permits bargaining over distribution of losses Consultation more likely to generate compensatory mechanisms supportive of reform

18

multiple veto points and fragmented parties. The Russian case is a powerful reminder that effective coordination and the creation of new institutions is not automatic; both Tanzi and Gimpelson cite conflicting centers of political authority as a major barrier to effective economic management and reform.

The advantages of consultative processes increase when reforms involve substantial institutional and administrative change. The decisiveness of centralized authority is useful when reforms involve discrete policy changes: adjusting goals and redeploying existing instruments to accomplish them. Unilateral executive action is far less useful when the reforms require new or restructured institutions or the cooperation, initiative, and monitoring of a large number of actors. Such coordination implies a complex division of labor, interdependence, and, to an important extent, voluntary compliance with organizational norms. In the absence of consultation and positive inducements, shirking, manipulation of information, and other behaviors can undermine successful implementation of the reform. In this regard, both Greskovits and Haggard, Kaufman, and Shugart argue that centralized authority in the Hungarian case was far more effective in adjusting fiscal policy than in restructuring fiscal institutions. Consultation also played a critical role in the evolution of the health reforms discussed by Nelson and Kornai.

Finally, the relative advantages and disadvantages of centralized decision making depend on whether the principal problems posed by the reform are ones of distributional conflicts or coordination and collective action. With coordination problems citizens are unwilling to act on widely shared preferences for the provision of a public good because they lack assurances that others will be impelled to contribute. In such situations, decision makers in systems with few veto gates can provide credible assurances that the supply of public goods will not be undermined by alternative sources of authority, and they can be more readily held to account in the event of failure.

Tanzi's discussion of tax-collection problems in Russia and Georgia provides a perfect example of the policy area in which such dilemmas are common. As Margaret Levi (1988) has pointed out, taxpayers are typically unwilling to comply in the payment of taxes if they know others are cheating. The creation of autonomous and impartial collection agencies beyond the reach of politicians can help solve this problem. Many other macroeconomic policy areas, including monetary policy and central banking, also involve coordination problems that are more easily resolved through centralized but accountable decision-making structures.

The advantages of centralized decision making decrease and the importance of representation increases in reforms characterized by strong distributive conflicts. Even these reforms, as Hausner and Nelson show, may require strong leadership to break stalemates and sustain the overall coherence of the reform, particularly during acute crises. Nevertheless, in democratic systems, distributive politics requires venues for negotiation, compromise, and forms of compensation. Particularly where the urgency associated with crisis is lacking, the process of change will necessarily be incremental, but there may not be good alternatives to gradualism within a democratic system, and particularly in democracies such as Poland's, which are characterized by multiple veto gates.

Conclusions

Despite the necessary policy, political, and institutional trade-offs that we have highlighted in this introduction, we should recall that the transition period in Central Europe has in large measure been one of hopes fulfilled. Contrary to earlier expectations, the transition to the market has not served to undermine democracy's prospects. Nor have democracies proved incapable and inept in making difficult policy choices. Russia and a number of the former Soviet republics still face very fundamental political and economic choices, and their future as capitalist democracies is by no means secure. But the difficult debates now faced by the Eastern European countries are not the fundamental ones of democracy and the market, but, as with the other advanced industrial and middle-income countries, how to define the mix between the two in a way that combines efficiency, fairness, and representation. In the effort to understand these choices we present the results of this collective project.

References

Aslund, Anders. 1992. *Post-Communist Economic Revolutions: How Big a Bang?* Washington, D.C.: Center for Strategic and International Studies.

Balcerowicz, Leszek. 1996. *Socialism, Capitalism, and Transformation.* Budapest: Central European University Press.

Barro, R. J. 1991. Economic Growth in a Cross-Section of Countries. *Quarterly Journal of Economics* 106: 407–44.

Berger, S., and R. Dore, eds. 1996. *National Diversity and Global Capitalism.* Ithaca: Cornell University Press.

Elster, Jon, Clauss Offe, and Ulrich Klaus Preuss. 1998. *Institutional Design in Post-Communist Societies: Theories of Institutional Design.* Cambridge: Cambridge University Press.

Fernandez, Raquel, and Dani Rodrik. 1991. Resistance to Reform: Status Quo Bias in the Presence of Individual-Specific Uncertainty. *American Economic Review* 81: 1146–55.

Fish, M. Steven. 1998. The Determinants of Economic Reform in the Post-Communist World. *East European Politics and Societies* 12, no. 1 (Winter): 31–78.

Garrett, Geoffrey. 1998. *Partisan Politics in the Global Economy.* Cambridge: Cambridge University Press.

Geddes, Barbara. 1995. Challenging the Conventional Wisdom. In L. Diamond and M. Plattner, eds., *Economic Reform and Democracy*, pp. 59–73. Baltimore: Johns Hopkins University Press.

Greskovits, Béla. 1998. *The Political Economy of Protest and Patience: East European and Latin American Transformations Compared.* Budapest: Central European University Press.

Haggard, Stephan. 1998. Interests, Institutions and Policy Reform. University of California, San Diego. Unpublished manuscript.

Haggard, Stephan, and Robert Kaufman. 1995a. The Challenges of Consolidation. In L. Diamond and M. Plattner, eds., *Economic Reform and Democracy*, pp. 1–12. Baltimore: Johns Hopkins University Press.

1995b. *The Political Economy of Democratic Transitions.* Princeton: Princeton University Press.

Havlik, P., ed. 1991. *Dismantling the Command Economy in Eastern Europe.* Boulder, Colo.: Westview Press.

Heller, William B., Philip Keefer, and Matthew McCubbins. 1998. Political Structure and Economic Liberalization. In P. Drake and M. McCubbins, eds., *The Origin of Liberty: Political and Economic Liberalization in the Modern World*, pp. 146–79. Princeton: Princeton University Press.

Hellman, Joel. 1998. Winners Take All: The Politics of Partial Reform in Post-socialist Transitions. *World Politics* 50: 203–34.

Kapstein, E., and Mandelbaum, M. eds. 1997. *Sustaining the Transition: The Social Safety Net in Postcommunist Europe.* New York: Council on Foreign Relations Press.

Klaus, Vaclav. 1992. *Dismantling Socialism: A Preliminary Report.* Prague: Top Agency.

Kornai, János. 1990. *The Road to a Free Economy. Shifting from a Socialist System: The Example of Hungary.* New York: W. W. Norton.

1992. *The Socialist System: The Political Economy of Communism.* Princeton: Princeton University Press.

1996. *The Citizen and the State: Reform of the Welfare System.* Discussion Paper No. 32. Budapest: Collegium Budapest.

1998. Preface: The General Trends and the Philosophy of Public Sector Reform. In L. Bokros and J.-J. Dethier, eds., *Public Finance Reform during the Transition: The Experience of Hungary*, pp. 25–44. Washington, D.C.: World Bank.

Kramer, Mark. 1997. Social Protection Policies and Safety Nets in East-Central Europe: Dilemmas of the Postcommunist Transition. In E. Kapstein and M. Mandelbaum, eds., *Sustaining the Transition: The Social Safety Net in Postcommunist Europe.* New York: Council on Foreign Relations Press.

Levi, Margaret. 1988. *Of Rule and Revenue.* Berkeley: University of California Press.

Murrell, Peter. 1992. Evolutionary and Radical Approaches to Economic Reform. *Economics of Planning* 25: 79–95.

    1996. How Far Has the Transition Progressed? *Journal of Economic Perspectives* 10: 25–44.

Naim, Moises. 1995. Latin America: The Second Stage of Reform. In L. Diamond and M. Plattner, eds., *Economic Reform and Democracy*, pp. 28–44. Baltimore: Johns Hopkins University Press.

Przeworski, Adam. 1991. *Democracy and the Market: Political and Economic Reforms in Eastern Europe and Latin America*. Cambridge: Cambridge University Press.

Rodrik, Dani. 1997. *Has Globalization Gone Too Far?* Washington, D.C.: Institute for International Economics.

Tanzi, V., ed. 1992. *Fiscal Policies in Economies in Transition*. Washington, D.C.: International Monetary Fund.

Tornell, Aaron. 1995. Are Economic Crises Necessary for Trade Liberalization and Fiscal Reform? The Mexican Experience. In R. Dornbusch and S. Edwards, eds., *Reform, Recovery and Growth: Latin America and the Middle East*, pp. 53–73. Chicago: University of Chicago Press.

Tsebelis, George. 1995. Decision Making in Political Systems: Veto Players in Presidentialism, Parliamentarism, Multicameralism, and Multipartyism. *British Journal of Political Science* 25: 289–325.

PART I

Fiscal Policy and Institutions

CHAPTER 1

The Politics of Labor-Market Adjustment: The Case of Russia

VLADIMIR GIMPELSON

By mediating the impact of macroeconomic stabilization and fiscal adjustment on the everyday life of the population, labor markets play an important role in determining the success of the transition to the market. After seven years of transition, however, the Russian labor market still seems to be performing quite differently from the labor markets in other transition countries. Hungary and Poland faced sharp declines in employment early in the transition. Unemployment rates there remain quite high even now, after several subsequent years of economic growth. The Czech Republic has little unemployment, but this must be set against slow economic restructuring and continuing government support to ailing enterprises.

In Russia, a large increase in unemployment had been widely expected even before the reform started. Nevertheless, open unemployment remained rather low until 1995, despite a 50 percent decline in production. In Russia, the standard trade-off between employment and wages was transformed into one between unemployment and underpayment with wage arrears. In 1996–98 wage arrears or significant delays in wage payments became one of the salient features of Russian economic and political development. They contributed heavily to rapidly growing public debt, thus eroding fiscal policy and generating even more political and economic uncertainty. To this extent, they became one of the determinants of the 1998 financial crisis.

I am extremely grateful to all members of the focus group, and also to Simon Clarke, Rostislav Kapelyushnikov, János Köllő, Hartmut Lehmann, Douglas Lippoldt, and Dan Treisman for valuable comments. I owe particular gratitude to János Kornai, Robert Kaufman, and Stephan Haggard, who helped me to shape my research and argumentation.

25

Why does the "Russian way" of labor-market adjustment (as it was described first by Layard and Richter 1994) deviate so much from that in most of the other reforming countries? There is a number of interdependent reasons. My explanation begins with the general fact that the Russian political leadership in 1992–97 was politically unable to take radical steps toward major structural reforms. Fearing the political implications of mass unemployment associated with enterprise closures and/or deep industrial restructuring, the government preferred to avoid radical fiscal adjustment and hardening of budget constraints. Moreover, political institutions offered strong incentives for inflating the total public-sector wage bill. Finally, the existing system of unemployment protection or enterprise-provided welfare and public fear of a potential unemployment catastrophe gave employees an incentive to keep their jobs at any price.

As a result, both the Russian government and society have preferred to avoid massive worker dislocation by attempting a "soft" labor-market adjustment. A policy of underpayment and underemployment has become a core of redistributive politics, shifting major social costs onto the politically and economically weakest groups in society.

In this chapter I explore the political and institutional factors leading enterprises to delay wage payment and to accumulate labor slack. I then examine the political feedback from the Russian way in labor-market adjustment, as reflected in electoral support for reforms and workers' protest.

"Great Contraction" without Unemployment?

The transformational recession (Kornai 1994) in Russia was much longer and deeper than had initially been expected by most observers. While muddling through with stop-go reforms for years, the country lost half of its industrial production and about 40 percent of its GDP.[1] By 1995 the decline still continued but at a slower pace. In 1997 the Russian economy at last appeared to be turning round, with GDP growing by 0.4 percent and industrial production by 1.8 percent. But in 1998 another steep decline occurred.

Massive unemployment might well have been expected as an immediate and inevitable consequence of such a long and deep recession.

---

[1] Column 8 in Table A.1 in the appendix shows that the estimated level of real GDP in 1997 was only 58 percent of the 1989 level. This means a slightly more than 40 percent decline, which was uncommon in the transition economies of Eastern Europe. Due to the economic collapse in 1998, Russia's GDP further deteriorated.

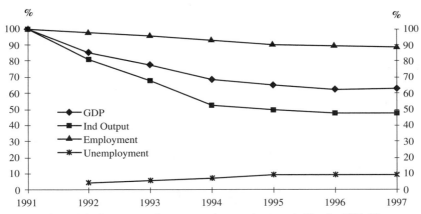

Figure 1.1. Output, employment, and unemployment in Russia, 1991–98.
Source: Goskomstat, various publications, and EBRD 1998.

Indeed, the situation could have been worse than in the Central and Eastern European countries, given the tremendous scale of labor hoarding in Russia prior to reforms. Yet, although the total social costs of the transition to capitalism were extremely high, mass unemployment came only after a delay. Figure 1.1 charts the major trends in output and employment over 1991–98, and shows clearly that the decline in employment lagged well behind the steep drop in output. Unemployment, according to the definition of the International Labour Organization (ILO)/Organization for Economic Cooperation and Development (OECD), rose from 4.8 percent in 1992 to 9.5 percent in early 1996, but did not top 10 percent until the following year. Not until early 1999 did unemployment climb to over 12 percent.

Because most Russian politicians viewed high unemployment as a major threat to political stability, they tailored all policies to avoid it. In 1992–95 job losses were held to a moderate level by stop-go monetary policies, insider privatization, and open and hidden subsidies to producers. In some regions, authorities also implemented "active" labor-market measures to protect existing jobs.[2]

The quantity adjustment has been partially facilitated by involuntary reduction in working hours, but this is not enough to explain why falling production did not lead to more extensive job losses. In 1992–93 reductions became a major substitute for layoffs and resulted in actual wage

---

[2] The trend in bankruptcies is revealing. The year 1994 witnessed only 240 bankruptcy cases in Russia, compared with 5,900 in Hungary and 4,285 in Poland.

27

cuts. In 1994–96, about 6–7 percent of the labor force was underemployed (*Russian Economic Trends* 1996: No. 2, pp. 105–6). The data do not indicate any significant increase in the rate of unemployment. Moreover, the proportion of the labor force working shorter hours seems to have decreased in 1997.

Thus, instead of mass and rapid dislocation leading to high unemployment, we can witness a very gradual employment change. This gradualism has provided economic and social actors with more time to adjust to changing labor-market conditions. On the one hand it decreased onetime costs, while on the other it prolonged the adjustment period and spread the costs across the wider population.

Wages: Real and Unreal

Price liberalization in early 1992 caused a drastic fall in real wages. But during 1992 and 1993, real wages seemed to recover somewhat. This slight upward trend lasted until the end of 1994, when a sudden jump in inflation caused a decline of about 25 percent. During the next several years, wage levels stabilized and then began to turn up in 1996 and 1997, even though output continued to decline for most of that period. A gradual rise in real wages halted only after the August 1998 financial crisis, when they nose-dived along with the national currency.

However, the statistics on real wage dynamics in Russia are misleading, because they do not measure the wages that are actually paid. Wage arrears form part of the more general and interrelated pattern of arrears throughout the Russian economy, in taxes, trade, and interenterprise debt (Alfandari and Shaffer 1996; Ickes and Ryterman 1993; Treisman 1998). Some observers blame overly tight monetary policy, low monetization, and inappropriate macroeconomic measures (Vaughan-Whitehead 1998: 28–29; Clarke 1997a). Following Kornai (1995), however, I believe, that the major determinants of all types of arrears lie in incomplete fiscal adjustment and lack of the political capability to ensure financial discipline. The budget constraint for firms taking on all types of debt remains soft. The civil code amended by Parliament in July 1996 stipulates that wage payments to employees have priority over other payments, but the government has persistently insisted that taxes be paid first.

The scale of delays in wage payments is well illustrated by public-opinion data (Table 1.1). The percentage of respondents who reported being paid fully and on time dropped from 62 percent in March 1993 to only 27 percent in January 1997. The proportion of those paid with delays over one month was only 7 percent in early 1993 but 40 percent in early

Table 1.1. *Wage Arrears in Russia (percentage of respondents paid with delay)*

Month	Paid on Time and Completely	Paid with Delay under One Month	Paid with Delay over One Month	Total
March 1993	62	31	7	100
December 1993	48	41	11	100
March 1994	38	43	19	100
June 1994	41	37	22	100
November 1994	40	41	19	100
March 1995	43	40	17	100
July 1995	48	40	12	100
September 1995	44		17	100
March 1996	31	45	24	100
May 1996	37	36	27	100
November 1996	29		39	100
January 1997	27		40	100

Source: VCIOM data, cited from Gordon 1997: 73.

1997. These figures imply that on average almost every family in the country was denied wages completely or partially for some time.

The buildup of wage arrears began in 1992, but became quite significant by mid-1993 against a background of stabilization of real contracted wages. As Figure 1.2 shows, almost any upward movement in contracted wages has been associated with the amassing of new arrears. Conversely, when contracted wages dropped sharply in late 1994 and early 1995, wage arrears followed the trend. There are, however, notable exceptions. Each December, real wages go up in partial compensation for previously accumulated debts; this reflects the traditional practice of paying a thirteenth monthly wage or additional bonuses. But in January the pattern of simultaneous movement of both trends resumes. Thus, wage arrears seem to reflect overestimates by employers (including both state and private firms) of their payments to workers. Real wage figures would show an even sharper downward trend if they were adjusted for accumulated real wage arrears.

Since mid-1993, wage arrears have been one of the major mechanisms of real wage flexibility. They grew in 1994 until midyear, resumed growth after mid-1995, and accelerated again in 1996. At the end of 1996, the stock of unpaid wages accounted for over 20 percent of monthly GDP or one month's total wage bill. This figure was an aggregate for all firms. In those actually having wage arrears, the stock of unpaid wages at the

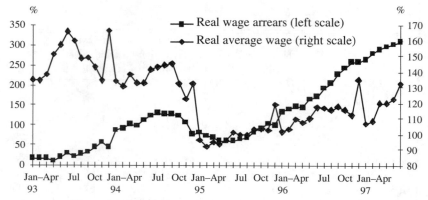

Figure 1.2. Real wages and wage arrears in industry, 1993–98.
Source: Russian Economic Trends, various issues.

end of 1996 was the equivalent of 275 percent of the monthly wage bill (*Russian Economic Trends* 1997: No. 1). By mid-1997 unpaid wages accounted for 55.3 trillion rubles, or 128 percent of the monthly wage bill. One-fifth of this was due to budget arrears and the remainder to firms' inability to pay (*Russian Economic Trends* 1997: No. 3).

In 1997 the government announced it would repay its debts to public employees as one of its priorities. By the end of 1997, due to a reduction in the budgetary arrears, the total stock of back wages had been reduced, although it remained significant. In January 1998, however, it began to grow again, and in March 1998 it was one of the underlying reasons why President Yeltsin fired the Chernomyrdin cabinet.

Wage arrears are widespread in sectors experiencing the most difficulty (e.g., machine building or the social sector) as well as in those which are doing better (e.g., oil and gas, construction, or private firms across all sectors). Geography also appears to be a factor: the farther a region is from Moscow, the higher the incidence of the accumulated wage debts.

But accumulated wage debts are allocated across firms and employees very unevenly, reflecting the position of different groups in the economy, their resources, and their bargaining power versus other groups of workers, managers, and the government. It appears that most of the arrears are shifted onto the least competitive and politically vocal part of the labor force (Desai and Idson 1998; Lehmann, Wadsworth, and Acquisti 1998; Earle and Sabirianova 1999). Significant intrafirm variation in wage arrears suggests discrimination within firms against those with less bargaining power (Earle and Sabirianova 1999). Better-paid employees have more political clout, because they can quit and move to jobs with lower arrears and higher paid-out wages. Lower-paid workers are concentrated in sectors and jobs offering limited exit options. They are less vocal and more likely to accept payment delays with acquiescence, even though wage arrears bring a much higher probability of poverty and destitution.

All this suggests that lower-paid employees suffer disproportionately more from nonpayment than those with higher wages. They are denied less in terms of the absolute amount, but significantly more in relative terms. The pattern seems to reflect a redistribution of the wage fund from the less competitive to the more competitive, or from relative losers to relative winners. Suffering from wage arrears also appears to be quite a persistent phenomenon: workers who had faced arrears once, in 1994, for example, had a higher probability of experiencing them again later in 1995 or 1996. This persistent vulnerability can be explained by low personal bargaining power and/or by commitment to an ailing firm or sector, factors that often coincide.

How to Stabilize? Do Not Pay Wages!

Wage arrears seem to have emerged as a by-product of tighter monetary policy. The decrease in the money supply imposed serious constraints on both public spending and enterprises' cash balances. In the absence of expenditure cuts or the enforcement of bankruptcy measures, disinflation[3] encouraged enterprises to take on all types of debts, including debts to workers. This assumption of debt has become a major means of softening budget constraints and keeping firms afloat.

Figure 1.3 shows the inverse relation between wage arrears and inflation. When inflation soared, the level of wage arrears stabilized or even went down. Each attempt to restrain the money supply was followed by a new wage arrears crisis. Since early 1992, Russia has gone through five major stages in its struggle for stabilization and five subsequent ups and downs in arrears.

1. January 1992 to mid-1993: In January, when prices were liberalized, real wages dropped drastically and inflation soared. Monetary policy was tight at the beginning of 1992, but laxity returned by midyear, fueling inflation. The labor market responded to monetary tightening with a slight increase in unemployment and some

---

[3] Table A.2 in the appendix shows that the gradual disinflationary process forced the inflation rate from a hyperinflationary level in early 1992 to 10.9 percent in 1997. However, the 1998 financial crisis caused a new price hike in the second half of the year.

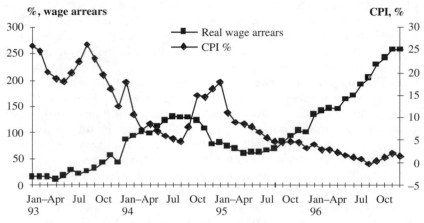

Figure 1.3. Wage arrears and inflation, 1993–98.
Source: Russian Economic Trends, various issues.

short-time employment emerged. Wage arrears appeared as well but remained at a rather low level.

2. Mid-1993 to mid-1994: In a new attempt to reduce inflation, monetary policy was tightened, borrowing on the bond market replaced inflationary sources of government financing, and most subsidies were cut. Unemployment still grew rather slowly, underemployment and real wages stabilized, but wage arrears started rocketing.

3. Mid-1994 to early 1995: There was a new loosening in monetary policy, and the monthly rate of the consumer price index (CPI) increase jumped from 5.3 percent in July 1994 to a peak level of 17.8 percent in January 1995. Trends in unemployment and underemployment showed no significant changes, but real wages plummeted by one-third between September 1994 and January 1995. Correspondingly, wage arrears almost halved.

4. Early 1995 to August 1998: Monetary policy became tighter once again. After reaching its peak in January 1995, the rate of CPI increase steadily went down. Monthly inflation did not rise above 3 percent between February 1996 and August 1998. A slight increase in unemployment by March 1997 was followed by a subsequent decrease; underemployment remained at about the 1 percent level and real wages due to be paid also seemed to recover somewhat. However, wage arrears grew rapidly.

5. From August 1998 onward: Sharp devaluation of the ruble, more lax monetary policy, and a rise in the rate of inflation have reduced

32

the real stock of wage arrears. Unemployment has crept up, but only at about the same pace as in earlier years.

Daniel Treisman has argued that the control of inflation from mid-1996 to August 1998 was attributable to specific, "nonorthodox" policies that compensated earlier opponents of stabilization and changed their incentives. First, initially pro-inflationary commercial banks were co-opted into the antiinflationary camp by the creation of a market for state securities, protected from foreign competition and offering extremely high rates of return. Second, "insolvent farms, enterprises, and state installations that demanded inflationary credits were appeased with free or cheap energy. This nonmonetary means of injecting liquidity into illiquid spots reduced the credibility of threats of mass strikes and civil unrest and stretched out the agony of restructuring into a politically less explosive pattern" (Treisman 1998: 264).

But "non-monetary" ways of keeping insolvent firms afloat do not provide cash to pay wages. The energy sector, which was heavily compensated with tax breaks, export privileges, and other perks, remained among the major debtors to the federal budget. Even when debts were repaid from time to time, firms then started to accumulate them anew. Workers who are not paid for months are no happier if their company also fails to pay its taxes.

How have households been affected by disinflation? High inflation taxes the whole population regardless of region, sector, or ownership type, but its major burden is put on low- and middle-income groups. Compared with high-income earners, these groups have fewer opportunities to protect their real incomes from erosion. As was shown by Granville, Shapiro, and Dynnikova (1997: 76), if in 1993–95 the monthly inflation rate was r percent, the monthly inflation tax reached $r/2$ percent. Over the year, it could account for an annual loss of up to 25–30 percent of monthly wages.

Wage arrears are also a kind of tax, but they affect households in a different way than inflation. First, 60 percent of employees experience no delays at all or only short ones. These people are "tax exempt" and low inflation provides a real gain for them. Second, those who are owed back wages are taxed very unevenly. As noted, most of the wage arrears are very heavily concentrated in particular economic sectors and regions, and among certain social groups. More competitive workers have higher wages and lower arrears, whereas less competitive workers have lower wages and higher arrears. For the latter, however, the choice is between wage arrears and unemployment. As we see, they prefer the former option. But in receiving delayed wages, they are taxed for

33

disinflation, whereas others pay little or nothing at all. In these cases, swapping inflation for wage arrears may have exposed them to even greater hardships than high inflation would have done.

Why Does the Government Tend to Set Unsustainable Wages?

Widespread arrears raise the question of how wages are set in the economy and why unsustainable wage claims emerge in the first place. If almost half of all firms are not able to meet their obligations, there is probably an upward bias in the wage-setting machinery; something pushes employers to set wages that are beyond the limits of their economic capabilities.

Alfandari and Schaffer suggest that wage arrears are in some sense an accounting fiction and present a way to reduce labor compensation. "In principle, managers always have the choice between paying a low wage (promptly) or essentially promising to pay higher wages with money the firm doesn't have (or the managers won't admit to having) – that is, to accumulate wage arrears. We suspect managers promise wages in excess of the cash they have available so as to turn workers' protests toward the government authorities in order to obtain financial assistance" (Alfandari and Schaffer 1996: 125).

When the flow of subsidies first showed signs of drying up, this might have well been one of the reasons for pushing up wage claims. The government itself, however, was also unable to meet its own obligations and was a major contributor to mounting wage debt, provoking other actors to follow suit. High inflation helped to meet these nominal claims by discounting them, but later, lower inflation raised the real value of unpaid wages. Over time, the trend became to some extent self-generating.

Various features of Russia's political institutions have played an important role in shaping the emergence of wage arrears. First, a persistent conflict between the government and the State Duma (the lower chamber of the Russian Parliament) has resulted in inflated expenditures. Second, fiscal-policy-making institutions are highly decentralized, and the Ministry of Finance has little control over off-budget funds. The Ministry of Finance has often been unable to resist lobbying demands within the government and the presidential administration, or to control fiscal policy and public spending in politically important regions.[4] Third,

---

[4] Regional expenditure and extrabudgetary funds together accounted for 59.4 and 57.8 percent of general government expenditure in 1995 and 1996, correspondingly (OECD 1997: 188).

34

an overpoliticized and unreformed tax collection system has contributed to losses in revenues.[5]

Let us look more closely at the basic institutional foundations of wage policy. The wage-setting institutions in the budget-financed, privatized, and private sectors differ. In budgetary-financed institutions (public education, health care, culture, and science among others) wages are based on a uniform tariff scale (UTS).[6] The statutory minimum wage is fixed by the president or Parliament and may change from time to time, albeit irregularly. Further regulation of wages and salaries in the public sector is in the competence of the government (Mikhalev and Bjorgsten 1996: 10).

According to the Russian Constitution, the government is accountable to the president, not the Parliament. The budget must be approved by the lower chamber, which is dominated by the Communist and nationalist opposition, but this role generally marks the limit of the Duma's power over fiscal policy. With limited direct policy influence or responsibility, legislators in the Duma have an incentive to adopt an expansionist stance. In this respect, moreover, Duma deputies are typically supported by the upper chamber of the Parliament: the Federation Council, which represents regional interests. Thus, Parliament has consistently raised expenditure, particularly increasing salaries, wages, pensions, and benefits.

The government, which is under pressure from the international economic organizations to limit budget deficits and set inflation targets at a low level, has resisted increases in social spending. Nevertheless, the government also has strong incentives to relax controls.

First, for both political and economic reasons, the government has attached considerable importance to meeting the scheduled deadlines in the budget cycle. This has pushed it to compromises with the legislature that raise expenditures. Although initial budget drafts have typically envisioned substantial limits on expenditure, they are blocked in the legislature, not only by Communists and other opposition groups, but also by pro-government deputies who lobby for particular regional and industrial interests. At that point, the budgets are referred to a reconciliation committee, where projected spending is usually inflated. The limited capacity of the government to raise revenues and collect taxes expands the gap. This has happened almost every year since the start of reforms,

---

[5] On the role of institutions of fiscal policy making, see Haggard, Kaufman, and Shugart, Chapter 3, and Tanzi, Chapter 2, in this volume.
[6] The UTS provides for eighteen grades, in which the first grade is equal to the minimum wage; higher grades are calculated by multiplying the minimum by increasing coefficients.

and 1998 is no exception.[7] Although most of the budgetary allocations are later reduced, due to insufficient revenues, they directly affect both the amounts and rates of wage claims.

Second, wage policy is also affected by a kind of political business cycle characterized by preelectoral promises.[8] During 1995 and the first half of 1996, a period of parliamentary and presidential electoral campaigns, there were seven minimum wage adjustments, a higher frequency of adjustment than at any other period of the transition. It could be accounted for only by electoral considerations, because inflation was no higher than in other periods, and growth had not resumed. Most of the promised increases could not be supported by available resources; tax collection, in fact, declined even further before and immediately after the election period.

The largest increase in wage claims was in the public sector. In the science sector, for example, the year-on-year growth in the real wages due to be paid was 12 percent. When the 1996 elections were over, the rate of wage growth in the economy fell from 15–16 percent in the second and third quarters (compared with the same period a year earlier) to 3 percent in the first quarter of 1997 (*Russian Economic Trends* 1997: No. 3, p. 52). However, the inflationary effect on wage claims had accumulated by late 1996, and this pressure was offset largely by arrears.

Once both general elections were over, the electoral campaign shifted to the regions. Since the autumn of 1996, almost all Russian regions have undergone elections of governors and regional and local legislatures. These campaigns were very expensive for regional budgets, and while no special studies exist on how regional elections affect economic policy, it is logical to assume that they increase the public-wage bill.

Regional governments continue to be very significant employers. They still run educational and health-care facilities and some housing, among other activities. Interestingly, against the background of general contraction, some parts of the public sector increased employment in the 1990s even in absolute terms. This clearly happened in public administration, education, and health (Gimpelson and Lippoldt 1997). Although the latter two sectors have relatively low wages, their total wage bill is expanding. Most of this employment expansion happens at the regional level and has to be financed from regional budgets. Regional and local

---

[7] As the OECD survey concludes in general (1997: 6), "The regular non-fulfillment by the Federal Government of its own budgeted allocations, due in part to unrealistic budgets that echo political confrontations between the Government and the Duma, has added fuel to the fire of escalating non-payment problems in the economy, also implicitly undermining overall efforts to promote the law and contract enforcement."

[8] On political business cycles in Russia, see Treisman and Gimpelson 1999.

authorities are likely to give priority to paying wages of those working in administration. Thus the latter are likely to gain relative to workers in the education and health sectors, not only with respect to employment and wages owed but also in terms of the wages actually paid out to them.

The Russian version of fiscal federalism also contributes to arrears. Rules for allocating financial transfers to regions are unclear and are the subject of constant bargaining between regional and central governments. In their tug of war with the federal authorities, regional officials may misallocate funds earmarked for public wages and then request new funds from the center. They may also cross-subsidize local consumers by raising energy and utility prices for federal consumers located in the region (e.g., military bases and defense plants). Faced with higher energy bills, federal consumers then go into arrears in their payments to energy suppliers. The electricity and utility sectors, in their turn, do not pay their coal or oil suppliers. This complex chain of arrears then becomes an occasion for requesting additional financial help from the federal government. The outstanding example of such center–region war over additional transfers is Primorsky Kray in the Far East. The economic policy of the regional administration is a kind of local populism based on pressuring Moscow for extra funds.

Why Do Private Employers Tend to Set Wages That They Cannot Pay?

Wages in employment not financed by the budget were completely deregulated in early 1992. Since then, firms have been free to set their own wages. Although the rate of union membership at large and medium-sized enterprises remains very high generally (officially it is about 70 percent of the labor force), this does not create any significant upward pressure on wages. Most wages are set by employers' fiat.

Private employers, however, may enter an unsustainable wage race for numerous reasons. First, the UTS designed for the public sector is used by many private employers as a guideline; thus, increases in the UTS indirectly affect the nonpublic sector as well. Second, uncertain or false market information may lead employers to overestimate the size of cash flows. For example, many privatized firms are under contract to budgetary institutions, and if the latter do not receive their funds in time, they do not pay their contractors either. Furthermore, the widespread barter deals leave firms short of cash. Here, firms may enter "virtual economy" pretending to have produced more value than they really have and, therefore, pretending to pay workers more than they actually can

(Gaddy and Ickes 1998). Third, the coordination between firms in wage setting is poor; firms try to retain and motivate skilled labor by paying an efficiency wage (Gimpelson and Lippoldt 1996; 1997). This generates "leap-frogging" by workers seeking higher wages, a common scenario wherever wages are set in a decentralized way.

Delaying wage payments also reflects "the relative power of managers in relation to workers, which the standard view suggests is greater in Russia than in Central and Eastern Europe" (Alfandari and Schaffer 1996: 133). This pattern is reflected in the fact that Russian managers place much lower priority on paying workers than Polish managers do, for example (128). This relative power of managers has its source not only in the weakness of trade unions but also in the inability of the state to enforce contracts and to punish violations of the labor law. "The more general the practice, the easier it may be to persuade workers that it is somehow legitimate, or at least not the management's fault. Costs of using arrears are inversely related to their prevalence due to a decreasing probability of punishment" (Earle and Sabirianova 1999: 18).

Small private firms do not hire labor from the pool of unemployed. Instead, they pull the best workers from state or privatized firms by offering much higher labor remuneration. Their offers are often based on the assumption of low nonwage labor costs, evasion of taxes, and social contributions. This competition between different types of employers results in upward pressure on wages in state and privatized firms and raises the average wage level in the economy.

Finally, if the government and large employers delay payment of legally contracted wages, and if this violation of laws is not punished, it creates clear incentives to all other employers to follow the practice. The result is an epidemic of wage arrears across all sectors and types of firms, even those that are profitable and face no liquidity constraints.[9] Nonpayment becomes a social norm among employers and shifts the whole system to a new equilibrium. Paying "on time and completely" becomes a collective good and exiting from the arrears trap requires the implementation of politically costly selective incentives (such as enforced bankruptcy of large firms or punitive fines for delaying payments).

Workers' Response to the Labor-Market Adjustment

One might expect that a situation where millions of employees are not paid for months would generate mass social unrest. In fact, although

---

[9] Indeed, firms with cash could make hefty profits by investing their wage arrears until the bond market collapsed in 1998.

Table 1.2. *Strikes in Russia, 1991–98*

Year	Number of Enterprises Where Strikes Were Registered	Number of Employees Involved in Strikes (thousand)	Number of Participants in Strikes per Enterprise	Days Lost per Employee Involved in Strikes
1990	260	99.5	383	2.1
1991	1,755	237.7	135	9.7
1992	6,273	357.6	57	5.3
1993	264	120.2	455	2.0
1994	514	155.3	302	4.9
1995	8,856	489.4	55	2.8
1996	8,278	663.9	80	6.0
1997	18,675	836.9	45	6.5
1998	12,456	530.7	43	5.4

Source: Goskomstat, various publications.

arrears have contributed to growing social tension and rising social protest, there has so far been little social unrest on a mass scale. Given the extent of the wage delays and nonpayments, this is surprising. Most strikes are localized in several particular sectors and regions. Wage arrears do cause some "wildcat" strikes or some individual actions from completely discouraged people. Russian newspapers report numerous cases of hunger strikes, blocking of strategic roads, and even suicides caused by extreme destitution. Yet the labor force causes less instability than constitutional stalemates, wars between various Kremlin clans, or the constant intriguing among Moscow political elites.

Table 1.2 reports on the dynamics of strike activity in the Russian Federation since 1991. The first peak came in 1992, when the toughest stabilization measures were introduced. A second and stronger wave of disputes came in 1995. Reporting on these data, Goskomstat, the Central Statistical Office of the Russian Federation, observes that the rising propensity to strike closely approximates to the growing incidence of wage arrears; 99 percent of all collective actions in the economy were directly induced by nonpayments. The trend continued in 1997–98 with miners and teachers becoming more and more militant. May 1998 was marked by a new explosion of miners' protests over unpaid wages, which involved blocking strategic railroads and stopping cargo traffic. Although the protests remained sectorally and geographically localized, they did increase the pressure on government and raised doubts about the capacity of the latter to resist growing fiscal pressures and wage demands.

On the whole, however, workers have accepted arrears with surprising tolerance. The strike movement during 1995 involved fewer workers in industrial disputes than were found in most affluent OECD countries. Moreover, breakdown of the data by sectors shows that the bulk of the actions have appeared in the coal industry, health care, and education. Although these sectors did face the most severe wage backlogs, their comparative militancy cannot be attributable entirely to the wage arrears. Coal miners, along with teachers and health-care workers, are the most militant sectoral group almost everywhere.

There are probably a number of reasons for the relative passivity of workers. First, as Connor (1995: 11) writes, "Labor, in Russia, is weak – a taker of prices, not a maker, and largely unable to exert strong influence over its environment." Second, employees are extremely scared by the possibility of losing their jobs and being pushed into unemployment. Third, labor market institutions do not seem to offer much help in coping with joblessness. Thus workers may consider alternatives such as underemployment and underpayment to be lesser evils.

Weak Voice

Despite the fact that about three-quarters of the labor force is still unionized, "Russian trade unions are too weak to dictate terms in a turbulent transition economy. Management has the upper hand in labor disputes" (Connor 1995: 8). As in other transition economies, trade unions in Russia are divided into "old" successors of the Communist unions and the "new" ones with "grass-roots" support that emerged at the beginning of the democratic transformation.

The Federation of Independent Trade Unions of Russia (FITUR) represents the former type of union and absolutely dominates the trade-union scene. In the dispute over back wages, they "have confined themselves primarily to political lobbying in collaboration with the employers on behalf of their particular branch of the economy" (Clarke 1997b: 2).

The "new independent" trade unions that emerged in the late 1980s as part of the rising democratic movement are confined to particular sectors or firms. Having limited mobilization capacity, they have adopted a strategy of pursuing individual employers through the judicial system, of providing legal advice, and of representing small groups of workers in court (Clarke 1997b). Their success in winning a number of cases has hardly affected the general trend. The low level of union voice and mobilization capacity in transition Russia also derives from structural changes within the labor force. Here I would mention the growing nonunionized private sector and the rising heterogeneity and segmentation within formally unionized labor.

More competitive employees have both exit and voice options at their disposal (Hirshman 1970) and exhibit a spectacular mobility to other jobs, particularly to those in the new private sector. Even if they stay with their current firm, their stronger bargaining power and louder political voice allow them to satisfy demands individually or within small groups in direct nonunionized disputes with management. This possibility creates incentives for more egoistic behavior.

Less competitive employees have a weak voice but still fewer options for exit. Underemployment weakens still further those who stay at ailing or nonpaying establishments, because those with bargaining power and voice are likely to quit. These people are dependent on managers' discretion and have nowhere to go. To accept wage arrears seems to many of them the cheapest option. They may believe that they at least save their jobs, will eventually get their wages in full, and can survive in the meantime by moonlighting.

However, the strong concentration of losers within a limited space or the same sectors and/or firms does create additional incentives for collective action. Underemployment increases the scale of social burdens imposed on them, but in many cases it also weakens a threat of layoff. Losers become locked in state-run firms, firms with monopoly power, infrastructure sectors (railways, public transportation, air controllers), public education, and health, which are more centralized, better organized, or heavily unionized. "Unions limited to losing groups in the public sector, as in the marketizing economies, can endanger reforms," warns Freeman (1994: 24). And as Nelson (1995: 356) writes, "Unions in strategic sectors may exercise tremendous economic and political leverage, even if the labor movement for the nation as a whole is not strong." This can partially explain the high militancy of miners' and teachers' trade unions, against a general background of impotence in the Russian trade-union movement.

Threat of Open Unemployment

Another reason why this particular form of labor-market adjustment is so easily accepted is linked to the actual and perceived threat of job loss. Fear of unemployment can reduce workers' demands and force them to be more tolerant to deteriorating terms of employment (Blanchflower 1991).

There was no open unemployment in Russia before the transition, but it was widely assumed that reforms would initially involve a very high rate of unemployment. These warnings came from proponents of reforms, as well as from opponents, although the political reasons and arguments differed. Proponents of reform pointed to the depth of the needed transformation and the scale of the existing distortions. Social-sector ministries, referring to these forecasts, lobbied for more resources and more power in economic policy making. Opponents of reforms manipulated the figures in an attempt to prevent the coming "national catastrophe" of shock therapy. The most pessimistic claims were supported by ILO experts, who favored piecemeal, socially oriented reforms over the orthodox prescriptions of the International Monetary Fund (IMF) and World Bank (WB) (Standing 1996).

All of these predictions overestimated the actual trend in unemployment rates (as discussed earlier). Because they were widely reported by the mass media, however, these forecasts increased public fears. So even before the reforms really got off the ground, the general public expected mass workers' dislocation. As the popular saying goes, "fear has big eyes."

In 1989, even before there was any hint of radical economic changes, public opinion perceived unemployment as a major problem. Half of those surveyed were afraid of losing their job. After 1992, about 70–80 percent of respondents were likely to admit to such fears. These proportions with these fears were very stable over the next five years (see Table 1.3) despite the modest level of unemployment that actually appeared. Thus, the extremely strong fear of mass dislocation and soaring unemployment in Russia penetrated into public opinion and workers' behavior. It became an additional factor pushing people to accept a low-wage model, of which wage arrears were a hidden part.

Labor-Market and Welfare Institutions

One of the goals for labor-market institutions such as the Public Employment Service (PES) is to assist the unemployed. The PES provides information on vacancies, helping with retraining, and arranging unemployment benefits for applicants. The more efficient the PES is, the easier it becomes for the unemployed to survive periods of joblessness. Consequently, the easier it becomes for them to accept unemployment.

A detailed account of the Russian PES performance has been given elsewhere (see, e.g., Standing 1996). For my purposes it is only important to note that it is not very effective. In addition to the red tape incurred when application is made to the PES, unemployment benefits remain very low and the benefits themselves are also in arrears in many regions. These arrears may last even longer than wage arrears. The prospects of

Table 1.3. *Perception of Unemployment (percentage of positive responses)*

Month	"People Are More Afraid of Losing Jobs"	"There Are Unemployed among My Relatives and Friends"	"There Is a Threat of Mass Layoffs at My Enterprise"	"I Am Likely to Lose My Job Due to Enterprise Closure or Employment Cuts"
November 1989	49	—	—	—
November 1992	70	—	—	—
April 1993	80	41	46	37
August 1993	80	43	47	41
December 1993	—	—	—	37
January 1994	82	51	48	—
May 1994	83	60	43	46
September 1994	—	—	—	38
November 1994	77	64	34	37
March 1995	81	66	35	43
January 1996	70	70	27	36
January 1997	—	—	37	50
September 1997	—	—	29	35

Source: VCIOM.

getting a new job through the PES are low as well, because most of the employers either do not report vacancies, or are reluctant to hire the unemployed. All this provides workers with additional incentives to stay with a current job, even if they are not paid on time. If they do, they can at least hope to get their wage sooner or later, and they encounter fewer restrictions on moonlighting.

Retaining existing jobs may also provide some in-kind compensation. It should be recalled that one legacy of the socialist period is that some welfare benefits to workers are still provided through enterprises. Their proportion is declining, but it is still significant enough to stimulate workers to stay at "any price."[10] This part of compensation is less flexible and paid even when wage cash is scarce. The larger it is, the stronger the incentives are to tolerate backlogs in wages. This institutional feature of the Russian labor market distorts price signals to employees, and so contributes to acceptance of nonpayment by employees.

---

[10] Enterprise related social benefits add about 5 percent to total labor costs in general but the larger firms that are most likely to be in arrears provide most of this amount.

Political Outcomes of Labor-Market Adjustment

We now turn to the political payoffs of the path chosen. Does the adjustment through underemployment and nonpayment help with political management of workers' tolerance of reforms? Or does it amplify tensions? Of course, we cannot answer this question fully, because we can only speculate about consequences of a counterfactual situation of low wage arrears and high unemployment. Nevertheless, it is possible to examine more closely some relationships between labor-market indicators and such political outcomes as labor militancy and electoral support to reformers in office. I argue that although wage arrears might possibly have cushioned the system against the shocks of contraction and stabilization during the early stages of the transition, nonpayment later became likely to trigger a political backlash.

Existing literature on the political economy of reforms in other countries deals exclusively with unemployment in its open, explicit form. Rising unemployment is often considered an outcome that can topple the government and derail reforms.[11] Adam Przeworski links this argument to the post-Communist reality: "There are good reasons why unemployment should turn people against reforms. Whatever else one may think about the communist economy, it did provide full employment. Moreover, full employment was the principal mechanism of income insurance. Hence, when unemployment appeared and began to climb, people found themselves not only without jobs but also without incomes and other services that were traditionally provided by places of work.... Hence the prospects of unemployment are frightening" (Przeworski 1996: 535).

For these reasons, Przeworski argues, mounting unemployment led to a sharp drop in support for reform in Poland (1993: 166). Meanwhile the exceptionally low unemployment rate in the Czech Republic contributed to the country's political and social stability in the early stages of transition. It helped to stabilize the Klaus government and served as an important component in the political compromise with trade unions (Stark and Bruszt 1998: 205, 211).

In the Russian case, as I argued at the beginning of the chapter, both the government and public opinion considered underemployment a

---

[11] In the introduction to a special issue of *Comparative Political Studies* on patterns of economic voting in Poland, Peru, and Mexico, Susan Stokes wrote, "Rising unemployment generated pessimism about the future and opposition to the government and reforms in all three countries.... Apparently, unemployment is such a catastrophic event that when people think the probability of losing their job is high, they interpret this unambiguously as bad news and hold the government accountable" (Stokes 1996: 514).

lesser evil than open unemployment. The social and political gains from the Russian way were explicitly stressed by Russian sociologist Leonid Gordon, who believed that "Russian society has groped for – partially deliberately, partially spontaneously – a few rational methods, that come with short-time employment, involuntary unpaid leaves, and the like. Transition to unemployment goes gradually here through partial employment, which is clearly tolerated by society more easily than a onetime layoff of many millions of employees. Moreover, underemployment does not always end in unemployment" (Gordon 1997: 70). This view was shared by some Western observers: "Amidst all the gloom, this avoidance of mass unemployment in the face of enormous structural shocks might seem to be the great achievement of the Russian transition" (Clarke 1997a: 42).

One way to measure the political implications of this adjustment mode is to look at labor militancy. As pointed out earlier, despite a dramatic deterioration in living standards and employment conditions, it has generally remained rather low (outside the mining and education sectors, which are very militant). Would it be higher under the alternative solution of higher unemployment? On the other hand, the underemployment-underpayment model does redistribute losses from stronger (more competitive) to weaker (less competitive) workers, and so is likely to segment the labor force and weaken the employees' voice even more. Even so, it is not at all clear that labor protest would increase under alternative conditions of high unemployment, because "bargaining power and militancy decline in hard times and increase in prosperity" (Nelson 1995: 363).

Figure 1.4 provides a schematic illustration of how unemployment and wage arrears can affect the labor force. One may assume that the general distribution of workers according to their bargaining power in the Russian economy (let us call them "weak" versus "strong") is skewed toward those who are "weak." Those heavily affected by wage arrears are to the left of the line AB. This line is almost vertical, since it separates the weakest. The line CD slopes and cuts off those who are affected by unemployment. Because high unemployment comes with more active use of bankruptcies and layoffs, it affects relatively "stronger" workers as well. Its effect is less selective, which is reflected by the fact that CD crosses AB and slopes. So wage arrears involve larger numbers of workers but are more selective toward those who are "weaker." In the case of unemployment, fewer but "stronger" workers are affected.

Elimination of wage arrears turns into unemployment – it turns the AB line anticlockwise. The incidence of unemployment increases, although the number of those unemployed will still be lower than the

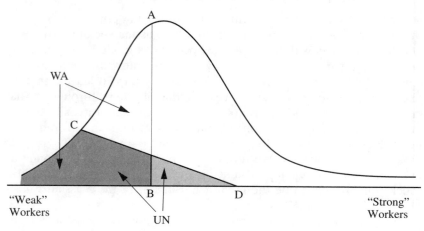

Figure 1.4. Effect of wage arrears versus unemployment on weaker and stronger workers.

number of workers owed back wages. The model thus suggests a political trade-off between two effects. Which is politically more manageable: to have fewer but stronger workers affected by unemployment, or to have more but weaker workers underpaid? To the extent that higher unemployment reduces the incidence of arrears across the Russian population, it is conceivable that it could actually boost political support for an incumbent government. Expanding arrears moves the AB line to the right, pulling in more stronger as well as weaker workers. This not only implies an increase in the potential for protest; it also substantially expands the size of the underpaid electorate.

Let us turn from this simplified picture to an examination of some electoral outcomes. During the transition period, Russian reforms have passed through a number of electoral tests. The most recent ones were the December 1995 parliamentary elections and the July 1996 presidential elections. By the end of 1995, underemployment and especially nonpayment of wages had emerged as hot public issues. Promises to pay the accumulated wage arrears became one of the cornerstones of Yeltsin's reelection campaign in 1996.

Some observers see the major factors that affected the electoral outcomes as located outside pure economics.[12] Wage levels, arrears, and

---

[12] Colton, in his study on economic voting in the 1995 parliamentary elections in Russia, concludes that "economic causes . . . merit a respectable but unsensational niche in our understanding of how Russian voters have behaved to date" (1996: 313–14). It is also argued that political values and preferences in Russia are quite strong and stable and have more influence on electoral outcomes than economic variables.

unemployment do matter, however, if only as second-order factors (Mau and Gasparyan 1997). Predictably, the likelihood of support for existing authority increases with higher wages and decreases with wage arrears. However, the impact of unemployment is surprising: the population in regions with higher unemployment is more likely to vote for the incumbent president. A study by Lissovolik and Nash (1996) shows similar results. Support for reformers is inversely related to wage arrears, but positively associated with both higher unemployment and average wage levels.

The elections to regional legislatures held in a number of regions in 1997 brought a clear victory to candidates associated with incumbent executives, enterprise managers, and businessmen, but not to the partisan politicians from left-wing parties. In a few regions where the left did win relative majorities the unemployment rates varied widely, and in some cases they were lower than the national average.

Thus the electoral evidence suggests that open unemployment has not been a major problem for winning or keeping office, while much more "electoral" tension has been brought about by wage debts. The incidence and duration of wage arrears are strongly and inversely correlated with voting for the incumbent president (Earle and Sabirianova 1999). In trying to cushion the negative political consequences of unemployment, the government may well have incurred political costs as high or even higher from wage arrears.

The positive association between unemployment and support for reformist incumbents does, however, pose a puzzle. If unemployment in Russia was and is considered by the population as the worst evil, as I argued earlier, then how can it be positively linked with support for incumbents? There are several possible ways to resolve this paradox.

First, as I have suggested, wage arrears (as an unemployment substitute) affect more people as voters than unemployment otherwise would. Second, low unemployment and high wage arrears indicate lack of economic restructuring. Restructuring, in turn, causes more unemployment, but expands the group of winners as well.

The distinction between winners and losers is more sophisticated than a sharp dichotomy between nouveau riches and the "new poor," which would include the unemployed. It is more useful to conceive of the distinction in terms of a continuum, in which the positions of relative "winners" and "losers" are dynamic and depend on many factors. Most of the people who experience unemployment are those with the least marketable skills. For them, losing a job does not come as a surprise; there is usually a prior history, a period of underemployment or underpayment, that conditions expectations about future prospects. In other words, this category of losers includes not only the unemployed but also "those who know that they cannot win" (Rychard 1996: 472).

Underemployed or underpaid workers with negative expectations are no less likely than the openly unemployed to have a negative perception of government policy, as various polls have documented. In such instances, a marginal increase in unemployment would do little to change either the proportion of voters who perceive themselves as losers or their attitude toward the government.

The situation is more complicated with the winners. If additional unemployment comes hand in hand with restructuring, the number of winners might be expected to expand. Potential winners are much less informed about their chances of actually becoming winners (Rychard 1996). Nevertheless, by divesting nonproductive or low-productive labor, firms may gain the breathing space to increase profitability and competitiveness. The pool of unemployed may in turn offer a relatively cheap source of labor and new opportunities for the creation of new jobs. All this brings more people into the group of winners or closer to it. The growing pool of those whom Rychard calls "winning losers" may thus eventually expand the proportion of "winning winners." Political attitudes under these circumstances may reflect Hirschman's (1981) famous "tunnel effect." The increasing number of actual and potential winners may offset the electoral opposition of the losers.

Conclusions

High unemployment is generally considered an almost inevitable consequence of the radical reform in the post-socialist economy. By introducing hard budget constraints through the enforcement of financial discipline and a tighter credit policy, the reforms speed up the exit of insolvent firms and the restructuring of those that remain in business. This creates labor redundancy and increases the potential for unemployment. With the "Great Contraction" of Russia's structurally obsolete economy, a scenario of very high unemployment seemed to be almost inevitable in the early stages of the transition.

Notwithstanding this plausible expectation, however, unemployment proved much lower than expected. Furthermore, it came after a significant delay and was accompanied by various forms of underemployment and underpayment. Nominal wages kept creeping up, and the inflation tax turned into nonpaid or delayed wages. This became a major adjustment instrument. Ultimately, wage arrears came to affect almost half the country's employees, and the social groups that bore the brunt of adjustment costs were the ones with the least marketable resources and weakest political voice.

Both political and economic factors were instrumental in producing this outcome. Political elites were afraid of causing high unemployment, which made them reluctant or unable to pursue structural reforms. The fiscal adjustment remained incomplete and fiscal discipline for enterprises was not applied, which in turn permitted unemployment to remain at relatively modest levels. Thus, although reliance on wage arrears allowed the government to move relatively successfully toward economic stabilization, it also reflected major delays in institutional and structural reforms.

Among the factors tending to push up nominal wages have been the country's political institutions, the political business cycle, and the design of federalism. Meanwhile, weak workers' voice, strong fear of unemployment, and a specific configuration of labor market and welfare institutions have allowed employers to discount inflated wage contracts.

The avoidance of high unemployment seems initially to have been the positive side of the arrears story. Arrears allowed political elites to cope with the "Great Contraction" and later to manage a tight monetary policy against a background of poor fiscal performance. This pattern resulted in relative political calm in 1995–97, with the most extreme forms of workers' dissatisfaction kept at bay.

The negative side of the policy has been that the postponement of institutional and structural reforms has increased pressures on public finances and on enterprise cash balances in the longer term. These pressures have contributed to a further deterioration in the fiscal performance of the economy. A new burst of wage arrears in the first half of 1998, as a result of an acute fiscal crisis, became a real threat to Russia's fragile political and social stability. It increased the militancy of the most cohesive segments of the labor force and intensified political pressure on the government. All this made its contribution to a full-blown financial and political crisis in August 1998, thus putting an end to more than two years of relative macroeconomic stability.

Might the crisis become a trigger for the long-awaited structural reforms? And if these reforms are implemented, will there still be room for "the Russian way of labor-market adjustment"? Answers to these questions are still to emerge.

References

Alfandari, Gilles, and Mark Schaffer. 1996. "Arrears" in the Russian Enterprise Sector. In S. Commander, Q. Fan, and M. Shaffer, eds., *Enterprise*

Restructuring and Economic Policy in Russia, pp. 87–139. Washington, D.C.: World Bank.

Blanchflower, David. 1991. Fear, Unemployment and Pay Flexibility. *Economic Journal* 101: 406–83.

Clarke, Simon. 1997a. Structural Adjustment without Mass Unemployment? Lessons from Russia. In S. Clarke, ed., *Structural Adjustment without Mass Unemployment? Lessons from Russia*, pp. 9–86. Cheltenham: Edward Elgar Publishing.

1997b. Trade Unions and the Non-Payment of Wages in Russia. University of Warwick. Mimeographed.

Colton, Tim. 1996. Economics and Voting in Russia. *Post-Soviet Affairs* 12: 289–317.

Connor, Walter. 1995. Labor in the New Russia: Four Years on. *Problems of Post-Communism*, no. 2, pp. 8–12.

Desai, Padma, and Todd Idson. 1998. *To Pay or Not to Pay: Managerial Decision Making and Wage Withholding in Russia*. Discussion Paper No. 9899-04. University of Columbia.

Earle, John, and Klara Sabirianova. 1999. Wage Arrears in Russia: An Exploration of Causes and Consequences. SITE, Stockholm. Mimeographed.

EBRD. 1998. *Transition Report 1998*. London: EBRD.

Freeman, Richard. 1994. What Direction for Labor Market Institutions in Eastern and Central Europe? In O. Blanchard, K. Froot, and J. Sachs, eds., *The Transition in Eastern Europe*, 2: 1–29. Chicago: University of Chicago Press.

Gaddy, Clifford, and Barry Ickes. 1998. Russia's Virtual Economy. *Foreign Affairs* 77: 53–67.

Gimpelson, Vladimir, and Douglas Lippoldt. 1996. *Labour Restructuring in Russian Enterprises: A Case Study*. Paris: OECD.

1997. Labour Turnover in the Russian Federation. In D. Lippoldt, ed., *Labour Market Dynamics in the Russian Federation*, pp. 17–55. Paris: OECD.

Gordon, Leonid. 1997. Polozheniye naemnykh rabotnikov v Rossii 90-kh godov (Workers in Russia in the 1990s). *Sotsialno-Trudovye Issledovaniya*, no. 7, pp. 1–99. Moscow: IMEMO.

Goskomstat of the RF (Central Statistical Office of the Russian Federation), Moscow. Various publications.

Granville, Brigitte, Judith Shapiro, and Oksana Dynnikova. 1997. Chem nizhe inflatciya, tem menshe bednost: pervye resultaty dlya Rossii (Lower inflation, less poverty: First results for Russia). In A. Aslund and M. Dmitriev, eds., *Sotsialnaya politika v period perekhoda k rynku; Problemy i resheniya*, pp. 63–88. Moscow: Moscow Carnegie Center, Carnegie Foundation for International Peace.

Hirschman, Alfred. 1970. *Exit, Voice and Loyalty*. Cambridge: Cambridge University Press.

1981. *Essays on Trespassing: Economics to Politics and Beyond*. Cambridge: Cambridge University Press.

Ickes, Barry, and Randy Ryterman. 1993. Roadblock to Economic Reform: Inter-Enterprise Debt and the Transition to Markets. *Post-Soviet Affairs* 9: 231–52.

Kornai, János. 1994. Transformational Recession: The Main Causes. *Journal of Comparative Economics* 19: 39–63.

——— 1995. *Highway and Byways: Studies on Reform and Postcommunist Transition.* Cambridge, Mass.: MIT Press.

Layard, Richard, and Andrea Richter. 1994. Labour Market Adjustment in Russia. *Russian Economic Trends* 3: 85–103.

Lehmann, Hartmut, Jonathan Wadsworth, and Alessandro Acquisti. 1998. Grime and Punishment: Employment, Wages and Wage Arrears in the Russian Federation. Paper prepared for the Conference on Labor Markets in Transition, University of Michigan, Ann Arbor, October 17–19.

Lissovolik, Yaroslav, and Roland Nash. 1996. Econometric Analysis of Electoral Data, 1995–96. *Russian Economic Trends* 5: 131–40.

Mau, Vladimir, and Michail Gasparyan. 1997. Ekonomika i vybory: opyt kolitchestvennogo analyza (Economics and elections: A quantitave analysis). *Voprosy Economiki*, no. 4, pp. 111–29.

Mikhalev, Vladimir, and Nils Bjorgsten. 1996. *Wage Formation during the Period of Economic Restructuring in the Russian Federation.* Paris: OECD.

Nelson, Joan M. 1995. Organized Labor, Politics, and Labor Market Flexibility in Developing Countries. In S. Horton, R. Kanbur, and D. Mazumbar, eds., *Labor Markets in an Era of Adjustment*, pp. 347–75. Washington, D.C.: World Bank.

OECD 1997. *OECD Economic Surveys: The Russian Federation.* Paris: OECD.

Przeworski, Adam. 1993. Economic Reforms, Public Opinion, and Political Institutions: Poland in Eastern European Perspective. In L. C. Bresser Perreira, J. M. Maravall, and A. Przeworski, eds., *Economic Reform in New Democracies: A Social-Democratic Approach*, pp. 132–98. Cambridge: Cambridge University Press.

——— 1996. Public Support for Economic Reforms in Poland. *Comparative Political Studies* 29: 520–43.

Russian Economic Trends. 1996. No. 2.

Russian Economic Trends. 1997. Nos. 1, 3.

Russian Economic Trends. Various issues, and monthly data from <http://www.hhs.se/site/ret/ret.htm>.

Rychard, Andrzey. 1996. Beyond Gains and Losses: In Search of "Winning Losers." *Social Research* 63: 465–86.

Standing, Guy. 1996. *Russian Unemployment and Enterprise Restructuring: Reviving Dead Souls.* ILO Study Series. Geneva: ILO.

Stark, David, and László Bruszt. 1998. *Postsocialist Pathways: Transforming Politics and Property in East Central Europe.* Cambridge: Cambridge University Press.

Stokes, Susan. 1996. Public Opinion and Market Reforms: The Limits of Economic Voting. *Comparative Political Studies* 29: 499–519.

Treisman, Daniel. 1998. Fighting Inflation in a Transitional Regime: Russia's Anomalous Stabilization. *World Politics* 50: 235–65.

VLADIMIR GIMPELSON

Treisman, Daniel, and Vladimir Gimpelson. 1999. *Political Business Cycles and Russian Elections, or the Manipulations of "Chudar."* Discussion Paper No. CIRJE-F-39. Faculty of Economics, University of Tokyo.
Vaughan-Whitehead, D., ed. 1998. *Paying the Price: The Wage Crisis in Central and Eastern Europe.* London: Macmillan.
VCIOM. *Economic and Social Change: Public Opinion Monitoring. Bulletin of Information*, Moscow. Various issues.

52

CHAPTER 2

Creating Effective Tax Administrations: The Experience of Russia and Georgia

VITO TANZI

During the central-planning period much of the economy was public and the private sector played a very marginal role. The role of the state was all-pervasive. To a large extent the government determined the wages and other incomes (including pensions) of individuals; the allocation of resources to various functions and activities; the investment-consumption breakdown; the allocation of jobs; and the relative prices and availability of products. The plan was the essential tool that the government used to carry out its economic decisions. Through planning decisions, the government could directly appropriate resources and use them in the ways it deemed desirable. It was difficult and unnecessary to separate an area that could properly be called *public* finance from *private* finance.

The transition to a market economy aims at replacing much public ownership with private ownership and many public decisions with private decisions.[1] It thus aims at reducing the role of the state in the economy and at changing the way that role is played. In the new environment, the state must get the resources that it needs by taxing individuals and private-sector activities and, to a much lesser extent, by borrowing; and it must play its role by spending those resources in the most efficient way.

In the preparation of this chapter, I received valuable support from Katherine Baer, John Crotty, and Allen Firestone. I am also grateful to Professors Stephan Haggard, Robert Kaufman, and János Kornai for their comments and to the participants at the March 27–28 seminar including George Kopits, who served as the formal discussant.
[1] The shift from a public-sector-dominated economy to a private-sector-dominated one in transition economies is shown in Table A.5 in the appendix. The table also gives a picture of how different the process of the private sector's increase was in the different transition economies. In 1995, however, the private sector in nearly all of the selected countries had a more than 50 percent contribution to the GDP.

To operate efficiently in market economies, governments need the support of various institutions as well as the implicit support of the taxpayers. Some of these institutions did not exist in centrally planned economies because they were not needed. Some existed, but only in a rudimentary or primitive form. At the beginning of the transition, some observers (see Fischer and Gelb 1991; Tanzi 1991) noted that the creation of these institutions would require a long time and that the process of transition would not be complete until these institutions were in existence. For example, Tanzi (1991) forecast that the creation of essential *fiscal* institutions might take at least ten years.

This forecast was not too pessimistic. Although ten years has almost elapsed, the creation of essential fiscal institutions is far from complete, and so far progress has been very uneven – with some countries, especially those closer to Europe, having progressed much further than the countries that originated from the breakup of the Soviet Union. Also, within the latter group some countries have progressed further than others.

We focus here on one important fiscal institution without which the pursuit of an efficient fiscal policy is not possible in market economies: the tax administration. We discuss in particular the experience of Russia and Georgia; in Russia progress had been relatively slow, whereas in Georgia it had been more rapid.[2]

The Importance of the Tax Administration

The disbanding of the planning mechanism and the removal of constraints to private-sector activities made it very difficult for the postsocialist countries to continue generating public revenues (Tanzi 1993). These difficulties stemmed from the fact that the transition to a market economy

1. Removed the controls that had existed, through plan directives, on the quantities produced and on the prices at which commodities were sold, thus reducing the information available to the government;
2. Sharply increased the number of producers in the economy through the creation of small private enterprises and other private-sector activities and through the breakup of state enterprises;
3. Removed the existing restrictions on the methods of payments

[2] Our discussion is based on developments up to the end of 1997.

within the economy by allowing enterprises to make payments in cash and to hold multiple bank accounts, rather than using just one account held with the monobank, making and receiving all payments through it as had been the case during central planning;

4. Eliminated the role of the monobank in collecting much public revenue, a role that was performed by simply debiting the accounts of the enterprises and crediting the account of the government with the monobank; and

5. Stimulated the growth of the most difficult-to-tax activities such as services, small enterprises, and independent contractors. These activities have led to booming unofficial economies, which are difficult to tax (Shleifer 1996; Kaufmann 1996; Johnson, Kaufmann, and Shleifer 1997).

In this situation, the fastest transforming economies in transition experienced a rapid fall in tax revenue, a fall that proceeded at a faster pace than government spending could be reduced (Tanzi 1991; Barbone and Polarkova 1996). The experience of the majority of the transition countries shows in fact that the share of tax revenue in GDP has been falling significantly (Cheasty and Davis 1996). In some of these countries the fall has been quite significant, creating serious macroeconomic difficulties. As one would expect, it is the taxes on the profits of enterprises that have fallen most rapidly. For example, in Russia they fell from about 9 percent of GDP in 1993 to less than 3 percent in 1997. In Ukraine the fall was from 11 to 5 percent of GDP.

In most of the transition economies there has been a lot of activism in creating or transforming the *statutory* tax systems. By now most of these countries have introduced a value-added tax, reformed the tax on enterprise profits, reduced taxes on imports and largely eliminated taxes on exports (Tanzi, Cheasty, and Kostial 1999), introduced personal income taxes, and enacted other significant tax policy changes. In general, the reform of the statutory tax system has advanced quite far, although the results so far are still not what one would wish to have.[3] Although in a broad and superficial sense, most transition countries now have tax systems that are characteristic of market economies, a closer look makes one realize that many changes in the structure of these taxes still need to be made. Furthermore, the codification of the tax laws and regulations is still an area where more progress is needed. Many of these countries, including Russia, have not been able to codify all their tax laws so as to make them more transparent and accessible to taxpayers.

---

[3] Hungary was the first of these countries to introduce a Western-style tax system.

Of course, tax laws can be largely taken as statements of intentions. In theory a country could change its tax laws by simply copying those of other countries or by asking foreign experts to write the country's new tax legislation. To some extent this is what has happened. There are no copyrights for tax laws. In practice, of course, the process is more complex because various vested interests and pressure groups lobby for changes that are advantageous to them, which results in a statutory tax system that is much in need of reform and improvement. This problem is not limited to transition economies but is particularly serious in countries where parliament and even the policy makers in the executive branch have been quite responsive to pressures coming from specific groups and where policy makers still reject the view that in a market economy most economic decisions must be made by the market.

Even when the statutory tax system is not too dysfunctional, it is of course up to the tax administration to render effective the policy intentions expressed in the legal documents represented by the tax laws. A poorly functioning tax administration can change the best-designed statutory tax system into a poor, ineffective one. When the tax system is not well designed to start with, the tax administration needs to be exceptionally good to cope with it. In many transition economies the interplay of poorly designed tax systems with primitive and inefficient tax administrations has produced results that are damaging to the development of a market economy. A booming underground or unofficial economy, for example, can be partly attributed to the high rates of the statutory tax system and partly to weak enforcement programs. Tax administration is thus clearly one of the essential fiscal institutions.

Some problems connected with the tax systems and the tax administrations of transition economies have been the direct result of political pressures and interference. In market economies, the tax system should be as neutral as possible, minimizing its interference with the decisions of private-sector agents. When the system is not neutral, the lack of neutrality should promote well-defined and desirable objectives, such as higher saving or an intentional reallocation of consumption or investment. Neutrality is generally encouraged through the use of broad tax bases and a limited number of relatively low rates. When the bases are narrow and the rates are high and multiple, the objective of neutrality is defeated. Neutrality is also defeated when tax expenditures and tax incentives are widespread.

In many of the economies in transition, a social-engineering mentality inherited from the past by many policy makers, combined with strong pressures from politically powerful groups for preferential treatment, has generated "Swiss cheese" tax systems, full of holes. Tax systems with these characteristics tend to be inefficient, hard to administer, inequitable, and often unproductive in terms of revenue. Furthermore, these characteristics make the tax system an object of continuous political debate because each pressure group wishes to improve its tax treatment. Of course, the tax systems of industrial countries are not immune from this problem, but in economies in transition the use of special treatment of taxpayers is far more extreme.

Pressures for special tax treatment of particular activities or groups may originate from different sources: some originate in Parliament and reflect the views of legislators that some activities or incomes deserve favorable treatment.[4] These politicians are simply not prepared to trust, or accept, the judgment of the market. Other pressures come from particular vested interests. These pressures may explain why agricultural incomes have been generally exempt from taxation or why the incomes of writers and other professional groups have been favorably treated. Sometimes demands originate from powerful, individual taxpayers for "customized tax incentives."

Pressures for preferential treatment directed to Parliament may result in changes in the legislation and in particular tax laws; those directed to the executive branch may result in special decrees that favor selected individuals or enterprises (Martinez-Vasquez and McNab 1997: 40). Such tax relief by decree is a characteristic of economies in transition and has generated major problems in some countries, such as Russia; it is relatively rare in traditional market economies. Pressures may also originate from local governments, especially in countries such as Russia and Ukraine where local governments are important. The pressures may also be directed to the tax administration itself and result in different interpretations of the laws or, more often, in lesser enforcement of particular laws for some taxpayers. These de facto tax incentives, which have no counterpart in the law, may have a significant impact. In particular cases policy makers may pressure the tax administration to go slow or go soft on some taxpayers.

Social or economic considerations, particularly the fear of unemployment, have resulted in preferential treatment of state enterprises, especially those which, because of their size, are important in providing employment and social services in some towns or regions. Because whole towns may depend on one enterprise, lenient taxation becomes an important form of subsidy to the enterprise and ultimately a way of keeping

---

[4] Members of parliament, first, reflect particular interests, as they are elected by particular groups of voters; and, second, many of them lack the relevant technical training in economic matters necessary to make good decisions.

employment high. Pressures have also resulted in the provision of tax incentives to foreign investors who may be fronts for nationals who export capital and repatriate it as foreign investment, thus benefiting from incentives. The fear that a foreign investor will go to a country more willing to provide tax benefits has been a stimulus to this special treatment.

A particularly damaging type of tax incentive has come in the form of tax arrears (see Gimpelson, Chapter 1, in this volume): enterprises simply do not pay taxes when due and, in periods of inflation, benefit from the erosion of the value of the liability due to the delay in payment. These enterprises may at the same time build arrears vis-à-vis their suppliers and workers. By not paying taxes, suppliers, and workers on time, an unprofitable enterprise can remain in operation, thus keeping unemployment down. At times, enterprises use tax arrears as a political instrument to force the government or the tax administration to grant them tax relief. Tax arrears have been and continue to be a major problem in Russia where, by the end of 1997, their accumulated total amounted to almost 6 percent of 1997 GDP, generating substantial revenue losses and thus contributing to higher fiscal deficits and continuing macroeconomic difficulties (see Gimpelson, Chapter 1).

Modern market economies that assign an important spending role to the public sector require high levels of taxation. For example, in industrial countries the share of taxes to GDP is around 40 percent or even higher. Such high tax levels can be achieved only if three conditions are present. First, taxpayers must be able to connect the benefits that they derive from public spending (free education, cultural activities, health care, roads, pensions) to the taxes they pay;[5] the more the taxpayers make this link, the greater will be their willingness to pay taxes. Second, the tax burden must be spread equitably among the population. Third, an effective tax administration must be created.

Meeting the first condition depends on the history of the country, the political process, the role of government, and the efficiency of public spending. History is very important. In countries where the government had traditionally been seen as alien and/or oppressive, taxpayers feel less enthusiastic to contribute spontaneously to the public coffers. In these countries it could take a long time before taxpayers saw the government in power as an embodiment of their collective interest.

The political process is also very important. Under a democratically elected government seen as pursuing the *public* interest rather than the

---

[5] Other aspects of the producers' and consumers' choice between illegality (tax avoidance, gray economy, etc.) and legality include protection against criminals, quick and efficient contract enforcement by the courts, and customer protection against cheating.

interest of special groups or regions, taxpayers feel more disposed toward paying taxes because they can make a connection between what they pay in taxes and what they derive in benefits.

The role of government and the efficiency of public spending are also relevant factors. The current role of the government is much influenced by policies or commitments undertaken by previous governments. When major political changes occur, the gap between what a government wants to do and what it is forced to do by these past commitments may become particularly large. This gap may then influence taxpayers' willingness to pay taxes.

In economies in transition this problem is aggravated by the fact that during the days of central planning taxes were largely hidden so that most taxpayers were not aware that, implicitly, they were paying high taxes. The average taxpayer never encountered a tax official. As János Kornai points out in this volume (Chapter 6), there was little awareness among the population of the burden of taxation. At that time the state was seen as a free good or, at least, costless. In the transition period, when the hidden taxes become explicit, taxpayers may find it difficult to understand the need for taxes. Their resistance to paying taxes becomes greater when public spending is seen as inefficient or when it is seen as benefiting particular groups rather than the general population.

The second condition required to achieve high tax levels is the perception that taxes are collected efficiently and equitably. If taxpayers come to believe that, because of widespread tax evasion or tax preferences provided to privileged groups, their payment is unfair, they will tend to evade taxes. The more the tax system is perceived to be unfair, and the less efficient the tax administration, the greater will be the government's difficulty in collecting taxes. Even when only one of these two aspects is lacking, however, the government may run into difficulties. An inefficient tax administration sends to the taxpayers the signal that evading taxes is an activity without serious consequences. Even when the tax administration is efficient, an unfair tax system encourages taxpayers to look for activities, including going underground, that allow some tax evasion.[6]

Because the tax systems in most of the economies in transition have been considered unfair, tax administrations have had a difficult time in establishing themselves as effective institutions and raising tax revenue. Thus, in most transition economies the ratio of tax revenue to GDP has

---

[6] In order to illustrate the propensity toward tax evasion Table A.6 in the appendix gives data about the share of the unofficial economy in selected transition countries.

fallen significantly. The two countries to be discussed here – Russia and Georgia – have shared this fate.

Creating Effective Tax Administrations

The Russian Experience

Creating a modern, effective tax administration and increasing taxpayer compliance have proven to be difficult tasks for Russia. Since its establishment in 1990, the Russian State Tax Service (STS) has faced obstacles in nearly all major areas: in defining its institutional role; in reforming and applying the tax laws; in obtaining the necessary budget resources and professional staff; and in controlling unethical practices within and outside of the tax administration. Despite some efforts to improve the effectiveness of tax administration, a fair assessment is that progress has been slow.[7]

Before the establishment of the STS the "tax administration" function had been very different and highly decentralized. Regional and local offices were supervised by their respective ministries of finance and by finance officers of the Republican Ministry of Finance. These offices did not formally "administer" taxes; rather, they controlled profit transfers from the enterprises to the accounts of the government and monitored the economic and financial performance of state enterprises, which were the major sources of revenue for the local, regional, and republican governments. Thus, what existed was really not a tax administration in the sense that the term is understood in market economies, and the skills of those who controlled these activities were very different from those required of officials in modern tax administrations.

In the early part of 1991, the government began implementing a new economic strategy, which required relying on genuine tax revenue for its financing. As a consequence, the tax system started being reformed and the STS was created within the Ministry of Finance. Later in 1991, the STS was separated from the Ministry of Finance and became an autonomous agency with ministerial rank. Much of the staff in the new agency was the same that had operated in the previous system. Since 1991, the STS has been responsible for administering all taxes (except those on foreign trade), including those imposed by the regional and local governments. Tax policy remains the responsibility of the Ministry of Finance.

---

[7] Examples of some of these efforts are the amendments to the value-added tax (VAT) law and selected improvements in VAT administration.

Four major obstacles have prevented the STS from becoming an effective institution: the unclear definition of its institutional role, the dispersal of responsibilities for some aspects of the tax administration among many government agencies, the lack of personnel with the necessary skills, and the lack of resources.

The problem of unclear assignment of property rights, so common in other areas of the Russian economy, has also affected the tax administration. In Russia, as in many other transition countries, the administration of taxes is linked to broader issues of economic transformation and corporate restructuring. In many cases, a company's failure to pay taxes due reflects serious financial problems that are closely linked to incomplete transformation. They reflect the inability of the enterprise to change its production toward products that the market wants and to produce them at competitive prices. Furthermore, the enterprise may still be responsible for social expenditures that should fall on the government. An enterprise's inability to pay taxes may also be the result of its inability to collect money due from other enterprises or even from the public sector itself.

In the existing system, tax administration has been used as a crude instrument for restructuring the economy and at times for sustaining employment. In fact, although the STS should allocate its maximum effort on registering, auditing, and enforcing collection from new enterprises and from all taxpayers with potentially positive tax liabilities, it has been required to administer to corporate taxpayers who are financially nonviable and unable to meet their tax obligations. As a consequence, the STS has become closely involved in corporate bankruptcy and financial restructuring cases. In addition to being administratively complex and resource intensive, these cases distract the STS away from its work of enforcing tax collection from financially viable enterprises and from bringing the growing number of new potential taxpayers into the tax net. It also draws the organization into politically sensitive areas, which tends to contaminate its basic functions.

The overlapping institutional responsibility for tax administration has also been a major obstacle to improving the effectiveness of the STS. In well-functioning market economies, the tax administration is the sole institution responsible for imposing taxes and for dealing with taxpayers. In Russia this is not so. For example, in dealing with tax arrears, a number of special commissions have been established *outside* the tax administration to handle different aspects of collection enforcement. These commissions were made up of high-level policy makers. This approach has undermined the STS's authority to enforce the tax laws, complicated tax administration procedures, defused accountability within the public sector for collection enforcement, and perpetuated the view that taxes are not rigid obligations but "soft" obligations subject to negotiation. More dangerously for a tax administration that should remain independent of politics, the approach has resulted in the involvement of officials at the highest levels of government, including, at times, the prime minister, in the resolution of individual tax cases. This contrasts sharply with the situation in market economies where tax administrations have much greater autonomy and where government officials usually do not get involved in their day-to-day operations.

In October 1996 the level of tax arrears reached about 5 percent of GDP.[8] At that time, the Emergency Tax Commission (VChK) was established by the president to resolve the largest federal tax arrears cases. Some twenty enterprises in the gas, oil, energy, metal production, transport, and manufacturing industries were selected for special attention because of their large size and large tax debts, which amounted to about 4 percent of GDP. The mandate of the commission was to negotiate settlement arrangements for the taxes due between senior government officials and representatives of the enterprises. The commission was chaired by the prime minister, and its work was supported by the STS, the State Tax Police, the Ministry of Finance, and the Bankruptcy Commission (the Mostovoi Commission).

The respective role of each agency in the enforcement process was as follows. The STS prepared detailed information on the tax liabilities of large tax debtors and on their financial situation. Once completed this documentation was transmitted to the Bankruptcy Commission, which reviewed the cases and evaluated whether there were grounds for restructuring the arrears or for starting bankruptcy proceedings. It might decide that a case warranted a higher level review before either restructuring or bankruptcy proceedings could be started. Then the case was referred to the Commission on Operational Questions (KoV), or, for more sensitive political cases, to the Emergency Tax Commission.

KoV was a high-level commission established directly under the Emergency Tax Commission. It was initially chaired by Anatoly Chubais, then deputy prime minister and former minister of finance. It was made up of the directors of major government agencies, including the STS. Its main role regarding tax arrears was to approve *voluntary* proposals by large enterprises for the restructuring of their tax debts. In other cases, the decision was to be made by the Emergency Tax Commission.

---

[8] This figure is the ratio of the stock of tax arrears accumulated through October 1996 to 1996 GDP.

The effectiveness of the two high-level commissions in collecting tax arrears and making decisions regarding delinquent taxpayers was marginal at best. Although the liabilities of some large debtors were settled, the stock of tax arrears continued to grow in 1997 and the number of enterprises with large tax debts grew from 1,120 in 1996 to 3,375 at the end of 1997. As of the end of 1997, bankruptcy proceedings, following review either by the VChK or the KoV, had been initiated *only against one enterprise*. The positive impact on tax compliance, especially for the largest taxpayers, seems to have been insignificant. On the other hand, because the failure to force payments by some enterprises was widely reported in the media, this information gave other companies the impression that not paying taxes was not a serious offense. For large enterprises it appeared that taxes were not a fact of life but obligations that could be negotiated and reduced.

Of course, the incomplete process of transformation has made an arm's-length approach to tax administration difficult to apply. Many of the large debtor enterprises either cannot or will not settle their tax liabilities because they are owed money by entities funded by the budget or because their major debtors are owed money by such entities. Furthermore, many of the large debtor enterprises enjoy a monopoly or quasi-monopoly position in the provision of goods and services or a monopsonist's position in employment in some areas. Thus, they may be too large to go bankrupt. This implies that enterprises do not take seriously their budget constraints. This "soft budget constraint syndrome" undermines the economic relationship that would prevail in a truly market-oriented economy (see Kornai 1995: chap. 6.)

It is debatable whether the most senior policy makers should be personally and almost routinely involved in resolving the tax debts of large taxpayers. They are likely to receive daily visits from the managers of the large enterprises and be pressed to be lenient with tax arrears. Their involvement inevitably creates risks of conflicting interests or political interference in the administration of cases that in market economies are handled by professional administrators who follow arm's-length principles and act according to well-defined rules and procedures. This political involvement perpetuates the notion that taxes remain "soft," to use Kornai's expression, and have not yet become parametric.[9] In late 1997, a step in the right direction was taken to revise tax legislation that grants the STS the authority to settle arrears cases for medium-sized enterprises.

Compounding the problems resulting from political interference in tax administration is the tax-related activity of criminal groups. Concrete

[9] For the concept of soft taxes, see Kornai 1992: 142.

evidence quantifying the extent of criminal interference in the assessment and collection of taxes is not available. However, many government officials and private businessmen have commented that the "protection payment" that organized crime groups often demand from small and medium-sized businesses to allow them to conduct their operations is equivalent to a tax. These protection rackets undermine businesses' willingness to take their tax obligations seriously and make the work of the tax administration difficult and even dangerous.

The absence of a clear specification of the tax administration's licenses and some other inadequacies have affected such basic functions as *auditing* and *enforcement*.

One of the major hindrances to the effective auditing of taxpayers is that auditors are often uncertain about their authority to demand specific records or pursue issues concerning specific sources of income. Taxpayers frequently exploit this uncertainty by denying inspectors access to all books of accounts or by promising to provide records at some later date without actually intending to do so.

The absence of legal clarity is most evident with respect to the sources of income. Tax inspectors, tax police, and managers at regional and local tax offices appear to be uncertain about their authority in these matters. Many of these officials believe that their rights to question taxpayers concerning matters relating to their source of income or financing are not clearly defined in the Law of Basic Principles of the Tax System. There are also questions regarding the STS's right to ask owners of companies about their personal asset holdings. As a result, STS's auditors tend to avoid questioning taxpayers about their incomes and asset holdings, even in cases where their businesses consistently report losses while the owners enjoy a comfortable or even a high standard of living. Audits tend to be conducted in a perfunctory manner, tax evasion is not reduced, and prospects for improvement in voluntary compliance remain dim. Under these circumstances, tax inspectors become less resistant to bribery, and corruption has been reported to be a major problem.

Regulations and procedures enabling the STS to enforce collection are also weak. In 1996 officials informally estimated that they would be able to recover less than one-tenth of the total tax arrears for the whole year. The reasons included legal obstacles in obtaining access to taxpayers' loan accounts, in which taxpayers often deposit funds to avoid tax payments; delays by the banks in processing collection orders issued by the STS; difficulties in liquidating nonfinancial assets seized as a result of nonpayment; and lack of coordination between the STS and the Tax Police in collection enforcement.

Quite apart from the political obstacles and the diffused mandate, modernizing the tax administration is very difficult because it requires challenging and replacing well-established practices and considerable financial resources. New personnel with dynamic and open-minded approaches and with new skills is required. These people must have the power and means to implement changes. The management of the STS has not exhibited these characteristics and has not shown much enthusiasm in changing or challenging existing rules, procedures, and laws. It has largely been made up of old-timers who have managed as in the pretransition era.

One example of this is in the area of taxpayer services. Few tax administrators, from senior STS managers to the tax officials who come into contact with the taxpayer, have recognized the importance of services in fostering voluntary compliance. There is a need for taxpayer education, through the supply of explanatory materials in the form of brochures, guides, and easy-to-use forms. Basic taxpayer assistance facilities are mostly lacking. A major change in the attitude of tax officials is required to make them become aware that collecting taxes also entails providing a service to the taxpayers.

The staff of the STS has grown considerably since it was established, from 60,000 nationwide to about 180,000 in 1997. In comparison with the personnel of the tax administrations of industrial countries, and given the size of Russia, the present staffing level is not particularly high. In spite of the increase in staff, the level of taxation has declined significantly. Since 1992, the share of total government revenue from taxation has fallen by about 18 percentage points, from 42 percent of GDP in 1992 to 24 percent in 1997.

There are several reasons for the decline in revenue, including the dramatic structural changes in the economy. However, the difficulties in the tax administration must have played a significant role. Many of the institution's tasks could be performed at considerably lower costs or eliminated.[10] In addition, the staff is highly decentralized across 89 regions and nearly 3,000 local offices. Of the staff of 180,000, only about 600 officials work at the headquarters in Moscow.

Local officials often face problems of allegiance between serving local and national objectives and usually pay more attention to taxes that go mostly to local governments. The dual subordination of tax offices to the national and the subnational governments reduces the control of the national tax administration over the tax administration staff. Martinez-Vazquez and McNab (1997) report that subnational authorities have the

---

[10] Procedures carried from the past still absorb much of the staff's time.

right to approve key appointments in territorial offices of the STS. Obviously, the appointees are expected to reciprocate the favor in some way.

Such a highly decentralized structure makes it difficult to introduce changes across the organization, and it is almost impossible to supervise operations and to ensure that officials are fully accountable for implementing tax administration laws and procedure for all taxes. There is, de facto, no clear line of authority between the deputy directors of the STS and the directors of the eighty-nine regional tax offices, and none of the national deputy directors is directly responsible for supervising the regions' operational activities. This responsibility is assigned to the director of the STS, who is already overwhelmed by many other duties.

In 1997, when new management was installed at STS, general budgetary difficulties increased, thus limiting the STS's ability to make changes in its organization and operations that required financial resources. During 1997 the STS faced serious difficulties in meeting its current operating costs. This situation made it more difficult to attract and retain highly qualified staff. Also, wage compression within the STS and the widening gap in salaries between the private and the public sector have led to an exodus of some of the most able individuals, who in some cases can earn ten times as much in the private sector.[11] The budgetary difficulties have also made it more difficult to finance necessary expenditures, such as auditors' travel.

Given the tight budgetary situation in Russia, a more efficient tax administration can only come from a major restructuring and reorganization of the STS. Such reorganization should aim at shifting resources from areas and tasks in which their productivity is low to areas where their productivity could be much higher. Such a reallocation of resources, however, requires major legal, administrative, and organizational changes, which would certainly run against strong vested interests. Only a major internal reorganization will transform the STS into a modern, professional revenue service capable of attracting and retaining high-caliber individuals and competently and efficiently administering the Russian tax system in a progressively more market-oriented economy.

A key aspect of the reorganization must be a review to evaluate whether the STS needs to have 2,800 offices and to identify the regions of the country that could generate the highest revenue. The results of such a review would most likely lead to the need to merge small tax offices that serve only a small number of taxpayers with those in

---

[11] During 1997, 10,000 inspectors are reported to have left the STS.

adjacent regions.[12] That would also increase the role of regional offices, especially in serving large taxpayers. Another aspect would be an evaluation of the staff of the STS to see whether it reflects the needs (legal, accounting, computational, and managerial) of a modern tax administration. It may require both layoffs and changes in the wage structure of the STS to be able to attract the required personnel. For political reasons, little willingness has been shown to carry out such drastic changes.

These political obstacles take various forms. First, regional and local powers are likely to oppose changes that reduce their influence on administrative decisions. Second, the Duma and the executive branch do not cherish the idea of firing many of the current employees of the STS. Third, the largest and most influential taxpayers, including large public conglomerates such as Gazprom, will continue to campaign to have access to the most senior government officials, thus bypassing the STS in order to settle, politically and to their advantage, their tax liabilities. At the regional level, the most influential taxpayers will continue to pursue the highest regional authorities to lobby senior government officials for a more lenient application of the tax and bankruptcy laws. If these political obstacles prove to be impossible to remove, the tax administration will continue to have limited authority, the customized application of the tax laws will continue, and the taxes will remain "soft," especially for large and politically powerful companies.[13]

The Georgian Experience

In April 1991, when Georgia declared its independence, creating a modern, effective tax administration was an even more challenging task than in Russia. At the time the State Tax Inspectorate, which in mid-1997 was renamed the Tax Inspectorate of Georgia (TIG), faced a task of Herculean proportions: the Soviet-era tax laws had to be reformed, budgetary resources had to be secured, the necessary personnel had to be hired, corruption had to be controlled, and the State Tax Inspectorate had to be drastically reorganized.

---

[12] Especially in small offices, contiguity between tax inspectors and taxpayers is likely to encourage corruption. However, this may be a problem everywhere because taxpayers are all assigned to permanent inspectors, who are rarely (or maybe never) rotated.

[13] A widely publicized example of the customized approach to taxation and tax administration is the Kamaz truck company located in the region of Tartarstan. The company, which has been an important source of regional employment, was placed in 1997 on the list of public companies considered eligible to be declared bankrupt by the Mostovoi Commission. After a personal appeal to the president of Russia by the president of Tartarstan, the decision was reversed and the company continued in operation.

As if this were not a sufficient challenge, soon after independence Georgia became embroiled for more than two years in political and civil strife, centered on the breakaway region of Abkhazia. Furthermore, the disruption of the traditional payments system and trade links with the rest of the former Soviet Union (FSV) contributed to the devastation of the economy. Georgia suffered from the sharpest economic decline among the FSU countries.[14] Between 1990 and 1994 the total contraction in the GDP reached the extraordinary level of 82.1 percent, which was much more than in any of the twenty countries reported in Mundell (1997: 74). During the 1990–93 period, Georgia's trade with other FSU countries fell by 89.2 percent (Mundell 1997: 87), while the general government revenue, as a share of GDP, fell from 33.8 percent in 1991 to only 2.3 percent in 1993; tax revenues almost disappeared. This decline, again, was the biggest among the FSU countries (Cheasty and Davis 1996: 9). The record fall in revenue resulted in very large budget deficits,[15] which were financed by monetary expansion, thus leading to a period of hyperinflation[16] and a sharp depreciation in the exchange rate.

Following the ceasefire in Abkhazia, the political and economic situation started to improve in 1994: a stabilization program with the International Monetary Fund (IMF) was implemented, a new currency was introduced, and a new constitution that gave the president strong executive powers was approved by Parliament in July 1995. In November 1995 Shevarnadze was elected president with an overwhelming majority. These political developments were very important from the point of view of reforming the country's tax administration.

The years 1996 and 1997 witnessed a dramatic change in the economic situation, and Georgia made substantial progress in the establishment of fiscal institutions. Both in the tax administration and in the public-expenditure management system, considerable progress has been made. This progress probably exceeded that of all FSU countries with the exception of the Baltic countries. The share of tax revenue to GDP rose from 2–3 percent in 1993 to about 10 percent in 1997 and after stabilizing the economy started growing at a very fast pace.

---

[14] Table A.1 in the appendix shows that Georgia suffered the greatest real GDP decline among the transition economies: even after three years of positive real GDP growth rates in 1995–97, the estimated level of real GDP in 1997 reached only a third of the 1989 level.

[15] Table A.3 in the appendix shows that due to the sharp decline in its government revenues in 1992–93 Georgia had one of the largest budget deficits among countries in the Commonwealth of Independent States (CIS).

[16] Inflation data in Table A.2 in the appendix give evidence of monetary expansion leading to hyperinflation. In 1993 the inflation rate in Georgia reached its highest level (7,487.9 percent) and remained extremely high until changes in the economic policy were introduced in 1995.

Compared with the situation in Russia, the budgetary and technical obstacles faced by Georgia in reforming its fiscal institutions were daunting. Budgetary allocations to the TIG were grossly inadequate to provide the facilities needed to support its work. No funds were allocated for the rental of office space and the purchase of supplies and equipment. The TIG had traditionally depended on municipal authorities to provide office space from their stock of housing, while funds for the purchase of supplies and equipment had come from the offices' portion of the incentive pay collected. This situation continues to date. In early 1995, under a structural adjustment credit, the World Bank provided funds for the purchase of computers and other equipment. These funds enabled the TIG to begin the computerization process with IMF assistance, starting with two local offices and the newly created Large Taxpayer Inspectorate (LTI).

Political obstacles have also surfaced in Georgia. First, in the 1993–95 period the criminal activities of a group called the Mkhedrioni siphoned off tax revenue that could have gone into the budget. This group seemed to enjoy a high level of political protection and actually had members assigned to major business enterprises to monitor operations and collect large protection fees, which were, in effect, a form of unofficial direct taxation. In 1993–94 the Mkhedrioni had become a monopoly for the importation and sale of petroleum, thus depriving the budget of important tax revenues.

Second, because local (municipal) authorities continued to allocate office space and provide utilities and other services, they sought a voice in the selection of heads of Regional Tax Inspectorates (RTIs) and in setting their work priorities, which resulted in the RTIs expending resources on enforcing the collection of low-yield local taxes and fees rather than on high-yield national taxes. Also, as a result of a new constitutional structure, since January 1997 the regional governors began to interfere with the day-to-day operations of the TIG officers in the region.

Third, the Tax Inspectorate of Georgia, the Chamber of Control, the police, and the public prosecutors have all claimed to have the authority to investigate the tax affairs of taxpayers. In late 1996 a presidential decree solved this problem by assigning to the TIG the exclusive right to investigate and control all matters related to taxation.

In spite of these obstacles, between 1994 and 1997 much technical progress was made, some with assistance from the IMF. Important steps included the registration of taxpayers, the issuance of taxpayer identification numbers, the organization of selected (pilot) offices for computerization, a comprehensive survey of taxpayers to identify those who had not filed a tax return in order to bring them into the tax net, and changes in the organizational structure of the TIG with a gradual move to a functional structure. After the November 1995 election, the government began to disarm the independent militia groups and to push harder for tax administration reforms in order to improve compliance and to reduce competition.

An important step was the creation of the LTI to focus on the large taxpayers, firms that account for the lion's share of total tax revenue. The LTI began with about 140 taxpayers under its control and expanded its activity to cover over 250 of the largest taxpayers in Georgia. The establishment of the LTI was strongly opposed by the regional governors, by the mayor of Tbilisi, and by the Tbilisi Central Office. This opposition was conveyed to President Shevarnadze but did not prevent the creation of an office that has proved very effective in many other countries.

Another important step was the adoption of a structure that organizes the activities of the tax administration along such major *functions* as filing and payment, collection enforcement, auditing, appeals, and taxpayer assistance. The new organizational structure reduced the power of regional and local offices and facilitated the introduction of other changes in the tax administration. Some offices were consolidated to reduce costs and to increase controls and efficiency.

Another important change was the development of a new tax code, passed by Parliament and signed into law by President Shevarnadze on July 6, 1997. The code included major changes in the value-added tax and in the corporate and personal income taxes. With the passing of the code, the TIG could begin computer processing of returns. The new tax code represents a major improvement in the transparency of the tax legislation of Georgia by consolidating and codifying in one document a variety of laws, directives, and decrees. Still, because of political opposition, some aspects of the proposed code (especially those related to the enforcement of compliance with the tax laws and to the power of the TIG to seize assets or place enterprises into bankruptcy) were considerably weakened. In Georgia, as in Russia, there still is much reluctance to separate tax administration from discretionary political decisions.

In conclusion, compared with Russia, Georgia made major progress over the 1994–97 period in creating an efficient, modern tax administration and establishing the institutions that make up the Public Expenditure Management System, a result of strong support from a politically powerful president. Still, the progress has been partial. There is a long way to go before Georgia can be said to have an effective, rules-based, and politically independent tax administration. Furthermore, its level of taxation is still too low to accommodate the growing needs of the country, and after 1997 the pace of change fell somewhat.

Concluding Remarks

Market economies need effective and efficient fiscal institutions to operate well. Because countries with central planning had had only embryonic tax administrations, they required both technical and political reforms to operate in a market economy.

The technical elements can be grouped into four categories. First, there is the need to establish a clear, legal framework within which the tax administration can operate. This framework must determine the legal powers, and the limits to those powers, for the tax administration. Thus, the politicians and others who hold political power must be willing to delegate this power to the tax administration as they have done in the majority of industrial countries. The recent controversy in the United States over the need for supervision of the Internal Revenue Service indicates that even in advanced market economies this issue is not a simple one. Second, there are important organizational decisions to be made. The current, prevalent view is that a tax administration organized along basic functional lines is best. In some countries a different organization (e.g., by tax) is still common. Third, there are aspects related to systems and procedures that must be followed in the operational work of the institution – for example, the proper use of computers, the places where tax payments are made, and the frequency of tax reporting. Finally, there are aspects related to measures that encourage voluntary compliance, such as taxpayer relations and simplicity of forms. In these technical aspects, Georgia has made more progress than Russia.

In terms of the establishment of a clear legal framework, in both countries there is no clear delineation of the legal powers of the tax administration and of taxpayers' rights. We have also seen that there is great reluctance to keep the tax administration independent from political interference. There is still too much involvement on the part of high-level public officials in the day-to-day work of the tax administration. Decisions that in market economies are routinely made by tax administrators are still made at a political level which subjects ministers to political pressures and affects taxpayers' compliance.

In terms of organizational issues, Georgia has made more progress than Russia, especially in setting up a large taxpayer unit. In both countries, however, budgetary constraints have put limits to how much reorganization could take place. It has also been difficult to get the right personnel, or to retain the most able individuals, given the level of official compensation that employees receive. In some cases, corrupt individuals have replaced honest ones, and corruption remains a major problem.

Attempts at introducing new systems and procedures, often with the help of foreign advisors, have been only partly successful and more in Georgia than in Russia. Russian administrators have resisted these attempts, perhaps on the assumption that foreigners do not understand the Russian environment and that Russian experts do not need foreign advice. In many areas of tax administration, work continues as it did during central planning. In both countries little effort has been made at making the payment of taxes convenient and much remains to be done to promote voluntary taxpayer compliance.

Of course, a well-functioning and politically independent tax adminis-tration assures taxpayers that they will be treated fairly when complying with their tax liabilities – that, for example, politically better-connected or more powerful taxpayers will not be able to escape their tax liabili-ties through favorable treatment. If an efficient tax administration exists in a country where the tax laws are also equitable and public revenue is efficiently and fairly used, all the conditions are in place to assure that rules are fair and prevail over discretion. In this situation tax evasion will be much reduced and tax obligations will be seen as parameters. Taxes will cease to be "soft."

In many countries, however, these conditions do not prevail. The tax laws may contain too many loopholes, tax preferences, or other special treatments for particular taxpayers. Or, at times, these special treatments are provided not by the law but by discretionary decisions. The use of tax revenue may also be seen as inefficient, and public spending may be seen as oriented toward special-interest groups. Tax obligations may not be seen as rigid parameters but as prices to be negotiated. This situation still prevails in many of the countries in transition.

Although Georgia has faced greater obstacles and difficulties than Russia, it has made greater progress. Several reasons may be advanced to explain this difference. First, in 1992–94 the situation in Georgia had deteriorated so much that citizens demanded a more stable environment and the provision of traditional government functions. In that period hyperinflation and criminal activities reduced the tax burden to about 2 percent of GDP, perhaps the lowest level in the world, and criminal groups appropriated some of the taxing functions of the government. The situation was unacceptable to most citizens. Second, and for the same reasons, a president was elected with an overwhelming majority indicat-ing that the population was willing to delegate broad powers to the pres-ident. In this environment Shevarnadze could exercise more control over the political establishment. Shevarnadze's strong control may be seen as authoritarian and thus undemocratic. However, given the circumstances, it helped establish institutions that would make a market economy possible.

In Russia, splits among parties and across branches of government and opposition from regional forces created strong centrifugal pressures. These pressures undermined the credibility of central government's claims that it could improve public welfare and enforce the collection of taxes. These pressures also resulted in greater difficulties to reform the tax administration. The tolerance of tax arrears, for example, is an indication that at this time the tax administration cannot be separated from broad developments in the economy and the political arena. The chapter has focused on tax administration; however, a similar story would be told if the center of attention had been the institutions (e.g., budget, treasury) that make up the public-expenditure management systems.[17]

References

Barbone, Luca, and Hana Polarkova. 1996. Public Finances in Economic Transition. *MOCT* 6: 35–61.

Cheasty, Adrienne, and Jeffrey Davis. 1996. Fiscal Transition in Countries of the Former Soviet Union: An Interim Assessment. *MOCT* 6: 7–34.

Fischer, Stanley, and Alan Gelb. 1991. Issues in the Reform of Socialist Economies. In V. Corbo, F. Coricelli, and J. Bossak, eds., *Reforming Central and Eastern European Economies: Initial Results and Challenges*, pp. 67–82. Washington, D.C.: World Bank.

Johnson, Simon, Daniel Kaufmann, and Andrei Shleifer. 1997. The Unofficial Economy in Transition. *Brookings Papers on Economic Activity* 2: 159–239.

Kaufmann, Daniel. 1996. *The Missing Pillar of a Growth Strategy for Ukraine: Institutional and Policy Reforms for Private Sector Development*. Discussion Paper No. 603. Cambridge, Mass.: Harvard Institute for International Development.

Kornai, János. 1992. *The Socialist System: The Political Economy of Communism.* Princeton: Princeton University Press.

1995. *Highways and Byways: Studies on Reform and Postcommunist Transition.* Cambridge, Mass.: MIT Press.

Martinez-Vazquez, Jorge, and Robert McNab. 1997. *Tax Systems in Transition Economies*. Working Paper No. 1. Atlanta: Georgia State University School of Policy Studies.

Mundell, Robert. 1997. The Great Contractions in Transition Economies. In M. Blejer and M. Skreb, eds., *Macroeconomic Stabilization in Transition Economies*, pp. 73–99. Cambridge: Cambridge University Press.

[17] This chapter covers a period that ended in 1997. After 1997 the tax administration of Russia has witnessed faster progress, while progress has slowed in the Georgian tax administration.

Shleifer, Andrei. 1996. *Government in Transition*. Discussion Paper No. 1783. Cambridge, Mass.: Harvard Institute for Economic Research.

Tanzi, Vito. 1991. Fiscal Issues in Economies in Transition. In V. Corbo, F. Coricelli, and J. Bossak, eds., *Reforming Central and Eastern European Economies: Initial Results and Challenges*, pp. 221–28. Washington, D.C.: World Bank.

    1993. Financial Markets and Public Finance in the Transformation Process. In V. Tanzi, ed., *Transition to Market: Studies in Fiscal Reform*, pp. 1–28. Washington, D.C.: International Monetary Fund.

    1994. Reforming Public Finances in Economies in Transition. *International Tax and Public Finance* 1: 149–63.

Tanzi, Vito, Adrienne Cheasty, and Kristina Kostial. 1999. The Fiscal Implications of Trade Liberalization in Transition Countries. In M. Blejer and M. Skreb, eds., *Balance of Payments, Exchange Rates, and Competitiveness in Transition Economies*, pp. 239–53. Boston: Kluwer Academic Publishers.

CHAPTER 3

Politics, Institutions, and Macroeconomic Adjustment: Hungarian Fiscal Policy Making in Comparative Perspective

STEPHAN HAGGARD, ROBERT R. KAUFMAN, AND MATTHEW S. SHUGART

During the 1990s, inflation and balance-of-payments crises in developing and transition economies created strong pressures for fiscal reform. In the early reform period, the policy debate centered on how rapidly to undertake fiscal adjustments; subsequent political economy analysis focused on the conditions under which governments were more or less likely to succeed in these efforts. However, a parallel debate typically ensued over the institutions and procedures of the budget process itself. How could these institutions be designed to effectively coordinate demands on government resources and bring them into line with overall macroeconomic objectives? In this study, we examine the politics of fiscal policy in Hungary since 1990, looking both at policy and at the design of policy-making institutions. Throughout, we seek to place Hungary's experience in the broader comparative perspective of other Central European and middle-income developing countries.

Effective fiscal policy making requires that governments respond quickly to crises with an appropriate – typically contested – combination of expenditure reductions and tax increases and that they reconcile competing demands on government resources with adequate revenues over the long run. We expect that the capacity of governments to perform these tasks will be related both to general features of the political system but also to the specific institutions and procedures surrounding the budget process.

We would like to thank Mark Allen, László Andor, László Bruszt, Ellen Comisso, László Csaba, Béla Greskovits, István Győrfi, Joel Hellman, Tibor Horváth, János Kis, George Kopits, Mihály Kupa, Csaba László, Péter Mihályi, Barbara Nunberg, Robert Palacios, Robert Rocha, and David Stark for their assistance. Our particular thanks go to János Kornai for his guidance, and Ágnes Benedict, Zsófia Ferenczhalmy, and Viktória Danics for their research assistance.

Fiscal-policy-making institutions vary in terms of the degree to which they centralize control over the planning, approval, and implementation of the budget. In centralized budget processes, finance ministries are delegated a central role in setting fiscal targets, clearing budget requests from other ministries, and monitoring implementation. In democratic systems, the legislature must approve the budget, and this fact plays into the government's calculations in crafting it; however, centralized systems provide relatively limited opportunities for legislators to amend government proposals, for example, by restricting the ability to increase expenditures (as in Korea and Chile). Decentralized fiscal institutions, by contrast, grant spending ministries and agencies greater independence through mechanisms such as special funds, earmarking, off-budget accounts, or independent capacity to borrow. Decentralized systems are also typically characterized by greater legislative discretion.

Centralized budget institutions may not always produce fiscal stability; in systems that lack transparency and accountability, centralization can increase opportunities for corruption and rent and revenue seeking. Nevertheless, highly decentralized fiscal systems are likely to face difficulty in conducting a coherent fiscal policy and therefore some degree of centralization is a necessary, if not a sufficient, condition for coherent fiscal policy (Alesina and Perotti 1995; Stein, Talvi, and Gristani 1998).

A variety of other factors also influence fiscal policy and policy-making processes. International pressures, including the strong pull of prospective European Union (EU) membership as well as demands emanating from international creditors and financial institutions, have had an important influence in Central Europe. Domestic interest groups have also played a direct role in certain areas, such as health reform. However, we adopt an institutionalist perspective that emphasizes how such international constraints and domestic interests are mediated by the constitutional design of government, electoral rules, and the party system. In democratic systems, major policy decisions must ultimately pass through representative institutions; the organization of these institutions and the incentives they provide for political parties, executives, and individual legislators thus play an important role in shaping the course of public policy. In Hungary and other transition societies, there has been considerable uncertainty and contestation surrounding basic constitutional arrangements. Nevertheless, these institutions have become more established over time, and it is increasingly possible to make general statements about how they affect the making of public policy.

Our orienting hypothesis is that both coherent fiscal policy and centralizing institutional reforms are more likely in constitutional and electoral systems that minimize the number of veto gates (i.e., the institutional points at which a proposed decision can be blocked); discourage party fragmentation; enhance incentives for intraparty discipline; and promote stable governments. Systems with these characteristics are more likely to act in a decisive fashion in the face of crises, face fewer problems in reconciling conflicting interests, and are more likely to delegate authority in ways that enhance the coherence of fiscal policy. Systems such as this contrast with those in which there are multiple veto gates; many smaller parties that complicate the formation of governing coalitions; incentives for legislators to buck party discipline and to placate special interests or narrow geographic constituencies; and a high possibility of government turnover between elections. Such systems are more likely to delay adjustment in the face of crises; to have difficulty in reconciling conflicts among competing parties, interest groups, and individual politicians; and to face collective action problems within the government in defining basic macroeconomic and fiscal objectives.

We begin by outlining the evolution of fiscal policy and institutions in Hungary since 1990, the outcome to be explained. We then provide a further elaboration of the propositions about Hungary's political system. In the following two sections, we contrast fiscal policy and policy making under the Antall and Horn governments. We conclude by placing Hungary in comparative perspective.

Fiscal Policy and Policy Making in Hungary: The Outcomes

The topic of Hungarian fiscal policy, and the pattern of economic reform in the country more generally, has been the subject of quite divergent evaluations. Bruszt and Stark (1997) point out that some aspects of the Hungarian reform, including the design of privatization and bankruptcy legislation, were much more radical than in the other Visegrád countries. David Bartlett (1997) has also emphasized the decisiveness of the Antall government across a range of policy areas, including monetary and fiscal policy, pointing to the advantages of a parliamentary system. János Kornai (1996a) reflects the more dominant view, however, that the advent of the Antall government in 1990 did not mark a significant break in the incrementalist (and, in Kornai's view, costly) "muddling-through" of the late Communist period. With respect to fiscal policy in particular, the Antall period was characterized by a drift that was not reversed until the Bokros package of 1995.

We can provide some insight into these controversies by looking at Hungarian fiscal policy and macroeconomic performance in comparative

Table 3.1. *General Government Balance, General Government Expenditure, and GDP Growth in Selected Transition Economies*

Country	1989	1990	1991	1992	1993	1994	1995	1996
General government balance, in percent of GDP								
Hungary[a]	−1.4	0.4	−2.9	−6.8	−5.5	−8.4	−6.7	−3.5
Czech[b]	−2.8	0.1	−1.9	−3.1	0.5	−1.2	−1.8	−1.2
Poland	−7.4	3.1	−6.7	−6.6	−3.4	−2.8	−3.6	−3.1
Slovakia[a]			N/A	N/A	−7.0	−1.3	0.2	−1.9
Slovenia[a]	0.3	−0.3	2.6	0.2	0.3	−0.2	0.0	0.3
General government expenditure, in percent of GDP								
Hungary			55.4	59.4	60.6	60.9	53.9	50.9
Czech[b]			N/A	N/A	41.9	43.3	42.8	41.8
Poland			49.0	50.4	50.5	49.6	49.9	49.2
Slovakia[a]			N/A	N/A	51.2	47.7	46.9	48.9
Slovenia			41.1	45.8	46.7	46.1	45.7	44.9
Growth in real GDP								
Hungary	0.7	−3.5	−11.9	−3.1	−0.6	2.9	1.5	1.3
Czech	1.4	−0.4	−14.2	−3.3	0.6	3.2	6.4	3.9
Poland	0.2	−11.6	−7.0	2.6	3.8	5.2	7.0	6.1
Slovakia				−6.5	−3.7	4.9	6.8	6.9
Slovenia	−1.8	−4.7	−8.1	−5.5	2.8	5.3	4.1	3.1

[a] General government includes the state, municipalities, and extrabudgetary funds.

[b] General government includes the state, municipalities, and extrabudgetary funds, but excludes privatization revenues.

Sources: European Bank for Reconstruction and Development, *Annual Report*, various issues, and *Transition Report Update*, April 1998, pp. 7, 51, 55, 64–65. For deficit and expenditure data, Czech refers to Czechoslovakia until 1992; for GDP growth, until 1991. After those dates, it refers to the Czech Republic.

perspective. Table 3.1 contrasts Hungary's performance with that of the other Visegrád countries and Slovenia, and supports Kornai's assessment of limited fiscal adjustment. Hungary had the largest fiscal deficits during the transition period. Despite deep recessions, Slovenia and the Czech Republic maintained relatively balanced central government accounts, while Poland and the Slovak Republic undertook dramatic fiscal adjustments. In Hungary, by contrast, deficits widened steadily after 1990, with some improvement in 1995 and 1996, the years of the Bokros package. Hungary also has the largest government of the five countries, and by a substantial margin; moreover, the size of the government actually increased under Antall. Hungary does have unemployment that is on a par with the other four countries, but consumption did not experience the dramatic fall seen in Poland; indeed, Kornai (1996a) argues that consumption in Hungary fell surprisingly little during the transition relative to the drop in GDP.

The Németh government initiated a stabilization in 1989 under International Monetary Fund (IMF) auspices. Antall inherited this program, undertook additional expenditure cuts in the 1991 budget (drafted in the fall of 1990), and appeared to have a budget that was broadly in balance, with little inflationary pressure. This fact had an important political effect; in contrast to Poland, the apparent fiscal balance and the absence of a crisis reduced the urgency of undertaking radical adjustments, even though some argued the case in forceful terms.

The aversion to rapid fiscal adjustment was strongly reinforced during the winter of 1990 by the strident reaction of taxi drivers to a sharp decrease in gasoline subsidies announced by Antall's first minister of finance, Ferenc Rabár. Protesting drivers paralyzed traffic in Budapest for days by blockading major bridges across the Danube River. The government quickly retreated from the price increases, and Rabár – a proponent of more radical adjustments – was removed from office (Greskovits, Chapter 4, in this volume). At a broader level, the taxi strike strengthened the government's preference for an incrementalist policy approach that would reduce the risks of destabilizing social protest.

Despite the earlier stabilization efforts of the Németh government and the apparent equilibrium sustained under Antall, however, the fiscal situation was far from healthy. First, the adjustment in public finances was partly illusory. Deficits were hidden on the balance sheet of the Central Bank, which was responsible for servicing the country's (and effectively the government's) large external debt. Antall did make progress in solving this problem by shifting to a more transparent system of government borrowing; as a result, however, interest payments took a steadily increasing share of total government expenditures, rising from approximately 3 percent of GDP in 1990 to a height of 8.5 percent in 1995. Trends in revenue were also troubling. Revenues began falling in 1989 and bottomed out during the deep recession of 1991 as a result of both cyclical and structural factors and the accumulation of substantial arrears on the part of firms (Schaffer 1995); between those two years, government revenue fell from nearly 60 percent of GDP to less than 52 percent, and it recovered only half of that loss by the mid-1990s.

The final problem was that expenditures did not adjust to these new realities. Political liberalization in the late Communist period had been accompanied by a continued expansion of various forms of entitlement, of which the pension system, health care, and a complex system of social assistance and family benefits constituted the three main pillars. At the time of the transition, Hungary was devoting a share of GDP to social welfare and transfers that was comparable to that of the most redistributive Scandinavian welfare states (Kornai 1996b). During the Antall period, this share increased steadily in both real terms and as a share of GDP, more than offsetting the dramatic reduction in direct subsidies during the early years of the transition and contributing to a growth in the primary deficit (exclusive of interest payments). By 1994 total transfers to households equaled approximately 20 percent of GDP, with pensions accounting for over half of that.

The Bokros package of 1995 marked a sharp reversal in these trends (Kornai 1996b). In 1995 a supplementary budget instituted an across-the-board freeze on expenditures, shifting the primary balance into surplus. In the 1996 budget, the government initiated an attack on a number of politically sensitive entitlements, including higher education, maternity benefits and family allowances, dental care, and the retirement age, and launched a discussion of more fundamental reforms of the pension and health systems. With revenues remaining roughly constant as a share of GDP, the 1996 budget deficit reached its lowest point since 1991. The deficit increased again in 1997, but this reflected the shift of quasi-fiscal Central Bank deficits onto the central-government budget, an important step toward greater fiscal transparency. Not all of Bokros's objectives were realized; reform of the pension and health-care systems fell far short of plans. However, the Bokros package constituted a break with the pattern of fiscal policy not only under Antall but in the early months of the Horn government as well.

Identifying the evolution of Hungarian budget institutions is somewhat more complicated than the stylized policy history just sketched, but we focus primarily on the extent to which the parliamentary majority acting through the prime minister and cabinet delegates power to the minister of finance and provides him with the authority to formulate and coordinate fiscal policy. Among the indicators we consider are the extent to which spending agencies, referred to in Hungary as Central Budgetary Institutions (CBIs), control their own revenues and expenditures; the number and weight of extrabudgetary funds; the role of semiautonomous social insurance funds (SIFs); the independent borrowing and lending authority of local governments; and the policy-making role of tripartite, corporatist bodies, including most importantly the governing bodies of the SIFs and the Interest Reconciliation Council.

During the late Communist period, policy making shifted away from more opaque party venues toward the government, and the influence of both the Ministry of Finance and the Central Bank increased relative to the spending ministries. However, other trends toward greater decentralization – such as the removal of the health and pension spending from the central budget into special accounts in 1989, the devolution of spending authority to local governments, the proliferation of extrabudgetary funds, and increasing independence on the part of specialized CBIs, including a shift into profit-making ventures – weakened the capacity to coordinate fiscal policy (Kopits 1993: 81).

This basic pattern of institutional change continued under Antall, and as in the late Communist period, had somewhat contradictory effects on macroeconomic policy-making institutions. The dismantling of the central-planning system continued, reinforced by a broad popular reaction against the Communist state; this served to strengthen the role of the Central Bank and Ministry of Finance vis-à-vis the old apparatus of the command economy. But these same political forces also strengthened the autonomy of spending institutions outside of the control of the Ministry of Finance. As was the case with fiscal policy more narrowly conceived, we see important changes in this institutional pattern after 1995 as well. The advent of the Bokros package was marked by initiatives to establish more centralized control over these autonomous spending institutions, although these efforts are still unfolding.

Institutional reforms under Antall included the dissolution of the Planning Office, with its extensive patronage ties to state-owned enterprises, and the corresponding decline in the influence of the branch ministries. In themselves, these changes enhanced the role of the Central Bank and the Ministry of Finance (Bartlett 1997). A Central Bank Law passed in 1991 did not grant the bank the degree of independence the reformers sought, but it did limit the bank's ability to finance public deficits. In combination with the effort to clarify the quasi-fiscal deficits of the Central Bank, these reforms increased the transparency of the budget process.

At the same time, a variety of institutional changes placed important constraints on fiscal policy making. Of course, the transition to democracy itself introduced an important new actor into the budget cycle, namely Parliament. The Law on Public Finance, which established a complex review process involving all standing committees, was passed in April 1992. This process provided an additional venue for the coalition partners to renegotiate portions of the budget, and served to delay its passage on several occasions (Kraxner 1995). However, Parliament's role did not constrain the government with respect to fiscal aggregates. Parliament is held to fairly restrictive timetables for review, and the capacity to amend is limited to the reallocation of funds within a given portfolio. Final budgets passed by the Parliament resemble quite closely those submitted by the government. As in most parliamentary systems, the key to understanding the passage of the budget lies in the level of intracoalition and intraparty cohesion.

More serious for the conduct of fiscal policy was a continuation and even acceleration of the decentralizing tendencies visible in the late Communist period. The 1992 Law on Public Finance condoned the proliferation of CBIs, over which the Ministry of Finance, and even the line ministries, had little effective control. Following the public finances law, the budget consisted of 31 chapters, under which fell 1,400 CBIs, 650 of which had budgetary autonomy and even control over their own cash flow. In addition, there were about 30 extrabudgetary funds, as well as 13,500 local budgetary institutions, of which 8,000 had budgetary autonomy. Not surprisingly, it proved extremely difficult for the Ministry of Finance to make informed estimates of overall revenues and expenditures and even to calculate the public sector's overall borrowing requirement. A striking indicator of the extent of decentralization is that of the 54 percent of GDP collected in revenues in 1995, only 28 percent was collected by the state budget, with the remainder flowing directly to other institutions: 12.9 percent to SIFs, 5.8 percent to local governments, 4.7 percent to extrabudgetary funds, and 2.4 percent to CBIs.

Two further institutional developments are of particular significance: the establishment of the Interest Reconciliation Council (IRC) in 1991, and the creation of a quasi-corporatist structure to manage the two major social insurance funds dealing with health and welfare in 1992–93. In principle, the Hungarian IRC – like similar corporatist councils established elsewhere – had the potential to steer overall macroeconomic policy through agreements among government, business, and labor. In practice, the IRC's role in Hungary was problematic. The body was not authorized to reach binding decisions on macroeconomic policy. Moreover, it would have been hampered in playing this role by the relative weakness of the participants. The employers' associations on the council did not provide substantial representation for new private firms and the capacity of the ex-Communist union federation, MSZOSZ, to make binding commitments for its constituent unions was limited. Nonetheless the IRC offered an alternative forum for debates that sometimes ran counter to the government's own preferred policies and thus increased the possibilities for stalemate over crucial policy issues.

The creation of the independent social insurance funds, which managed fully a third of general government expenditures, also had potentially detrimental effects for fiscal policy. The initial creation of the funds in 1989 was to be coupled to an ambitious restructuring of the health-care and pension systems, but this failed to materialize. The discretion of the pension and health managers was relatively limited by fiduciary responsibilities, but health fund officials exercised wide decision-making power with respect to health spending, including control over treatment strategies and the location of health facilities. The general budget was obliged to cover deficits incurred by either fund, which was not only costly but limited the transparency of decisions. Perhaps most important, however, is the fact that the corporatist structure of the funds meant they became centers of organized opposition to health and pension reform. In principle, they could be restructured by an act of Parliament assuming that the Constitutional Court did not come to their defense. But the very access they offered to representatives of the MSZOSZ and the health-care profession served to magnify the influence of groups opposed to reform.

The continuing decentralization of the budget process naturally became a target for reform under the Horn administration, and the Bokros package was accompanied by a number of institutional initiatives. Perhaps the most successful to date has been the establishment of a treasury, which centralized government accounts, improved the Ministry of Finance's control over both the allocation and use of resources, and reduced the discretion of agency heads and local governments. Consolidation of extrabudgetary funds constituted a second important step; the number of funds was reduced during the first year of the program from over thirty to only five. In an important accounting move, finally, the balance sheet of the Central Bank was cleaned up, increasing the transparency of fiscal data.

As we have already noted, however, progress was much more limited on reform of the health and pension systems, and of the institutions that ran them. In 1997, the government did succeed in passing a pension reform law that established a private pension pillar as a supplement to the pay-as-you-go (PAYG) system, but strong opposition organized by the managers of the Pension Fund came close to blocking the legislation. Discussion of the issue in the IRC substantially diluted Ministry of Finance proposals, reducing the weight of the private pillar within the system. Reorganization of the Health Insurance Funds constituted an even greater challenge because of the power (and income) the fund granted to health-care providers, medical associations, and local politicians. Notwithstanding the problems this fund posed for fiscal coordination, the Horn government was unable to challenge its authority.

Political Arrangements and Public Policy: General Principles and the Hungarian Case

The evolution of fiscal policy and policy-making institutions has been affected by two institutional features of the Hungarian political system: the basic constitutional arrangements and characteristics of the party system. Constitutional systems can be distinguished most fundamentally in terms of the number of major veto gates. The Hungarian Parliament is a unicameral body, and the cabinet is exclusively responsible to it. Unlike most Latin American systems and Poland, the president has no veto over legislative proposals. And, unlike Czechoslovakia prior to the breakup in 1993, Italy, and some other countries with parliamentary systems, Hungary has no upper chamber where potentially conflicting preferences must be accommodated. As long as the prime minister can sustain a legislative majority in the single chamber, the government will ordinarily be able to pass its policy initiatives into law. In fact, the constitutional provision for a unicameral legislature, in combination with features of the electoral law to be described later, was designed in part to offset the strong pressures toward political and regional decentralization that had otherwise characterized the process of democratization in Hungary.[1] In addition, the provision for a constructive vote of no confidence – requiring that an alternative government be elected by a majority at the same time that the incumbent government is turned out – makes it somewhat more difficult to replace governments between elections.

Although these provisions stengthened central authority, the reaction against the overwhelming executive power of the Communist state also led to the establishment of a second important veto gate, the Constitutional Court. This institution, as well as those in a number of other Central East European (CEE) countries, has been granted authority that goes significantly beyond that of the United States Supreme Court. The Hungarian Constitutional Court not only may review and overturn any law it deems in violation of the constitution, but it can take such action on its own initiative without reference to cases appealed from lower levels of the judicial system. It could be argued that Parliament ultimately controls the court through its appointment powers and its ability to change the constitution itself. However, once appointed, judges are independent and Parliament has been unable or unwilling to muster the two-thirds majority required to curb the court's power (Dethier and Shapiro 1998). As we shall see, the court has played an important role in the economic policy-making process, particularly with regard to welfare entitlements (Sajó 1996).

Within this constitutional framework, both policy adjustment and institutional reform depend on the extent to which the electoral and party systems produce stable and cohesive legislative majorities. In these

---

[1] János Kis, one of the leaders of the democratization movement, refers to concerns about the dangers of a "Weimar-type" situation (interview).

respects, Hungary provides a mixed picture. On the one hand, the overall effect of Hungary's complex electoral system is to exaggerate the representation of larger parties. Nearly half the seats are elected in single-member districts (SMD) by a two-round majority-plurality formula, and the rest of the seats – filled via proportional representation – only slightly counteract the effects of the SMDs.

The conditions for intraparty discipline also appear to be present. The party-list section of the electoral process employs closed lists, meaning that there is no opportunity for the voters to alter the rank ordering of candidates established by party leaderships. The SMDs also pit parties against each other in each district, in the sense that each party is represented by only one nominee. In contrast to Japan prior to 1996, Brazil, and Poland, the system does not establish intraparty competition, which creates incentives for politicians to provide particularistic favors to voters in order to distinguish them from copartisans.

The combination of unicameral parliamentarism with at least potentially strong and cohesive parties has been a theme in a number of political analyses of Hungary's reforms (Bartlett 1997; Bruszt and Stark 1997). These analyses tend to emphasize precisely the characteristics we would predict of Westminster and Westminster-like systems, including decisiveness, the capacity to undertake wide-ranging (although not necessarily popular) reforms, and a concentrated decision-making process centered on the cabinet and the prime minister.

On the other hand, however, we find a number of features of the party system have periodically pulled Hungary in a different direction, contributing to indecision, stalemate, and a reduction in the discretion of top decision makers. Perhaps the most important of these, especially during the Antall period, is the very newness of the party system and the lack of strong intermediate associations and interest groups. Cohesive parliamentary majorities rest not only on electoral and governmental institutions but also on voters having strong identification with parties and with party labels as meaningful signals of a specific basket of policies. Such signals are likely to be weak where most parties are very recent creations with no stable roots in society. One would still expect that, over time, electoral competition would lead to stronger parties and a greater focus on national issues, but the possibility of an extended period of much less coherent partisan competition cannot be ruled out.

A second important consideration is the fact that the party spectrum has not lined up strictly on a single issue dimension: both economic issues and what might be called "the national question" divide the electorate. Systems with two main issue cleavages tend to generate three parties or blocs of parties (Taagepera and Grofman 1985) and that was true in

Hungary. At the time of the transition, the party system was divided among the left, principally the Socialist Party, the successor to the former ruling party, the liberal parties, of which the Alliance of Free Democrats (SZDSZ) was the largest force, and the national conservative parties, including the principal party in the 1990–94 government, the Hungarian Democratic Forum (MDF) and its coalition partners, the Independent Smallholders and the Christian Democrats. Owing to these multiple issues, even in the SMD runoffs, voters are rarely confronted with "straight fights" between two candidates. As a result, the voters do not face clear choices among competing potential governments as in Westminster systems. In fact, most districts have been won with less than a majority of the votes cast (although there were many more straight fights in 1998 than in 1990 or 1994).

Because of multiple issue dimensions and the absence of any one party with a near majority of the votes, Hungary's governing coalitions have contained parties likely to be at odds on at least one policy dimension. This constituted an important impediment to timely and coherent policy decisions and increased the risks of political stalemate.

A third consideration muting intraparty discipline is the very existence of single-member districts. On the one hand, such districts are like closed lists, in the sense that each party nominates only one candidate per district and voters are thus faced with a categorical choice. On the other hand, such districts also allow the legislators elected from them to serve as the delegate of a locality. Parliamentarism – and the concomitant role of legislative contests as simultaneous executive contests – tends to inhibit members' ability to attend to local matters (Cox 1987; Shugart and Carey 1992). But in the context of weak party labels and the possibility that main party contenders will not be matched in straight fights, candidates in the SMDs might very well seek to carve out niches for themselves not simply as local representatives of the party but also as servants of a local constituency. As a large literature shows, such a propensity may result in greater attention to local issues, such as casework and pork (for reviews, see Carey and Shugart 1995; Cain, Ferejohn, and Fiorina 1987).

The conditions just outlined – weakly rooted parties, a multidimensional issue space with three blocs of parties, and multiparty competition in SMDs – might help explain the propensity for progovernment parties to construct oversized coalitions or to strike bargains with the opposition. Both the Antall and Horn coalitions contained more parties than necessary for a parliamentary majority. Horn's Socialist Party had the legislative seats to form a majority government on its own without the Free Democrats, but included them in the government nonetheless.

Somewhat counterintuitively, the formation of oversized governments signals government weakness rather than strength, because it reflects the anticipation of intraparty and intracoalitional conflicts.

These institutional arrangements and political structures have implications for fiscal policy and the institutions of public finance. The following hypotheses focus attention both on differences between Hungary and other transition and developing countries, and on differences between the Antall and Horn governments.

In parliamentary systems with limited veto gates, it should be easier to implement rapid and comprehensive changes in both policy and government organization than in systems with multiple checks and balances. Radical changes have, of course, also been implemented in systems with multiple veto gates, including presidential ones, but usually only after severe crises have opened windows of opportunity for "extraordinary politics" in which executive authority is substantially enhanced (Carey and Shugart 1998; Haggard and Kaufman 1995). In parliamentary systems, crises are also important spurs to reform. Ceteris paribus, however, governments that are less constrained by multiple veto gates are more able to act decisively, even when crises are less severe (Grilli, Masciandaro, and Tabellini 1991; Roubini and Sachs 1989). We return to this point in our discussion of the Bokros stabilization package.

Where parliamentary governments and their cabinets are formed on the basis of relatively stable legislative majorities to which they are directly accountable, policy is more likely to emanate directly from the cabinet than from the legislature itself. Plenary sessions of the legislature and legislative committees are less important venues for decision making than in presidential systems where executives and legislators are separately elected and serve independent terms, or in parliamentary systems with short-lived cabinets (Lijphart 1984; Powell 2000).

The decisiveness and cohesiveness of policy in parliamentary systems still depend heavily on intracoalitional and intraparty discipline. The most decisive and cohesive system is presumed to be the classic Westminster one, with two dominant parties, single-party parliamentary majorities, and strong internal party discipline. However, parliamentary governments, including those in Hungary, are often formed on the basis of coalitions and may even be formed in the absence of a legislative majority (minority government). When the legislative coalition is cohesive and stable, the main decisions will be made at the prime ministerial and cabinet level. Policy will reflect the political incentives of the rank-and-file politicians in such a system to support the broad policy initiatives of the leadership; at the limit, such systems should resemble the Westminster model. In this circumstance, the prime minister and backbenchers alike should have an interest in a budget process that is relatively centralized, with power typically delegated to a budget agency within the Ministry of Finance with strong influence over the other ministries.

By contrast, when coalitions are fragmented and/or the constituent parties are themselves undisciplined, policy will be more prone to drift or deadlock. Under these conditions, incentives of government leaders and rank-and-file politicians are less likely to be in alignment, so policy will reflect more difficult bargaining either between the prime minister and the leaders of other parties in the coalition, or between party leaders and their own rank and file, or both. Under these circumstances, it will prove more difficult to take decisive action and policy will be less coherent.

Such circumstances also reduce the likelihood that the prime minister will be able to delegate decision-making authority to centralized budget agencies. The pressures of a fragmented coalition will thus create incentives for the prime minister to shift fiscal decisions to corporatist venues outside the parliamentary framework, thereby involving directly in policy making the organized interests that form the constituencies of parties or factions within the government.

The Antall Period

We begin our examination of the propositions just outlined with a discussion of the underlying economic situation the Antall government faced. We have already noted how the apparent absence of a fiscal crisis at the time of the transition tended to reinforce the Antall government's caution. However, in 1991, the crisis triggered by the collapse of the Council for Mutual Economic Assistance (CMEA) changed the context of the political debate. The dramatic fall in output and the corresponding emergence of problems of unemployment made it politically more difficult to undertake fiscal adjustments and strengthened the voice of those arguing against the imposition of austerity. But the crisis also made the underlying fiscal problems of the government more apparent to key technocratic actors.

Precisely because Hungary had been an early reformer, a network of well-trained economists associated with the University of Economics occupied important positions of junior leadership under the Németh government, where they had also gained experience in working with the international financial institutions. These officials, who remained influential after the transition, included György Surányi, the first Central Bank president under Antall; Mihály Kupa, the minister of finance from

1991 to 1993; Lajos Bokros, the minister of finance from 1995 to 1996; and a large number of second-level officials within the Central Bank and the Ministry of Finance. Though far from homogeneous in their outlook or politics, these economists provided the major impetus for fiscal adjustment and the centralization of fiscal institutions.

As we show in more detail later, these technocrats were not constrained by well-organized domestic interests, as they were in many Latin American countries or in Poland. Policy choices and institutional design were thus heavily dependent on the views of the prime minister and on bureaucratic rivalries and personality conflicts that unfolded within the executive branch itself (Greskovits, Chapter 4, in this volume). But the fiscal decisions of the prime minister and his advisors could not be made independently of parliamentary approval, and their freedom of maneuver appeared to narrow as the government's legislative coalition began to unravel. Particularly after the post-Communist "honeymoon" had faded, the decisions of the prime minister and cabinet were constrained by the constitutional arrangements we have outlined, the electoral dynamics that brought the government to office in 1990, and the particular coalitional and party weaknesses under which it labored.

Antall's MDF was one of three major right-wing Christian parties and had been cobbled together in 1987 out of a group of populist-nationalist intellectuals who enjoyed the tacit protection, even sponsorship, of the reform wing of the Communist Party (Tőkés 1996: 199). While clearly in opposition, the party was not deeply rooted in the kind of social movement that propelled Solidarity to office in Poland. In the first round of elections in March, the party was the top vote getter, but, as Table 3.2 shows, the initial fragmentation of the party system meant that it held this status with only 25 percent of the vote, only 3 percentage points more than its closest rival, the Free Democrats.

The second-round elections appeared to clarify political alignments somewhat, even though most districts continued to feature at least a three-candidate competition. Running on a platform that argued explicitly for a more gradual approach to the transition than its liberal protagonists, the MDF secured a decisive victory, winning 43 percent of seats to the Free Democrats' 24 percent. However, this result reflected the elimination of smaller parties during the first round, votes by disaffected Socialists opting for the lesser of two evils, and the disproportionality in the electoral system itself; abstention in the second round was high, with only 45 percent of voters taking part. In sum, the MDF's support was relatively shallow, in no way reflected a majority of votes (not even a majority of votes cast in runoffs), and was predicated on electoral promises of gradualism and caution.

Table 3.2. *Electoral Outcomes, 1990 and 1994 (percentage)*

| | 1990 Elections | | 1994 Elections | |
| | Party-List | | Party-List | |
Parties	Votes	Seats	Votes	Seats
MDF (Hungarian Democratic Forum)	24.7	42.7	11.7	9.8
SZDSZ (Alliance of Free Democrats)	21.4	24.4	19.7	17.9
FKgP (Independent Smallholders Party)	11.7	11.0	8.8	6.7
MSZP (Hungarian Socialist Party)	10.9	8.6	32.9	54.1
FIDESZ (Alliance of Young Democrats)	8.9	5.7	7.0	5.1
KDNP (Christian Democratic Party)	6.5	5.4	7.0	5.1
Independent and other	15.9	1.8	12.9	0.5

Lacking the seats to govern on its own, the MDF turned to two "historic" conservative parties with roots in the pre-Communist past, the Independent Smallholders and the Christian Democrats, resulting in a slightly oversized coalition. Over the heads of its coalition partners, the MDF also negotiated a pact with the opposition to avoid recurrent legislative stalemate with respect to constitutional issues requiring a supermajority (Tőkés 1996: 397).

An oversized coalition and a pact with the opposition might appear to enhance the government's freedom of maneuver. However, as we noted, these factors masked substantial problems among the coalition partners and within the parties themselves. First, the coalition had little or no programmatic coherence. The government did not produce a common platform until four months after it took office, and, as Csaba (1995: 222) argues, the document that finally emerged "was a collection of good intentions, not an operational policy document."

Second, the parties themselves were not cohesive entities. This problem was a general one that affected all parties, and can be seen in indicators of legislators' loyalty; about 14 percent of MPs elected in 1990 later left the parties under whose labels they had been elected. However, lack of cohesion appears particularly marked among the two largest coalition partners, the MDF and the Smallholders. Throughout the first Parliament, the most significant cleavage within the MDF was between its populist and nationalist "founding fathers," who tended to retain influence within the party, and Antall loyalists, whose influence stemmed mainly from Antall's backing and positions within the government. These factional conflicts did not initially harm the party's functioning in Parliament (Szarvas 1995; Pataki 1992), but they did undermine the government's ability to present a clear public image with respect to economic policy.

With the crisis of 1991–92, and as elections began to loom, the intra-party problems became more intense. In August 1992 a prominent MDF leader, István Csurka, wrote a long chauvinist tract in which he argued among other things that the government was complicit in a Jewish-liberal international conspiracy, in which the IMF played a central role. Following a national and intraparty uproar, Csurka and several other deputies were expelled from the party, but the problem of indiscipline continued. Over the course of the entire first Parliament, nearly 20 percent of the MPs elected under the MDF label left the party, a rate notably larger than in most stable parliamentary systems. The Independent Smallholders were particularly prone to internal fragmentation. In February 1992 the party's presidium voted to leave the government, but fully thirty-five of forty-five Independent Smallholder deputies chose to remain loyal to the coalition (Pataki 1992).

The Course of Fiscal Policy

The failure to cut the overall size of the state and to adjust to the reduced flow of revenue was arguably a result of the severe recession and wide-ranging structural reforms the government had launched. However, as early as the formulation of the 1992 budget estimates in the fall of 1991, there were signs of politically motivated optimism in the government's projections. During 1992 the danger signals became increasingly clear as spending dramatically outran estimates, and revenues lagged; for 1992 as a whole, the fiscal deficit jumped from 2.9 to 6.8 percent of GDP (Table 3.1). The need for adjustment became increasingly evident, both to economic officials within the government and to the World Bank and IMF.

During the preparation of the 1993 budget in the fall of 1992, Minister of Finance Mihály Kupa proposed a package of measures that combined adjustments in the value-added tax (VAT) and other revenue enhancements with a freeze on expenditures of public institutions at their nominal 1992 levels. Continuing recession placed an important con-straint on a deep fiscal adjustment; nevertheless, the Kupa package was probably the last chance for the government to address growing macro-economic imbalances ahead of the 1994 general election. Béla Greskovits (1998) provides a detailed analysis of the political dynamics of the Kupa reform, and suggests that the outcome was strongly influ-enced by politics within the government's own coalition.

On the surface, there was evidence of widespread social protest to the VAT increases both from civic associations and new social movements, including a series of hunger strikes by activists. Opposition also came from unions, the best organized of which was MSZOSZ. However, Greskovits argues that the new civil organizations that formed the base of opposition were of dubious representativeness and uncertain membership; moreover, the government was aware of this fact. Although the MSZOSZ had inherited the property and organizational infrastructure of its Communist predecessor, it remained weak in terms of membership and mobilizational capacity. In the early transition period, there were some local work stoppages, but few countrywide strikes.

For Greskovits (1998: 224), "what the government really may have been afraid of was less the civil and labor protests than the fragmentation of the coalition in the face of the austerity program and the budget for 1993." It is important to emphasize that while the opposition signaled its dislike of the plan early, some of the most vehement resistance came from within the ruling coalition itself, including the deeply divided Smallholders and the Christian Democrats. In the fall of 1992, the right wing of the MDF was calling for fundamental change in the government's economic policies. "Reformist technocrats around Minister of Finance Mihály Kupa were increasingly threatened by MDF extremists, who hinted at the necessity of cleansing the Treasury of 'narrow minded financial experts'" (Greskovits, 1998: 212). Parliament failed to act on Kupa's broader policy guidelines (Kraxner 1995: 139).

It was only against this backdrop of policy conflict that the government responded positively to a call from the unions to negotiate a social pact through the IRC, deflecting pressure away from intracoalitional and intraparty tensions and seeking alternative sources of support for Kupa's reforms. Within the IRC, the government was able to negotiate an adjustment package, but only at a substantial cost. Unions won a number of important concessions on the elimination of wage controls, a central part of the government's stabilization efforts; on wages in the education and health sector, both major components of government spending; and on the minimum wage. In return, the government secured a modified tax reform and increased contributions to the unemployment benefit fund, measures that fell far short of what was needed.

There is no need to detail the difficulties surrounding the preparation of the 1994 budget, except to note that Minister of Finance Kupa was ousted in February 1993, and that elections loomed. Greskovits (Chapter 4, in this volume) argues that Kupa's eventual dismissal had more to do with the threat he posed to Antall's authority within the bureaucracy than to opposition within the parliamentary coalition. However, the new minister of finance, Iván Szabó, held heterodox economic views that appeared to be more closely aligned with those of the party leadership and consonant with the process of political caution of the preelection period. With the government severely weakened by Antall's failing health, the runup to the election was characterized by a slow-moving but nonetheless full-blown fiscal crisis.

Institutional Reform

A similar interplay between coalitional politics and technocratic reformers marked the efforts to reorganize fiscal institutions under Antall. Efforts to strengthen the role of the Ministry of Finance and the Central Bank were advanced by many of the same economists who pursued these objectives under Németh, with the World Bank and IMF providing important intellectual templates for the process (Kopits 1993). Bartlett (1997: 171) argues that the efforts of the domestic reformers were initially facilitated by the change of regime and by the authority of a prime minister with strong partisan support. As noted earlier, however, these officials faced important constraints within the governing coalition, and in several respects, they lost ground to the creation of new decision-making centers that were altogether outside their control. These developments can be seen by analyzing the political influences on several key elements of fiscal and macroeconomic policy making including the organization of the budget and fiscal process within the government, the creation of extrabudgetary funds and their managing bodies, and the use of the IRC as a corporatist body.

Fiscal policy making is but one component of macroeconomic policy making and is strongly affected by the conduct of monetary policy. The Central Bank Law of 1991 stipulated that the National Bank of Hungary (NBH) may make its monetary policy independently of the government and limited its ability to finance the government to 3 percent of planned government revenues by 1995; moreover, the prime rate was to serve as the base for determining the pricing of these loans, reducing the heavy subsidies that had characterized the bank's lending to the government in the past. However, following the introduction of extensive amendments to the government's proposed legislation by a member of its own party, the independence of the NBH was made somewhat more ambiguous. For example, the final version of the law requires the bank to support the government's economic program and to coordinate financing of the budget deficit both with the semiindependent Central Bank Committee and with the Ministry of Finance.

The 1992 Public Finance Law helped to rationalize the fiscal decision-making process by setting timetables and procedures for the preparation and passage of the central budget. This legislation was preceded,

93

however, by the passage of a Law on Local Government pushed by the Free Democrats and factions of the MDF that sought to weaken control of central ministries. This legislation seriously constrained the budget process by granting substantial spending autonomy to local self-government without corresponding specification of the services for which they were responsible (Kupa, interview).

We have already noted how the welfare fund was separated from the general budget in 1989 by Ministry of Finance reformers who sought to establish health financing on an insurance basis. Neither the Németh nor the Antall governments, however, were willing to run the political risk of taking this crucial final step, thus continuing the fiscal strain that welfare expenditures caused. Further legislation under Antall established separate pension and health funds in 1992 and compounded the problems of fiscal management. The legislation left the Social Insurance Funds (SIFs) relatively free from "hard budget constraints," yet enhanced their political independence by placing each under the control of union representatives elected by the population at large.

As we would expect, Antall was reluctant for both institutional and partisan reasons to give control of the two funds to directly elected union leaders, and the legislation encountered opposition from Mihály Kupa in the Ministry of Finance and from World Bank advisors. But Antall faced strong pressure from groups in a position to threaten his ruling majority. The Christian Democratic minister of welfare and his parliamentary colleagues were strong advocates of the fund legislation, motivated in part by a desire to emulate what they perceived to be the main features of Western European corporatist models (Kupa, interview). The Free Democrats also strongly supported funds with directly elected union managers, in part because they viewed direct elections as an opportunity to increase the power of the non-Communist union movement. Although the Free Democrats were not members of the governing coalition, Antall needed their cooperation for the two-thirds majorities necessary to back judicial reforms, media laws, and privatization legislation that remained on the agenda. In addition, the party constituted a potential reserve of votes that might offset defections within the coalition (Kis, interview). A third source of support for the funds, ironically, came from the ultranationalist and strongly anti-Communist right wing of the MDF itself, which also sought to limit the control of the prime minister in these important policy areas.

A final irony of this story is that the logic of coalitional politics led to an outcome that none of these actors had preferred or anticipated: the overwhelming predominance gained within the funds' governance structure by representatives of the old Socialist union movement, the

MSZOSZ. The weakness of the organizational links between party politicians and grass-roots movements permitted this miscalculation. Without a means of gauging the relative strength of competing forces within the union movement, the government badly overestimated the extent to which Communists had been repudiated by the union rank and file while underestimating the preferences the electorate had for maintaining welfare entitlements.

The establishment of the IRC was less controversial, and with some important exceptions, it had a less significant impact on the fiscal policy process.[2] When he enjoys a strong majority or cohesive coalition, the prime minister in a parliamentary system like Hungary's is not likely to be interested in using such a corporatist mechanism. But the problems were deeper. As already noted, the socialist unions and the business associations on the council were not tied closely to their constituencies and could not make binding commitments on their behalf. Thus, unlike corporatist bargaining councils in Western Europe, deliberations within the IRC did not routinely have a major influence on fiscal policy making under Antall. The exceptions came at moments when the ruling coalition was severely divided over policy issues. Under Antall, the best example came with the package of tax reforms proposed by Mihály Kupa in 1992, when the government turned to the IRC as a forum for redesigning the proposal (Greskovits 1998). As we have seen, however, the IRC effectively weakened the government's initiative, while failing to build any broad social consensus for an alternative.

The Horn Government

The general elections of 1994 brought Hungary's reformed Socialist Party to power but also marked a shift toward a more stable and predictable pattern of party politics. The Socialists emerged with a decisive victory, winning 32 percent of the party-list votes and an absolute majority (54.1 percent) of parliamentary seats. This led some analysts to argue that the system had evolved in a bipolar direction (Ágh 1996: 27). Our analysis of voting in the second-round runoffs does not bear this out entirely; although the Socialists were clearly the leading party, the runoffs were not characterized by straight fights and no single coalition of parties

---

[2] As a point of contrast with the Hungarian experience, however, it is worth noting that it took a good deal longer to establish such a council in Poland, despite the comparatively greater strength of the Polish union movement. An important reason was that Walesa hoped to consolidate his own position as interlocutor of the movement and, as a president with veto power, was able to block legislation until 1994 (Orenstein 1996).

formed a coherent alternative. But after four years of parliamentary experience, the six parties that gained continuing representation in the Parliament had established sharper ideological and electoral profiles. More important, and in contrast to 1990, one party – the Socialists – had emerged with a clear responsibility for governing, a fact we would expect to encourage a more streamlined and centralized policy-making process.

A complicating element in this picture was the decision of the Socialists to govern through an oversized coalition with the Free Democrats, a decision driven at least in part by concerns about how their leadership would be viewed in the West. Domestic political calculations also came into play, however. The presence of a liberal coalition partner provided Horn an additional degree of freedom in managing his own left wing; the Socialists were deeply divided along factional lines, with a small liberal wing on one side, a left wing linked to the old Communist unions on the other, and the more moderate faction led by Gyula Horn in the center. Despite these divisions, the Socialists were a far more disciplined legislative party than the MDF; for example, only three Socialist deputies voted against the controversial stabilization budget to be discussed shortly (Ágh 1996: 23). As we shall see, neither this coalition nor the internal discipline of the Socialist Party precluded bruising battles within the governing coalition; still less would it ensure that the government preferences would prevail in the reform process. Nevertheless, it created the basis for a more cohesive government than the one forged under Antall.

The Course of Fiscal Policy

Hungary's macroeconomic situation continued to deteriorate in the runup to the 1994 election. Despite some growth and a decline in inflation in 1994, large current-account and fiscal deficits made the recovery unsustainable. During 1994 the general government deficit ballooned to over 8 percent of GDP, and the current-account deficit reached almost 10 percent,[3] higher than Mexico's in the period preceding the peso crisis. Given the apparent improvement in general economic performance during 1994, the general public did not fully perceive the implications of these problems, but broad segments of the policy elite were aware that the incoming Horn government faced formidable policy challenges.

---

[3] See Table A.4 in the appendix. According to the current-account balances data for transition economies, Hungary in 1994 showed one of the worst performances.

In analyzing the course of fiscal policy, it is necessary to distinguish several phases. The first nine months of the Horn administration was characterized by indecision and drift. This was followed in March 1995 by the initiation of the tough stabilization program known as the "Bokros package." Finally, we must consider the efforts by Bokros and his successor Medgyessy to establish a more centralized budget process during 1996 and 1997.

During the initial period, the long delay in framing a policy response occurred despite the warnings of Horn's first minister of finance, László Békesi, about the seriousness of the macroeconomic situation. Békesi, a leader of the liberal faction of the Socialists and an ally of the Free Democrats, had proposed an adjustment package similar to the one eventually instituted under Bokros, but he was unable to gain the backing of the prime minister. Instead, the issue of adjustment was delegated to the "social partners" represented in the IRC, and they remained unable to agree on a workable program or a realistic budget for 1995.

The failure of the government to take more decisive action was attributable to a number of factors. The decision to delegate to the IRC and the social partners reflected commitments the Socialists had made during the electoral campaign, and several months of negotiations – from May to July 1994 – were required to conclude the coalition agreement with the Free Democrats. Most important, however, internal coalitional divisions created strong incentives for Horn to avoid taking decisive steps; reliance on the IRC was one way of doing this. On the one hand, Horn was reluctant to delegate extensive authority to Békesi, who was a rival for leadership within the Socialist Party and had substantial support from the Free Democrats as well (Greskovits, Chapter 4, in this volume). At the same time, as in 1992, the shift of decision-making responsibilities into the IRC provided a means for the prime minister either to deepen backing for reform among his political supporters or to evade responsibility for inaction were it to eventuate.

For the reasons already discussed, however, Horn was ultimately in a better position than Antall to gain command of his coalition; in some respects, his position was even reinforced by the nine-month standoff over stabilization policy. The deadlock served to undercut Békesi as a rival for the party leadership and reduce the influence of his backers within the Free Democrats; Békesi resigned at the end of January 1994. It is also likely that both the Socialist left wing and their union allies on the IRC were weakened by their inability to forge a workable alternative to Békesi's proposals. By March 1995 this opening allowed Horn to appoint a new economic team, led by Lajos Bokros, with a strong commitment to deep and painful macroeconomic adjustments.

An external catalyst – the Mexican crisis of December 1994 – played an important role in this change of policy and ministers of finance. Concerned with the policy drift in the postelection period, both the IMF and the European Bank for Reconstruction and Development (EBRD) had refused requests for assistance prior to the crisis. In the aftermath of the peso meltdown, high-level talks in Germany emphasized even more strongly that European governments were not prepared to provide the kind of financial backing that Mexico had received from the United States. This refusal placed substantial pressure on Horn, who placed a very high priority on taking Hungary into Europe.

The need to establish credibility with external creditors also substantially increased the leverage Bokros could exert over Horn. Bokros was able to make his appointment as minister of finance conditional on the concurrent reinstatement of György Surányi, who had been removed in November 1991 by Antall, as head of the Central Bank. In the ensuing period, Bokros's insistence on full government backing of his adjustment program was repeatedly reinforced by threats to resign.

However, it is also important to emphasize the significance of a stronger parliamentary majority and greater prime ministerial authority in permitting Horn to provide this backing. While external pressures were undoubtedly crucial, the appointment of Bokros and Hungary's stabilization initiative did not come until almost three months after the Mexican devaluation, in part because of the coalitional divisions that prevailed during that period. Conversely, as Horn consolidated his position in the early part of 1995, he was able to move more decisively than executives who faced comparable challenges in other countries. In some presidential systems of Latin America, reform initiatives came at a much more acute stage of crisis, when hyperinflation induced the acceptance of strong executive action. In Russia and Brazil executives facing fragmented legislatures were unable to respond quickly to the external shocks of 1998 despite the real threat of financial collapse. In Hungary, despite growing concerns about the country's deteriorating fiscal and current-account position among technocrats and in the international financial press, there were no immediate signs of economic deterioration that would have alerted the mass public, or even politicians, to the need for reform. What was unusual about the package adopted under Horn was that it was primarily intended to preempt a more serious macroeconomic crisis.

The program was announced without prior consultation with the other ministers or the parliamentary leaders. Its key features included a temporary 8 percent surcharge on imports, designed to raise revenue as well as slow the deterioration of the current account, a 9 percent real devaluation, and an across-the-board freeze on spending, including tough limits on nominal wage increases in the public sector.

The more controversial issues included structural reforms, such as efforts to roll back entitlements in university education, maternity leave, and family allowances. Despite strong protest and the resignation of the minister of welfare, the cutbacks in entitlements were passed by the governing majority in the emergency budget legislation of May 1995; this step served to break the political taboo against welfare reform (Kornai 1996b). Many of these measures were overturned or delayed by the Constitutional Court. The wage and spending cuts allowed the government to cut deficits significantly anyway, but as we will suggest again, the insertion of the Constitutional Court into the debate had important implications for subsequent efforts at welfare reform.

A more effective instrument of fiscal adjustment proved to be the restraint on the wage bill that followed the 9 percent devaluation of the forint. While the devaluation contributed to an inflation estimated at over 28 percent in 1995, the Ministry of Finance imposed a limit of about 15 percent on nominal wage increases in the public sector. In contrast to the previous period, this decision was made unilaterally by the Ministry of Finance, without attempts to negotiate the assent of the unions. It was not clear initially that this component of the package could be implemented, and the IMF delayed signing an agreement for over a year in part because of concerns about whether the government would be able to hold the line. In fact, real wages dropped by over 12 percent in 1995, despite the protests of the unions and the Socialist left.

In contrast to the emergency measures undertaken in 1995, the budget for the following year (formulated and passed in the fall) was designed in conjunction with an IMF agreement and coordinated by the Ministry of Finance to calibrate spending priorities more carefully through consultations with the relevant ministries. The government's proposal sailed through the Parliament fairly smoothly, with only three Socialist deputies and one Free Democrat withholding their support.

These developments coincided with other signs of the weakening position of the dissident factions within the coalition. In the fall of 1995, Free Democrats and reform-oriented factions of the Socialists defeated a proposal to establish a new deputy prime minister for economic affairs, to be filled by Sándor Nagy, the former head of MSZOSZ and the leader of the left wing of the Socialist Party. This was followed in November by a Socialist Party congress, which reaffirmed the existing leadership in office and voted by a large majority to support the Bokros stabilization program (Ágh 1996: 21).

The Drive to Institutional Reform

Despite these victories, it remained unclear whether the government would be able to follow its initial steps with the establishment of more lasting and rationalized fiscal institutions. The institutional reform initiatives that accompanied the Bokros package sought to rationalize the management of public expenditures, eliminate or establish control over the centers of decentralized decision making inherited from the late Communist and Antall periods, and thus increase the transparency of intergovernmental transfers. The proposed reforms drew on the recommendations of a committee formed several months earlier under Békesi, but they gained further momentum after the initiation of the Bokros package.

Not surprisingly, efforts to implement this agenda were beset by controversy, and several major initiatives were defeated or delayed. Nevertheless, the government did put a number of significant reforms into place. Among the most important was the establishment of a central treasury, which was organized in 1995, formally established in January 1996, and given full legislative authorization in 1997. The newly established treasury was mandated to handle all fiscal flows and to disburse funds on an as-needed basis to CBIs. Decisions on the coverage of local governments were postponed until after the 1998 elections, leaving important possibilities for fiscal leakage at the local level. But the treasury did impose hard budget constraints on CBIs, which were deprived of the opportunity to utilize "free" government resources in the financial markets while accumulating debts to the central government. Consolidation of the extrabudgetary funds constituted a second important step. The number of funds was reduced during the first year of the program from over thirty to only five. In an important accounting move, finally, some remaining liabilities on the books of the Central Bank were transferred to the general government budget.

Although these steps are significant, the government had a much more mixed record in confronting the more important, politically salient, and controversial reforms of the health and pension systems. The Health Fund, which exercised wide discretionary authority over expenditures, posed the most immediate problems for fiscal management. Bokros had initially hoped to abolish it entirely and finance health expenditures fully from the central budget, but he was blocked almost immediately. The fund was not only the stronghold of powerful health-service organizations, but was also suspected of using its discretion to channel financing to politicians from the Socialist and other parties and to distribute patronage to local government. The showdown came during the preparation of the 1996 budget, when Bokros resigned rather than accept deficit projections by the Health Fund that he considered wildly unrealistic. His successor, Péter Medgyessy, followed with more incremental steps to increase the transparency of the fund and to regulate the delivery of services. Nevertheless, in the aftermath of the confrontation with Bokros, the decision was taken to defer further attempts at more fundamental reform until after the 1998 general election.

Efforts to reform the pension system met with somewhat greater but still partial success. The political story behind this process has been analyzed in detail by Joan Nelson in this volume (Chapter 8), and thus can be briefly sketched here. The initiative took shape while Bokros was still minister of finance, with encouragement and advice from the World Bank. As initially designed within the Ministry of Finance, the reform envisioned the establishment of a privatized "pillar" that would be approximately twice the size of the existing PAYG system. The proposal encountered strong opposition, however, both from the Ministry of Welfare and the Pension Fund, each of which developed counterproposals that defended the pay-as-you-go system. By the time Bokros resigned in March 1996, the process appeared stalemated.

In April 1996 the new minister of finance Medgyessy tried a different tack. Meeting with representatives from welfare and with key Socialist Party leaders, he agreed that if the others would publicly announce their acceptance of the principle of a private pillar, the Ministry of Finance would abandon the specifics of its own proposal and negotiate all "details." The cooperation of the Ministry of Welfare was enhanced by the appointment of more moderate officials at the staff level, and subsequently by Horn's appointment of a new minister, Mihály Kökény. From April to December, a new proposal was crafted by working groups that included personnel from the Ministries of Welfare and Finance, as well as from the World Bank.

Managers of the Pension Fund, however, remained hostile even to moderate proposals for privatization and became the principal leaders of the opposition during a period of public debate that followed. As has been the case with other severely contentious issues, bargaining over the reform was shifted into the IRC, where the social partners made substantial modifications of the government's plan with respect to both the indexing of pensions and the size of the private pillar. Although even these compromises were opposed by fund managers, they were sufficient to gain acceptance from the union representatives on the IRC.

Pension reform legislation was finally passed in 1997, but its implications are unclear. On the one hand, it has made Hungary one of the first of the transition economies to include a private pillar as part of its pension system. Demographic projections indicate, moreover, that the reform will have an important long-term impact in easing the strain that the pension system placed on public finances (Palacios and Rocha 1998). On the other hand, in the course of the long bargaining process, the final bill left almost all of the existing work force within the PAYG pillar and provided concessions on indexation that increased fiscal burdens in the short run. To soften union opposition to the reform, finally, the government acquiesced to a substantial increase in the leverage that existing union leaders could exert over the funds. Under the terms of the new agreement, union leaders would be allowed to appoint fund managers instead of being required to submit their candidates to direct election.

To a significant degree, the difficulties encountered in the pension and health reform can be explained by the fact that the Horn administration had already undertaken a very substantial reform package; one could thus expect some natural limit to the process. The decision to postpone the health reform, moreover, is consistent with a modified electoral-cycle hypothesis under which coalitional cohesion on particular issues tends to fall as elections approach and the incentives of coalition members to compete with one another begin to outweigh those pushing toward cooperation. It is important to underline as well that the Parliament is not the only veto gate in the Hungarian system. As we have seen, the Constitutional Court played a conspicuous role in deflecting the 1995 initiative, and the possibility that it might again intervene could have been a deterrent to more radical reform measures in 1996 and 1997.

Nevertheless, the mixed outcome of this part of the reform effort suggests how even prime ministers who control cohesive legislative coalitions can be constrained by the interactive effects of political institutions and constituent interests. Given Horn's political constituencies, the formation of independent governance structures in health and pensions posed a substantial limit to the government's freedom of maneuver. In challenging health and welfare entitlements, Horn was taking on commitments to these constituencies made both by the late Communist government and by his own political party; and these commitments were now protected by the institutionalized influence of interested parties: the health-care profession in the one instance and the labor unions in the other. Similarly, the IRC offered an important point of access to groups whose influence might have been more limited in other venues. In principle, the government's disciplined majority gave it the power to reverse earlier decisions with relative ease, but the congruence of interests between Socialist Party factions and the interests organized through these bodies would have made such a decision politically costly.

In contrast, the Orbán government that came to power in May 1998 appealed to anti-Socialist voters and did not operate under these political constraints. Although a detailed discussion of its policies is beyond the scope of this chapter, the initial measures of the new government were indicative of the fact that Horn's dilemmas with the funds were political rather than constitutional. In July 1998, the Orbán coalition of Young Democrats, Smallholders, and the Hungarian Democratic Forum passed legislation that eliminated both funds as self-governing bodies, appointed a new state secretary to supervise their reorganization, and dismissed the head of the health fund. Authority over the funds was first placed in the prime minister's office but later transferred to the Ministry of Finance – a further step toward centralization of the budget process. Policy toward the IRC was defined in the spring of 1999. A paper issued by the Finance Ministry declared that it did not consider the council a decision-making body, that it should be seen as only one of several such councils, and that it enjoyed no monopoly on interest representation. These measures indicate that the prime minister could wield substantial power when freed from the political constraints of his predecessor. As we suggest briefly in the conclusion, the ability of the government to move so decisively may reflect a longer-term trend toward the formation of two relatively stable partisan blocs within the framework of a parliamentary constitution.

Conclusions and Comparative Context

Although myriad factors have shaped Hungary's transition to the market, we have focused on the contributing role of politics and political institutions. We have argued that there are features of the Hungarian political setup that provide the basis for strong government, including a unicameral parliamentary system with a strongly majoritarian electoral system. While these institutional features make decisive government possible, we have also argued that much depends on characteristics of, and developments in, the party system: the capacity for decisive policy action and institutional reform rests on the cohesion of the ruling coalition. Both the drift in fiscal policy and the continuing tendency toward decentralized budget institutions under Antall reflected deep and worsening intracoalitional and intraparty rivalries. Conversely, under Horn the fiscal adjustment and the initiation of important institutional changes, such as the treasury reform, were made possible by a more cohesive and stable legislative coalition.

These findings run counter to conclusions drawn from broader cross-national research on reform in transition economies, some of which shows that progress toward reform varies positively with party fragmentation and weak executives. In a recent article, Joel Hellman (1998) provides an important summary and discussion of these findings. The governments that are most vulnerable to electoral and coalitional pressures are more likely to undertake radical reform, he argues, because they are least likely to be captured by enterprise managers and other elites who gained during the first round of partial reforms but who oppose the elimination of remaining market distortions. Using the EBRD measures of reform, his regressions show that progress is correlated not only with the extent of political freedom but also with the number of parties in the governing coalition (r = .72) (Hellman 1998: 204).

Our analysis of Hungary is consistent with Hellman's general argument that democratic reforms reduced the vulnerability of fiscal and monetary authorities to groups linked to the old planning apparatus. We find entirely plausible, moreover, that reform would tend to lag among Central Asian republics ruled by personalist, ex-Communist dictatorships that deploy political and economic resources derived from the old Soviet system; these are typically among the slowest reformers in Hellman's statistical sample.

When we consider variations among democratic systems, however, we are skeptical about the challenges that Hellman's findings pose to the generalizability of our argument about coalition politics and constitutional veto gates. One reason for our skepticism derives from the relatively close correlation between Hellman's indicators of reform and the historical background and geographic location of the countries in the sample. The fast reformers are the Baltic and Visegrád countries. Next are the rest of Eastern Europe, Russia, and most other European ex-Soviet republics. The Central Asian republics are ranked at the bottom. Although this pattern does have exceptions, it suggests that Hellman's findings may be driven less by institutional arrangements and party politics than by other factors, including initial conditions and opportunities to enter the European Union. Most former Soviet republics were disadvantaged in this regard, whereas the high score that Hungary received during the Antall period reflected in part both the prior history of reform Communism and the political and economic influence arising from proximity to Western Europe.

More important for our analysis is the way the countries in Hellman's sample are ranked in terms of the independent variable: the number of parties in the governing coalition. According to his measure, parliamentary governments in countries such as Hungary include a larger number of coalition partners than the slower reforming countries of Russia, Ukraine, and most other former Soviet republics. This seems to indicate either that our analysis of fiscal reform under the Horn government in Hungary has overemphasized the importance of cohesive legislative majorities and a strong executive, or that Hungary is a deviant case.

But such a conclusion would hold only if we were to accept the validity of Hellman's measures of the size and composition of the governing coalitions. These measures, however, are based on debatable judgments about what should count as a party, and how to identify the governing coalition; and they do not consider the question of internal party discipline. Such measurement problems can be especially problematic in presidential systems such as Russia and Ukraine, which are characterized not only by exceptionally high levels of fragmentation in the party system, but also a low level of intraparty discipline and a multiplicity of veto points. Reform in such countries is slow not because governments answer to fewer coalition partners than in Central Europe and the Baltics, but because they have narrow and undisciplined bases of legislative support and must rely instead on the backing of extraparliamentary coalitions of "oligarchs." If one accepts this alternative view, our analysis of the Hungarian experience would be quite consistent with the general pattern: reform accelerated in Hungary because, unlike in most former Soviet Republics, the Horn government could count on a disciplined parliamentary majority and faced a relatively limited number of institutional veto gates.

Questions about our argument can be raised not only by findings from large-n regressions but also by reference to experiences among the smaller set of more comparable Central European countries. Within this set, the Polish case presents perhaps the most serious challenge. Polish governments maintained fiscal restraint and initiated a pension reform, despite a larger number of veto gates and very fractious multiparty politics, a success attributable in part to international pressures and the packaging of reform programs. In assessing the impact of constitutional and party institutions in that case, however, it is again necessary to look closely at initial conditions and the policy process itself. Although an extended discussion of the Polish case is well beyond the scope of this chapter, a few brief comments can serve to illustrate this point.

Poland's success in fiscal reform owes much to the political and economic crisis conditions in which the Solidarity government first assumed power. In contrast to the Horn government in Hungary, the initiation of radical macroeconomic adjustments was undertaken in Poland during a period of hyperinflation and "extraordinary politics," which temporarily concentrated substantial authority in the hands of the executive. As Polish parties fragmented in the early 1990s, the adjustment program stalled and the IMF temporarily suspended its support (Johnson and Kowalska 1994). The Hana Suchocka government did correct course, but fiscal brinkmanship continued and she herself was ousted in a vote of no-confidence. Under the succeeding Socialist–Peasant governments, which still faced a president with opposed preferences and with veto power, fiscal pressures were eased by the resumption of growth and increasing public revenues. Nevertheless, pressures to increase spending were not brought under control until 1995, when the election of a Socialist president and the appointment of a Socialist prime minister reduced the number of veto players in the Polish system. At this point, Polish politics began to exhibit somewhat greater resemblance to parliamentary politics in Hungary.

The pension reform analyzed by Hausner in this volume (Chapter 7) underscores the importance of skillful packaging of reform and political negotiations; these factors were crucial in gaining broad backing for the reforms across almost the entire spectrum of political parties in the Polish Sejm. It should be noted, however, that this success was achieved not during the turbulent Solidarity years but under the relatively more stable Socialist–Peasant governments. As Hausner also stresses, moreover, success would not have been possible without the establishment of an initiating authority that bypassed normal ministerial and parliamentary channels and set the agenda for debate and negotiation.

Within the more limited framework of the Hungarian case itself, finally, we would argue that our comparison between the Antall and Horn governments shows reasonably well that the cohesion of parliamentary coalitions does make a difference – and in the expected direction. We have also seen that even with the establishment of a solid parliamentary majority, the Horn government did not achieve all that it set out to do, particularly with respect to the reform of the pension and health systems. As Joan Nelson points out in this volume (Chapter 8), the ambiguous nature of the government's achievements rests in part on the inherent difficulty of these "second stage" reforms; there is less technical consensus on them, they are administratively more complex, and they take more time to implement. However, we also found that institutional factors played a key role in understanding the course of these reforms. First, despite strong legislative support, some key provisions of the government's reform efforts were overturned by the intervention of the Constitutional Court. Second, the reforms were made more difficult by institutional initiatives taken under the much weaker Antall government, including particularly the governance structures of the two social insurance funds. These governance structures serve to underline our argument that a straightforward interest group analysis of the course of reform is subtly misleading. The political weight of both unions and the health-care profession came not from their independent organizational capabilities; this is particularly true of the unions, which are in fact quite weak. Rather, their influence came from institutional arrangements in which they were disproportionately represented, and from political alliances with the ruling party.

Looking forward, we may speculate about the way the politics of reform and economic policy making might evolve in the aftermath of the defeat of the Socialists and Free Democrats and the installation of a new governing coalition under Viktor Orbán. Of course, a number of factors exogenous to the political realm will influence the direction of further reform in Hungary, including the shocks that began to emanate from the world economy in 1998, the timing and nature of entry into the European Union, and the longer-run effects of the reforms already initiated. However, we base our speculation not on the future course of the international or domestic economies, but on possible developments in the political system. First, much will depend on how organized interests evolve. In major sectors such as labor there are ongoing signs of fragmentation and weakness, parallel perhaps to similar trends in advanced industrial states. This weakness poses problems for the evolution of corporatist mechanisms such as the IRC, because fragmentation makes any bargains struck through them more difficult to sustain. Decentralization and local politics, to which we have given only passing attention, will also play an important role in the politics of fiscal policy and reform. In other settings, we have found that the devolution of greater authority to local government naturally exerts a centrifugal force on the fiscal system, as provincial and municipal politicians seek to gain greater autonomy and freedom of maneuver vis-à-vis the center (Willis, Garman, and Haggard 1999). This tendency is enhanced in countries in which national legislators have incentives to be attentive to local political forces; in Hungary, such incentives exist through the SMD legislators. This might become more muted, however, by increasing rationalization of the party system and the exigencies of national government formation.

A key question for Hungary's political future is whether the party system continues to revolve around three major blocs (Socialists, Liberals, and Nationalists), whether other, postmaterial issues become salient, or whether we see the evolution of two relatively stable blocs that compete along a single dominant issue dimension. Some aspects of the political situation that emerged after the 1998 elections seemed on the surface to point to the first of these possibilities. The resurgence of the traditional

Smallholders and the Young Democrats' shift toward "identity politics" indicates the continuing strength of cultural as well as economic issues in Hungarian politics. As noted earlier, if strong crosscutting economic and ethnonationalist cleavages persist, it would complicate the policy-making process within the governing coalition. Under such circumstances, Orbán could find it difficult to maintain fiscal discipline in the face of pressure from populist currents within the Smallholders Party. The emergence of other salient issue cleavages would naturally tend to fragment the party system further, although this seems less and less likely.

On the other hand, the emergence of two major blocs divided along a single cleavage dimension may be more likely than appeared to be the case throughout most of the 1990s. In the 1998 elections, there was a tendency for parties to form preelectoral coalitions that involved strategic withdrawals in advance of the runoffs.[4] This indicates a "settling down" of the party system and a clearer connection between voters' choices and the formation of governments. Were such a change to occur over the long-run, it would produce a system with "Westminster" features: weak blackmail potential for smaller parties and more cohesive governing coalitions. Under situations of deep social and economic divisions, such systems can in theory polarize as in Jamaica in the 1980s. However, the general prognosis here is positive. While governments of this kind would be somewhat less representative of the full variety of social interests, they would be more decisive – as reflected in the reform efforts of the Horn government and in Orbán's actions toward the social funds and the IRC – and potentially more oriented toward the broad policy preferences of the Hungarian electorate.

References

Ágh, Attila. 1996. The Year of Two Elections. In S. Kurtán, P. Sándor, and L. Vas, eds., *Magyarország politikai évkönyve 1995* (The political yearbook of Hungary 1995), pp. 16–29. Budapest: Demokrácia Kutatások Magyar Központja Alapítvány.

Alesina, Alberto, and Roberto Perotti. 1995. *Budget Deficits and Budget Institutions.* Working Paper No. 5556. Cambridge, Mass.: National Bureau of Economic Research.

Bartlett, David. 1997. *The Political Economy of Dual Transformations.* Ann Arbor: University of Michigan Press.

Bruszt, László, and David Charles Stark. 1997. *Postsocialist Pathways: Transforming Politics and Property in East Central Europe.* Cambridge: Cambridge University Press.

---

[4] We are indebted to Kenneth Benoit for this observation (personal communication).

Cain, Bruce E., John Ferejohn, and Morris Fiorina. 1987. *The Personal Vote.* Cambridge, Mass.: Harvard University Press.

Carey, John M., and Matthew S. Shugart. 1995. Incentives to Cultivate a Personal Vote: A Rank Ordering of Electoral Formulas. *Electoral Studies* 14: 417–39.

eds. 1998. *Executive Decree Authority.* Cambridge: Cambridge University Press.

Cox, Gary W. 1987. *The Efficient Secret.* Cambridge: Cambridge University Press.

Csaba, László. 1995. Hungary and the IMF: The Experience of a Cordial Discord. *Journal of Comparative Economics* 20: 211–34.

Dethier, Jean-Jacques, and Tamar Shapiro. 1998. Constitutional Rights and the Reform of Social Entitlements. In L. Bokros and J.-J. Dethier, eds., *Public Finance Reform during the Transition: The Experience of Hungary*, pp. 448–75. Washington, D.C.: World Bank.

EBRD. *Annual Report.* Various issues. London: EBRD.

1998, April. *Transition Report Update.* London: EBRD.

Greskovits, Béla. 1998. *The Political Economy of Protest and Patience: East European and Latin American Transformations Compared.* Budapest: Central European University Press.

Grilli, Vittorio, Donato Masciandaro, and Guido Tabellini. 1991. Political and Monetary Institutions and Public Finance in the Industrial Democracies. *Economic Policy* 13: 41–89.

Haggard, Stephan, and Robert R. Kaufman. 1995. *The Political Economy of Democratic Transitions.* Princeton: Princeton University Press.

Hellman, Joel S. 1998. Winners Take All: The Politics of Partial Reform in Post-Communist Transitions. *World Politics* 50: 203–54.

Johnson, Simon, and Marzena Kowalska. 1994. Poland: The Political Economy of Shock Therapy. In S. Haggard and S. B. Webb, eds., *Voting for Reform: Democracy, Political Liberalization, and Economic Adjustment*, pp. 185–242. New York: Oxford University Press.

Kopits, George. 1993. Hungary: A Case of Gradual Fiscal Reform. In V. Tanzi, ed., *Transition to Market: Studies in Fiscal Reform*, pp. 65–91. Washington, D.C.: International Monetary Fund.

Kornai, János. 1996a. Paying the Bill for Goulash Communism: Hungarian Development and Macro Stabilization in Comparative Perspective. *Social Research* 63: 943–1040.

1996b. *Adjustment without Recession: A Case Study of the Hungarian Stabilization.* Collegium Budapest Discussion Paper No. 33. Budapest: Collegium Budapest.

Kraxner, Erika. 1995. Parliamentary Discussion and Committee Preparation of the Finances Act. In A. Ágh and S. Kurtán, eds., *Democratization and Europeanization in Hungary: The First Parliament, 1990–1994*, pp. 135–48. Budapest: Hungarian Center for Democratic Studies.

Lijphart, Arend. 1984. *Democracies: Patterns of Majoritarian and Consensus Government in Twenty-One Countries.* New Haven: Yale University Press.

Orenstein, Mitchell. 1996. Out of the Red: Building Capitalism and Democracy in Post-Communist Europe. Ph.D. dissertation, Yale University.

Palacios, Robert, and Roberto Rocha. 1998. The Hungarian Pension System in Transition. In L. Bokros and J.-J. Dethier, eds., *Public Finance Reform during the Transition: The Experience of Hungary*, pp. 177–219. Washington, D.C.: World Bank.

Pataki, Judit. 1992. Hungarian Government Midway through Its First Term. *RFE/RL Research Report* 1: 18–24.

Powell, G. Bingham, Jr. 2000. *Elections as Instruments of Democracy*. New Haven: Yale University Press.

Roubini, Nuoriel, and Jeffrey Sachs. 1989. Government Spending and Budget Deficits in the Industrialized Countries. *Economic Policy* 8: 99–133.

Sajó, András. 1996. How the Rule of Law Killed Hungarian Welfare Reform. *East European Constitutional Review* 5: 31–42.

Schaffer, Mark E. 1995. *Government Subsidies to Enterprises in Central and Eastern Europe: Budgetary Subsidies and Tax Arrears*. Discussion Paper No. 1144. London: Centre for Economic Policy Research.

Shugart, Matthew S., and John Carey. 1992. *Presidents and Assemblies; Constitutional Design and Electoral Dynamics*. Cambridge: Cambridge University Press.

Stein, Ernesto, Ernesto Talvi, and Alejandro Gristani. 1998. *Institutional Arrangements and Fiscal Performance: The Latin American Experience*. Working Paper No. 6358. Cambridge, Mass.: National Bureau of Economic Research.

Szarvas, László. 1995. Personnel and Structural Changes in the First Hungarian Parliament. In A. Ágh and S. Kurtán, eds., *Democratization and Europeanization in Hungary: The First Parliament, 1990–1994*, pp. 201–8. Budapest: Hungarian Center for Democratic Studies.

Taagepera, Rein, and Bernard Grofman. 1985. Rethinking Duverger's Law: Predicting the Effective Number of Parties in Plurality and PR Systems – Parties Minus Issues Equals One. *European Journal of Political Research* 13: 341–52.

Tőkés, Rudolf. 1996. *Hungary's Negotiated Revolution*. Cambridge: Cambridge University Press.

Willis, Eliza, Christopher Garman, and Stephan Haggard. 1999. The Politics of Decentralization in Latin America. *Latin American Research Review* 34: 7–56.

Interviews

Kis, János. Philosopher; 1990–91, Chairman of SZDSZ. November 19, 1997.

Kupa, Mihály. Economist; 1991–93, MoF. November 19, 1997.

CHAPTER 4

Brothers-in-Arms or Rivals in Politics? Top Politicians and Top Policy Makers in the Hungarian Transformation

BÉLA GRESKOVITS

Leadership in the Hungarian Economic Transformation

Between 1990 and 1998 Hungary became a market society where the freedom of internal markets, foreign trade, and private-sector entry matched the standards of the Organization for Economic Cooperation and Development (OECD). In 1998 three-quarters of productive capacity was operated by private owners. New institutional and legal infrastructure compatible with the market economy replaced the direct and indirect bureaucratic coordination of the socialist system (Kornai 1992: 97). However, the implementation of the market-oriented strategy was difficult. The reform process seemed to be fragile and indeterminate.

On the one hand, harsh initial conditions, the collapse of the Soviet markets, and policy failures meant ever-present macroeconomic challenges for politicians and policy makers. Between 1990 and 1993 Hungary suffered from the transformational recession (Kornai 1994) followed by a short-lived recovery at the high cost of macroeconomic imbalances in 1994. Mounting current-account and fiscal deficits in 1995 were corrected by a draconian stabilization and adjustment package, which brought about falling investment and living standards, stagnation, social dislocation, and political protest. By 1997 Hungary returned to growth.

On the other hand, the rules, institutions, and conflicts characteristic to democratic politics had an immense impact on the economy

I am thankful to László Bruszt, Valerie Bunce, László Csaba, Vladimir Gimpelson, Stephan Haggard, Robert R. Kaufman, János Kornai, Kamilla Lányi, and Joan M. Nelson, for their comments and suggestions on an earlier version of this essay. Collegium Budapest provided generous funding, and a supportive scholarly and human environment for my project.

111

throughout the whole period, underlining the idea that creating capitalism after Communism is an eminently political project. This fact generated a number of political economy interpretations of economic policy making and institution building in Hungary. Alternatively, or in combination, these explanations highlighted the role of initial economic conditions, inherited behavioral and political patterns, and the impact of external actors, of emerging domestic political institutions, and of domestic coalitions.

My question is, How important a part did political leaders and their ambitions play in Hungary's economic transformation?[1] Specifically, how did leaders influence the dynamics of economic transformation programs, economic policy-making institutions, and their governments' capacity to reform? Thus I explore the explanatory power of the personal element, of micro level politics. I accept as a point of reference that the leaders' strategies are shaped by legacies, external constraints, political institutions, and societal interests. But I am intrigued by another set of causal links: are these constraints and opportunities also shaped by personalities, ideas, political profiles, and relationships, and if they are, in what way?

I address these questions in a comparative case study of Hungary's two successive governments, focusing on eight persons who held key positions in them: two prime ministers, József Antall (1990–93) and Gyula Horn (1994–98), and their six ministers of finance (hereafter, MoF), Ferenc Rabár (1990), Mihály Kupa (1990–93), Iván Szabó (1993–94), László Békesi (1994–95), Lajos Bokros (1995–96), and Péter Medgyessy (1996–98). My account is based on my interviews with the MoFs and other actors, media coverage of events, the MoFs' programs, other documents, and the literature on the subject.[2] The next section starts by comparing the two prime ministers' political leadership profiles. The third section takes a closer look at the personal and institutional conditions and outcomes of the policy-making process under the Antall government, while the fourth section outlines the corresponding story under Horn.

Methodologically, my inquiry originates in the literature on the political economy of policy reform and leadership.[3] Writers on these topics

---

[1] My question is similar to the one put in Domínguez 1997.

[2] I am indebted to my interview partners who shared with me their views and knowledge of the events and processes. Mária Csanádi generously shared her own interviews, which provided me with valuable background information.

[3] Representative works of the political economy of policy reforms include Bates and Krueger 1993; Haggard and Kaufman 1992, 1995; Haggard and Webb 1994; Nelson 1989, 1990; and Williamson 1994.

usually assume that if reforms are to succeed politicians must delegate concentrated executive authority to policy makers, and mobilize political support for their programs. In my essay I provide evidence that in the course of Hungarian transformation this frequently happened. Whenever the Hungarian prime ministers allied with their top policy makers and supported them, the result was the acceleration of reform measures and the expansion of control of the MoF over the policy-making machinery. I also found that the prime ministers were not always ready to behave as "brothers-in-arms" with their MoFs. Often, their relationship was full of tensions. In part, these tensions were inherent in their different political roles. The prime ministers' efforts to maintain the balance between political feasibility and economic rationality occasionally contradicted reform goals, and resulted in the limitation of the power of top policy makers.

However, the MoFs, especially when they attempted to implement comprehensive reforms in hard times, viewed their control of executive power as a sine qua non of success. Moreover, the MoFs often had their own bureaucratic and political ambitions, which the prime ministers sometimes interpreted as challenges to their own power and authority. Whether the prime ministers could cope with such tensions depended in part on how much they trusted their top technocrats. To a great extent, trust was a personal matter. It depended not on purely rational calculations but on personality traits and the "chemistry" of the leaders' relationships.[4]

To the extent that the ambitions of prime ministers' and their MoFs' clashed, or that the "chemistry" of mutual trust was absent for other reasons, the stage was set for conflicts, mistrust, and rivalry rather than alliance. If rivalry at the top prevailed, economic reforms were aborted, slowed, or watered down; the MoF's bureaucratic power was circumscribed by the prime minister; and the challenger was ultimately fired from the government. Instances of both alliance and rivalry between top leaders are evident in the course of Hungary's transformation and did indeed make an impact on the dynamics and the bureaucratic institutions of policy reform.

My second finding concerns the sources and explanations of recurrent patterns of alliance and rivalry. In a political institutionalist perspective, leaders backed by large, cohesive, and disciplined majorities in the legislature provide more support to reform programs and are more likely

---

[4] The "chemistry" may depend upon the complementarity or conflict between their ambitions, preferences, and behavior and may ultimately decide if they like or dislike, trust or mistrust each other. I am indebted for this interpretation to János Kornai.

to delegate power to their top policy makers than leaders with fragmented or reckless partisan background (see Haggard, Kaufman, and Shugart, Chapter 3, in this volume).

My findings on the Hungarian case challenge this argument in terms of its general validity. I found that radical and risky reform steps could be undertaken under the politically fragmented Antall government whenever the prime minister trusted and supported his top reformer. Specifically, when Antall – who valued his strong position more than his role as a party chief – felt his authority was reinforced by the coordination and credibility provided by his top policy maker, he did not hesitate to support him even against partisan pressures from his own fragmented coalition. Yet, his alliance with his reformers ended when he suspected them of challenging his own authority as prime minister. Thus policy makers with excessive bureaucratic and political ambitions were sooner or later identified as rivals and lost both the prime minister's support and their power.

Conversely, the political cohesion and discipline of the Horn coalition was not sufficient for radical reform when the prime minister mistrusted his MoF in charge. Horn, who behaved like a party boss, refused to support any radical policy changes advocated by policy makers who were also rivals in his own party. In the beginning of his term Horn thus fought out his partisan rivalries before implementing a comprehensive economic package, despite the cost of the delay to his credibility and Hungary's economic stability.

Leadership thus mattered – political leaders were important in Hungarian economic transformation – as did the ideas, ambitions, and strategies of the Hungarian policy makers selected to key decision-making positions. The availability of strong coalition support could both be substituted for and offset by the quality of leadership. Whereas Prime Minister Antall's leadership occasionally counterbalanced the effects of coalitional fragmentation, and proved to be the ultimate source of political support to reforms and reformers, Prime Minister Horn's leadership ambitions from time to time undermined reforms and reformers, even if the political support of a cohesive coalition was available to him.

The more general lesson for political economy is that the contribution of leadership to economic reform cannot be mechanically inferred from the leaders' coalition background. Rather, these variables must be studied both separately and in interaction with each other (and with other important factors mentioned).

Yet, how important was leadership in Hungary's economic transformation? Was this influence evenly strong over the whole period? I do not think it was. One way to point out the limits of my explanation is to contrast my argument with that presented by Haggard, Kaufman, and Shugart in their contribution to this volume (Chapter 3). In the area of fiscal policy and institutional reforms, these authors contrast the slow and contradictory advance under Antall with the radical and decisive thrust under Horn. They conclude that the secret of success lies in the cohesive majority of the Horn government, whereas political fragmentation under the Antall government contributed to policy drift and failure. I agree with Haggard, Kaufman, and Shugart that the pace of reforms was slower under Antall than under Horn, especially between 1995 and 1998. Although Antall was a strong leader he did give in to particularistic pressures and antireform forces in his fragmented coalition toward the end of his term.[5] I also agree that after Prime Minister Horn eliminated his challengers, his cohesive political coalition proved to be an asset for decisive reform steps. In this sense while Haggard, Kaufman, and Shugart point at the "general trend" my argument explains the "deviations."

Moreover, these authors also argue that as political institutions are consolidated, they will increasingly shape the opportunities and constraints available to political leaders. In conformity with this argument I found that leadership did not have an evenly strong effect over the whole period. Rather, the *institutional fluidity*[6] characteristic of the first few years of Hungarian economic transformation enhanced the personal influence of Antall, a strong leader, whereas Gyula Horn based his personal power on his standing in his party and the coalition. Thus I believe the future belongs to party builders, power brokers, and coalition managers. This is one lesson I have to offer to forthcoming Hungarian governments.

---

[5] The acceleration of reforms in the Horn period was first highlighted by Kornai (1997), who considered the 1995 Bokros package as a decisive break with the gradualist transformation strategies followed by both the Antall government and by the reformist governments of Hungarian state socialism. But Horn could proceed with the transformation faster because of the crucial measures undertaken by the Antall government. For instance, privatization could dramatically accelerate under Horn, because his predecessor had passed laws on financial institutions, accounting, and bankruptcy, and by restructuring many firms and making them attractive for foreign investors. Similarly, the Horn government could achieve remarkable results in the banking privatization because the Antall government's bank consolidation program created favorable conditions for a rapid sale of the Hungarian banks to foreigners in 1996–98. The implementation of these measures was costly in fiscal terms and politically risky. Yet, they were implemented – greatly contributing to the poor fiscal performance of the Antall government – and alongside other reforms they paved the road for the rapid advance of the economic transformation between 1995 and 1998.

[6] I am indebted for this formulation to Valerie Bunce.

A Sketch of József Antall's and Gyula Horn's Political Leadership Profile

In order to explain the conditions and limits under which Hungarian political leaders were willing to delegate executive power we have to understand who they were. Both Antall and Horn were prime ministers and party leaders at the same time and sought to reconcile the administrative and partisan aspects of their roles. However, they had quite different attitudes about the relative importance of bureaucratic and party politics. To put it briefly, Antall was more a prime minister than a party chief, whereas Horn was more a party boss than a prime minister. This difference is evident in their socialization and political career paths, in the political opportunities and constraints they exploited when in office, and in their behavior while prime ministers and party leaders.

There is anecdotal evidence that Antall's main ambition was always to become the Hungarian prime minister and he had been consciously preparing for this mission (Beke 1993: 18). Given this ambition, it was of secondary importance to him which party would actually support him politically: in 1988–89, it could have equally been the Smallholders, the Christian Democrats, or the Hungarian Democratic Forum (MDF) (Révész 1995: 30–32). When Antall entered politics in 1988–89, he "shopped around" in the emerging political market. He chose the MDF, and joined the party as a latecomer at a time when its success as a movement seemed to be on the wane. Antall ideologically transformed the MDF into a conservative Christian Democratic Party, and forced through organizational changes that enhanced his authority. Antall and the MDF needed each other, in short, for strategic political reasons. For Antall the MDF was a means rather than an end to his political ambition. For the MDF, Antall enhanced its prospects for electoral victory.

Horn followed a rather different career path. He has always been a party politician. In 1989, it was his party position which allowed him to become minister of foreign affairs in the last Communist government. After the transition, Horn's major achievement was to turn his Hungarian Socialist Party (MSZP) from the marginalized loser of the 1990 elections to the powerful winner of the 1994 elections. Unlike Antall, who could become party chief because he was (regarded as) influential and powerful, Horn became prime minister in 1994 because he had proved a capable party boss from 1990 to 1994. For the MSZP, Horn was less indispensable as a prime minister than an integrative party leader, even after 1994.

It is also striking how much the two prime ministers differed in their ways of exploiting and shaping initial political opportunities and constraints. Their first, crucial steps of political institution building both reflected further contrasts in their leadership profiles. Apparently unconstrained by any partisan accountability, in 1990 Antall signed the "founding pact" cementing his strong position not with the members of his coalition but with the major opposition party, the Alliance of Free Democrats (SZDSZ). Moreover, despite their protests, he never signed a formal coalition agreement with his coalition partners. Thus, while Antall based his power in part on the opposition, he was never formally accountable to his own coalition. By contrast, Horn's authority as a prime minister was constrained from the beginning by a detailed, formal agreement with his coalition partner, the SZDSZ. As a consequence, Horn was held accountable not only to the MSZP, but to some extent even to the SZDSZ. Thus both Antall's and Horn's career ambitions were reinforced by the incentives and constraints stemming from the framework they created.

Finally, there is ample information on how Antall acted as the "prime minister of the MDF" and of the coalition parties, whereas Horn typically behaved as if he were Hungary's and his government's "party boss." In dealing with the MDF, Antall pushed through a new, centralizing statute for the party (Beke 1993: 55). He repeatedly threatened the MDF that he would resign as prime minister unless he was elected party chairman. He then filled the MDF's presidium with members of the government, and the coalition parties' leadership with politicians personally loyal to him (Révész 1995: 120). Horn, in turn, was widely known for his style of "acting out" from his role as a prime minister. He often shocked his government with personal promises made to various MSZP constituencies – workers, pensioners, public servants – mostly without any prior consultation with his cabinet. Whereas we see an element of "presidentialism" in Antall's flotation over the parties, Horn was deeply enmeshed in party politics.

In this context a final point can be stressed: coalition management posed different tasks for Antall and Horn. Antall could rise above parties because their divisions in terms of ideology, policy preferences, and societal interests were less clear-cut than those in the MSZP. The MDF's supposed segmentation into "national liberals," "Christian Democrats," and "populist nationalists" was more a reflection of how Antall wanted to see his party than of reality (Révész 1995: 132). In contrast, the MSZP really had a liberal wing supported by opinion-leading intellectuals, the media, some MSZP oriented business interests, and the SZDSZ. While many of the MSZP's constituencies, rank and file, and MPs did not have clear-cut ideological and policy preferences and were loyal to the party and Horn, the party also had a strong left wing based in the post-Communist union federations.

The "interest groups" played different roles under the two governments. Under Antall, they were either not yet in place – private business was just in the process of creation – or were not represented in his coalition. By contrast, both the trade-union elite and the post-Communist business-managerial elite had a strong representation in the MSZP. Thus Antall faced stronger extraparty pressures between 1990 and 1994; whenever he wanted to get in touch with the lobbies, he had to leave the party-political arena and be a prime minister rather than a party chief. Under Horn, interest-group influence appeared in the form of intraparty pressures.[7]

Prior to sorting out the implications of these differences I want to highlight one similarity. As a consequence of his pact with the SZDSZ Antall could create the legal and institutional framework of a chancellor's system of governance, which provided him with almost unconstrained power over his government. This arrangement was also maintained under Horn. Thus in constitutional terms both Antall and Horn were strong prime ministers. But what accounts for the variation? My argument is that the conditions under which the prime ministers were willing to delegate executive authority to their policy makers were different, and this was in part due to the contrasts in their leadership profiles.

Antall, much more than Horn, tried to shield the core of his political mission and his governance against partisan pressures. Often his appointments were either nonpartisan, or if they had significant positions in any of the coalition parties, they were safely under his control. Furthermore, in contrast to Horn, nothing was more alien to Antall's administrative strategy than to neutralize political rivals by co-opting them to top policy-making posts.[8] Antall strengthened his position by *excluding* his potential competitors from bureaucratic power, and by co-opting persons who he potentially could rely on as allies, in extreme cases even against his coalition.

The political profile of Horn contributed to different patterns of trust and authority. Personal loyalty or bureaucratic capacity were important for Horn as well, especially after 1995. But Horn more often than Antall

---

[7] Clearly, however, the variation of the task of coalition management also reflected the two leaders' profiles. Because of his vision of "proper" democracy and his mistrust of post-Communist elites, Antall deliberately tried to keep his party safe from their direct presence and influence. Horn's political socialization in the Kádár regime made him feel more comfortable with the idea of MSZP as the political organization for a multitude of social interest groups from trade unions to business associations and pensioners' organizations.

[8] For example, neither István Csurka, the leader of the MDF's extremists, nor József Torgyán, the chairman of the Smallholder Party, ever managed to capture decision-making authority, although both of them repeatedly and forcefully expressed their demands for more influence.

used appointments or the restructuring of economic policy-making administration to smooth over partisan rivalries within the MSZP, or between the MSZP and the SZDSZ. Thus trust played a less central role than in his predecessor's case. Rather, Horn was occasionally forced to choose and support top policy makers because of their own political position or in response to an economic emergency.

What do these differences imply for our understanding of the politics of economic transformation under Antall and Horn? The main arena of Antall's and his MoF's interaction was the administration, which was relatively insulated from party politics. Moreover, his decisions originated more directly from personal or bureaucratic motivations than from his exposure to partisan pressures. Horn's efforts to maintain his power in the MSZP and the coalition penetrated his bureaucratic decisions. Hence, although leadership and bureaucratic politics seem relevant for understanding decision making under Antall, party politics gives a better insight into the relationship between the top actors under the Horn government. These differences can be seen by examining the MoFs' influence on policy making during the two periods.

Interaction at the Top under the Prime Minister Party Chief József Antall

The Policy Drift of 1990

Hungarian economic policy making in the 1990s was divided at its birth. Antall's first government did not have one top policy maker but four influential actors in top positions: Ferenc Rabár, MoF; György Matolcsy, head of the Economic Policy Secretariat of the Prime Minister's Office; Béla Kádár, minister of international economic relations; and Ákos Péter Bod, minister of industry and trade. Accordingly, their institutions emerged as alternative centers of policy making. None of them was subordinated to another, and each had both operational powers and a say in the strategy. Policy coordination was to take place in the Economic Cabinet, the administrative body of economic ministers headed by the MoF, but this group was empowered only to prepare and advise; decisions were made by the government.

Predictably, competing policy views soon emerged, which was reflected in the incoherence of government programs. For example, the "Program for National Revival," the official program of the Antall government approved in September 1990 embraced contradictory policy proposals rather than advocating a clear strategy. MoF Rabár's first draft of the government's economic strategy for the coming three years had been submitted to and rejected by the government in August 1990. This professionally coherent and comprehensive, radical scenario could have become the first serious medium-term policy document of the government. Much in line with János Kornai's radical proposal of macroeconomic "surgery" (Kornai 1990), Rabár advocated radical reforms including budget cuts, sharp devaluation, fast liberalization of prices and trade, and a rapid transition to convertibility (Rabár, interview). His program was criticized by Matolcsy, Kádár, and Bod for its radicalism and lack of attention to political considerations. As a consequence the draft budget for 1991 reflected a more moderate approach to economic change.

By early December 1990, the Ministry of Finance prepared a new medium-term policy draft, a slightly softened but better elaborated version of Rabár's plan. However, the draft budget, along with its underlying philosophy, was criticized by Matolcsy, but this time for its lack of radicalism. In Matolcsy's rival proposal presented in late October 1990, economic change was to be accelerated. Also, more attention was given to supply-side policies such as tax reform and the acceleration of privatization. Matolcsy's plan, however, could not get government support either (Petschnig 1994). Tired by their rivalry and by the absence of a politically and administratively viable program, Antall accepted Rabár's resignation and fired Matolcsy in November 1990.

How could this rivalry and the resulting policy deadlock devour the honeymoon period of Hungary's first democratic government? One explanation would put the stress on factors such as the uncertainty inherent in the transformation, the lack of the prime minister's administrative experience, or the proximity of municipal elections. While these factors were important, the paralysis of decision making was partly due to the administrative structure set up by Antall and was exacerbated by the strategies of the top policy makers.

Antall was not simply dragged into these personal and policy rivalries; rather, they were an unintended side effect of his own administrative design. Antall's decision to divide policy-making authority deviated significantly from the proposals of the original MDF program. All the top policy makers in his first government were trained economists, spoke several languages, and had medium-level administrative positions as heads or deputy heads of research institutes. However, none had independent political standing.[9]

---

[9] None of his policy makers were Communist Party members (except Matolcsy, who used to be a member, but did not have any higher function). Nor were they members of the Hungarian Democratic Forum (except Bod who, similarly to Antall, was a latecomer

But most interesting is the fact that Antall placed policy rivals in key positions, even though disputes over the economic chapter of the MDF program had already revealed the nature and depth of their conflict over strategic issues (Rabár, interview).

Why these people, why such decision-making institutions? A possible explanation is that the prime minister was uncertain about economic strategy, found it too early to delegate exclusive decision-making power to any of them, and wanted to let their rivalries play out. An alternative explanation would highlight Antall's own precarious political situation. In the summer of 1990, however, he was in full control of both the MDF and the coalition. Later, at the turn of 1990–91, he did not hesitate to delegate decision-making authority to his next MoF, Mihály Kupa, despite the fact that the political situation in the coalition was more tense.

Rather, we need to assess the strategies pursued by the rival policy makers in "selling" their views to the prime minister. A consensus on what was to be done in the economy could not emerge because the distance between the rival views was so large that it effectively ruled out their reconciliation. However, these differences did not primarily reflect professional disagreements. It was not Kádár, originally the most ardent opponent to Rabár's "monetarism" and radicalism, who emerged as his major challenger, but Matolcsy, whose views had originally been the closest to Rabár's (Rabár, interview). Matolcsy in turn changed his policy stance from that of moderate opposition to Rabár's radicalism to proposing a radical alternative. These shifts did not help to provide the prime minister with a clear picture of choices.

As to the political strategy of policy makers, we do not see much difference. None of the four based his program's viability on his own political resources or efforts. Not only did they lack political resources of their own, but they did not consider building up political support for their programs an important part of their job. As Rabár remembers in a different context, "At the time I did not attribute any real significance to the media, to public opinion, or to influencing public opinion. I was extremely naive" (Rabár, interview). All of the rivals counted on Premier Antall's backing, and left the task of generating political support exclusively to him. The rivals' inattention to politics did not make Antall's decision easier.[10]

---

in the party). The candidates' loyalty was reflected merely by the fact that they became advisers to the party, and participated in preparing the economic program in 1989–90.

[10] In sharp contrast to the "Guidelines" and the "Program for National Revival," the "Fast Program" or Rabár's three-year strategy consisted of politically difficult measures combined with tight deadlines for implementation. The latter was first presented to the

Still, the prime minister could have resolved the stalemate. Even if a formal division of authority was absent in Antall's bureaucratic model, it might have been possible for one agency to assume leadership. In principle, the Ministry of Finance with its rather well-trained, numerous, and experienced staff seemed the logical candidate for policy leadership.[11]

Given the bureaucratic resources of the MoF, it is even more puzzling how Matolcsy, with his staff of but fifteen to twenty in the prime minister's office, could regularly challenge his rival. I believe this could happen essentially for two reasons: first, for most of 1990 the financial bureaucracy was in a state of disorganization; second, Rabár's lack of administrative experience, the enormous pressure of day-to-day tasks, and his short time spent as MoF implied an underutilization of the bureaucratic capacity available in his ministry.

In the bureaucratic arena Matolcsy fought a sort of administrative guerrilla warfare based on informality, ad hoc committees, and networks centered around his Economic Policy Secretariat. Into his ad hoc committees he invited competent, second-ranking bureaucrats from several ministries. Exploring his position as personal adviser to the prime minister, and using a network of experts, businessmen, and journalists, he began to produce alternatives to the MoF's policy proposals. Rabár (1991: 674) wrote that:

[By] building up a partly informal organization (frequently involving the experts of the Ministry of Finance) the Secretariat pursues autonomous economic policy. . . . Whenever the Ministry of Finance elaborated a proposal the Secretariat responded with a counterplan. . . . Of course, on the basis of informal contacts and ad hoc committees the Economic Policy Secretariat could be much more flexible than the machinery of the Ministry of Finance, which besides handling operative issues had to prepare a great number of laws.

When Rabár assumed his position, his ministry was at the start of a long and difficult process of reorganization following its merger with the Central Planning Office. The ministry lost its most capable experts to private firms, banks, and other state institutions. Rabár tried to stop the brain drain and decrease uncertainty, but he personally did not deal much with the details of reorganization (Rabár, interview). Neither did he attempt to expand his control over other bureaucratic agencies or

government shortly before the local elections of 1990, whereas Matolcsy started to advocate his program of accelerated economic reforms just a few days after the political trauma of the 1990 taxi-driver blockade.

[11] The more so that, at least in principle, Antall respected the long tradition, that the Ministry of Finance is a *primus inter pares* among government agencies (Szabó, interview).

policy functions. To the contrary, he accepted that short-term policy measures and the formulation of the privatization strategy would belong to the prime minister's office and, personally, to Matolcsy.

In late June 1990 Rabár organized an ad hoc "think tank" for outlining Hungary's three-year transformation strategy. Irrespective of their formal bureaucratic positions, he invited experts whom he thought were capable of discussing strategic issues. In this way, Rabár could generate input to the professional core of a radical and comprehensive program, but he did not have much time for administrative "deepening" involving the lower echelons of his own bureaucracy and cooperation with other agencies. As a result, Rabár entered the decision-making phase with a document that was not any more processed through the administration than his rival's, which, by contrast, had the advantage of exposure to a variety of interests. Rabár regressed to the role of but one of the advisers to his own government, failing to utilize the administrative advantage inherent in his position. Hence Rabár failed not only because he was a radical, but also because he was politically isolated, overwhelmed by crisis management, and administratively inexperienced.

Trapped in a personal and policy rivalry partly of his own making, and probably bored both with economic policy and endless debates, Antall did not permanently ally with any of his top policy makers, and did not empower any of them with exclusive authority. This became explicit in the decline of the power and efficiency of the Economic Cabinet. As noted by Rabár (interview),

The government sessions were characterized by very peculiar procedures. We began to argue, repeating our earlier disputes in the Cabinet, the prime minister and the rest of the government patiently listened, and finally, typically before any agreement was reached he asked, "Should we take a vote then?" So the government took a vote, which could easily mean that if the minister of industry and trade or the minister of international economic relations allied with the minister for environmental protection or the minister of welfare, they together could outvote the MoF in a personal income tax matter. This was exacerbated by Antall's behavior, who never voted against the majority. . . . He always supported the majority, although those questions were far from being typical subjects of democratic decisions; rather they were professional matters.

The Kupa Program: Temporary Alliance between the Premier and the MoF

The experience of 1990 set a learning process in motion. Antall might have learned the lesson that the paralysis of economic decision making posed a political risk, and that economic policy success implied a break with his predecessors' professional, political, and administrative strategies. In December 1990, as part of a substantial reshuffling of his government, Antall nominated Mihály Kupa as his new MoF. A few days later the MDF reelected Antall as its chairman. The fact that Antall chose Kupa before his leadership in the MDF was formally secured revealed that Antall's administrative decisions did not hinge on the MDF's political support; rather, Antall's image and indispensability gave him substantial power over personnel and policy (Beke 1993).

His choice also signaled a new pattern of relationship between him and his top policy maker: that of an *alliance*. Antall expressed his commitment to Kupa not only in the MDF and the coalition, but also in bureaucratic politics. Parallel to Kupa's nomination the prime minister eliminated the Economic Policy Secretariat in his office. He assured Kupa that the Economic Cabinet would be responsible for economic matters, his program would be the sole program of the government, and privatization would be under the MoF's control. Kupa had reasons to feel he was a superminister of the economy. This was most explicit in the changing relationship between the Economic Cabinet and the government. Without altering the legal status of the cabinet, Antall firmly allied with his MoF during the government sessions. As Kupa (interview) put it, the Economic Cabinet became

the forum of reconciliation of interests, which meant that we had to process all the debated issues through it, and if we could not agree, to go back again and again, even five times if necessary. Practically, you could not submit debated issues to the government. In general, roughly until mid-1992 the Economic Cabinet had enormous power. Whatever had been suggested by the cabinet was also accepted by the government.

Why did Antall trust Kupa more than any of his earlier policy makers? Most probably because Kupa appeared to be committed to, and well prepared for, a bureaucratic and a limited political role, which initially seemed compatible with the prime minister's ambition to improve his own and his government's reputation and performance. First, Kupa had bureaucratic skills, and the financial bureaucracy, which was also more consolidated in early 1991 than half a year earlier, accepted him.[12] He inherited the milder, December 1990 version of Rabár's program. On this base he built up his own program. The Kupa program advocated the elimination of remaining subsidies, price and trade liberalization, tight fiscal policy, a variety of privatization schemes including those based on

---

[12] In 1988–89 he was head of the department in the Ministry of Finance, responsible for the introduction of the VAT reform and the reform of public finances.

the initiatives of management, further steps toward currency convertibility, the promise of sectoral strategies for structural change, and a comprehensive reform of public finances. By transforming the inherited elements to what became known as the "Kupa program," he substantially improved the professional, administrative, and political viability of that medium-term policy document. This meant essentially three things: a further break with Rabár's radicalism, some minor concessions to various political and interest groups, and modifications that made the program tractable for legislative and bureaucratic implementation (Petschnig 1994: 66–68; Kupa, interview).

However, Kupa also introduced two innovations. While he, like his predecessor, was politically dependent on the prime minister, he also tried to secure political backing for his program and himself outside the government. His program was embraced by two opposition parties, the SZDSZ and the Alliance of Young Democrats (FIDESZ), because of its technical merits. From the start, he also built up good contacts with the media. Within the government, Kupa utilized the bureaucratic capacity in his ministry while also expanding his administrative reach to other policy areas and bureaucratic bodies, most importantly with respect to privatization. Kupa's efforts to generate political support for the government's strategy and to coordinate the economic bureaucracy initially made him an attractive ally for Antall. But Kupa's actions might have also signaled to the prime minister another lesson: that a potential challenger was in sight.

Recurrent Rivalry in 1992–93

According to Kupa the first serious signs of mistrust began to materialize in the first half of 1992, at a time when the economic situation was perceived as relatively stable. Kupa felt he was less needed than he had been in hard times. However, Kupa lost the most important administrative battle, the one for controlling privatization, in late 1991. Moreover, it was also in 1991 that he attempted to establish an autonomous political standing, which was a big mistake. After running in a single-member district, he became an MP. He also had a passionate debate with the prime minister on how to deal with the strike threats of trade unions, and he also intervened in foreign affairs, the prime minister's own favorite policy domain (Kupa, interview).

In the battle over privatization policy, Kupa had struggled for control of the State Property Agency from early 1991, with limited success (Kocsis, interview). A new proposal drafted by the MoF envisioned three options for implementation. As Kupa (interview) remembers,

125

One put the MoF in charge of privatization, because of his neutrality: he had no other interest than fetching a fair price. . . . However, we knew that this was not going to be feasible, the MoF had too much power anyway. . . . The second possibility was to delegate the control to the minister of industry and trade, Ákos Péter Bod. . . . To tell the truth . . . we wanted to help the Ministry of Industry to acquire some power. By this move we also hoped to secure Ákos Péter Bod's consent to and support for the economic policy. . . . But all this failed, because Antall ripped off the whole government by appointing Tamás Szabó as minister of privatization, which was only the third option in the bill, and we never really supported it.

Tamás Szabó's appointment as minister of privatization in January 1992 meant multiple challenges to Kupa's monopoly over economic policy. The fragmentation and decentralization of economic decision making – the rivalry of programs, persons, and institutions that characterized the first year of Antall's premiership – recurred. In part, this was a reflection of intensified partisan pressures on economic policy. Kupa (interview) reflects that "this was similar to the way Horn bypassed Békesi's program with his own scenario of 'dynamic expansion,' or the more recent Matolcsy strategy of 'sustainable growth' at seven percent."

However, it was not simply the MDF's and other coalition members' demand for a strategy of growth, improving living standards, and accommodating particularistic interests in the privatization that urged the prime minister to reconsider his relation to Kupa. Rather, the partisan advocates of administrative and policy alternatives became more effective, because of the prime minister's declining trust in Kupa. Tamás Szabó, Kupa's main rival, drew on party support and his personal ties to the prime minister; he was a deputy chairman of the MDF and at the same time Antall's political and personal intimate.

As a minister without portfolio, Tamás Szabó had his institutional home in the prime minister's office. From there, he began to challenge Kupa's role by setting up the Working Group on Economic Strategy (WGES) with the task of preparing a document on Hungary's growth strategy. The working group consisted of top- and lower-level bureaucrats from various ministries save for the Ministry of Finance; Ákos Péter Bod, then head of the National Bank; and Antall's personal domestic and foreign advisers (Petschnig 1994: 70). Just as Matolcsy had challenged Rabár, Tamás Szabó fought with Kupa and the Ministry of Finance by heading an ad hoc committee hosted and backed by the prime minister.

By late March 1992 the committee had prepared a document that stressed the necessity of growth and paid less attention to macroeconomic and external balance than did the Kupa program. In order to secure the financial resources, the program did not rule out further indebtedness. This is how Kupa (interview) remembers the program, its purpose and impact:

This was a real scandal for – although I cannot prove this – it was most probably Antall himself who gave the order for the preparation of the WGES program. I first encountered the program at a meeting of MDF MPs in Balatonkenese. I remember Imre Kónya, the leader of the MDF faction who chaired the meeting, sarcastically asking me, "Tamás Szabó will soon present something, will you be ready to react to it?" Actually, I was: it was easy for me to annihilate it. . . . In essence, it was nothing but a partisan action in the sense that it was twice discussed by the MDF faction and the party leadership. However, when it was submitted to the government with the assistance of my secretary of state Zoltán Nagy, I managed to eliminate the most dangerous proposals, such as creating owners through the free distribution of shares, or the incentives for "unlimited growth."

The WGES program was rejected by most economists for its emphasis on growth and its inconsistency and irresponsibility regarding external debt. Faced with the strong professional opposition, Tamás Szabó retreated from the document (Petschnig 1994: 70–73). By early 1993, the time the new MoF, Iván Szabó, had assumed his office, the WGES program was not considered as a serious government document (Szabó, interview). However, the WGES program also included the government's new philosophy of privatization, and this more or less remained in place. Reflecting the prime minister's and MDF's wish to accommodate the interests of public firm managers in privatization, the WGES document said, "We have to learn to accept politically that the main force of the new Hungarian bourgeoisie will be the 'nomenclature-bourgeoisie'" (cited by Petschnig 1994: 73). Meanwhile, another (then secret) government document pointed out, "The goal to be achieved by the acceleration and expansion of privatization is not the maximization of cash receipts but the creation of a broad and powerful domestic class of owners facilitating an efficient economic system" (cited by Voszka 1998: 65).[13]

These were, essentially, Tamás Szabó's twin tasks in privatization: both to accelerate it and to use it to mobilize political support. The peak year of privatization under the Antall government was 1993, both in terms of equity sold and of receipts, showing that Tamás Szabó performed both tasks with remarkable energy. László Lengyel, however, suspects that Tamás Szabó's enthusiasm and success turned into a trap for him later

---

[13] Table A.7 in the appendix shows that by 1997, Hungary has privatized more than 50 percent of its medium-sized and large enterprises, primarily by selling them to foreign investors, which was uncommon in other transition countries.

on. He began to dream about a new strategic superministry of the economy under his control and to flirt with MDF extremists (Lengyel 1993: 99). The prime minister became suspicious, so he put an end to Szabó's leadership ambitions. In the end Szabó joined the club of the victims of excessive bureaucratic and political ambition. Even earlier, following Antall's reshuffling of his government in early 1993, his rival Kupa also became a member of the club.

Iván Szabó, a Minister of "Industry and Finance"

With Iván Szabó, Kupa's successor, a new period started in the relationship between the political leaders and their top policy makers. The last year of the Antall period[14] was characterized more by alliance and cooperation than rivalry and bureaucratic tug-of-war. What explains the peace? Many Hungarian analysts share the view that in the preelection year of 1993 the governing elite's interest in political survival became dominant over its divisions; cooperation for reelection was the main agenda in 1994. In this view Iván Szabó was a political appointee whose task was to orchestrate election economics: fostering growth and job creation through increased public spending, distributing election gifts, and postponing unpopular measures to the next term. Alternatively, one may argue that by spring 1993 Antall was already too ill to control politics, while his successor, Péter Boross, considered his position as transitional; there were no big conflicts about power and policy, but in the meantime the economy ran out of control.

I believe that both arguments capture important elements of truth, but neither is fully valid. First, although Antall had been in poor health by early 1993, he was careful enough to empower someone whom he trusted. Iván Szabó was no less Antall's man than Tamás Szabó. Second, although he was a politician (a vice-chairman of the MDF) Szabó's motives were not simply electoral. His policy preferences should be seen in the broader context of the debate on growth versus external balance. In several of his speeches Iván Szabó admitted that as an MDF man he sought to implement social democratic policies, and despite the mounting macroeconomic problems and the warnings of the economics profession, he really believed these policies were feasible.

Iván Szabó had been Antall's minister of industry and trade. In his new position of minister of finance, he was dissatisfied with the lack

---

[14] After Antall died in the fall of 1993, his deputy and minister of the interior, Péter Boross, became prime minister for the remaining few months till the May 1994 elections.

of communication between the fiscal and the macroeconomic planning units:

The toughest debates always took place when the draft budget was prepared. There I had to recognize that for the fiscal departments it was very difficult to accept the idea of putting the stress on the prospective gains from economic activity. For them, the costs were a hundred percent certain, but they did not calculate the gains because they were uncertain. In this sense, they approached the problem not as economists, but much more as accountants who think that if expenditures are certain and revenues uncertain, the business will necessarily run into loss. (interview)

Iván Szabó felt his mission was to popularize the "economic" approach and to bridge the gap between the economic strategists and the fiscal technocrats in his ministry and the economic bureaucracy in general. In his ministerial conferences he acted as "mediator" between the conflicting approaches, invited a few experts from the Ministry of Industry and Trade to leading posts in the Ministry of Finance, and revitalized his advisory body of about forty experts, including engineers, bankers, managers of public firms, and owners of private enterprises. Such a body had helped him while he was the minister of industry and trade, and he asked them both to prepare and to discuss their own proposals and to comment on his policies, including the plans to establish a treasury (Szabó, interview). He also believed he was better prepared to cooperate with other bureaucratic agencies and to understand their specific problems than were his fiscal technocrats. To elicit communication within the bureaucracy, he also brought together representatives of the Ministry of Industry and Trade, the Ministry of Agriculture, the minister of privatization, and the National Bank in his office for strategic meetings with his own colleagues.

While Iván Szabó tried to accommodate various bureaucratic interests, unlike his overly ambitious predecessor Kupa and his successor Békesi, he accepted that privatization was controlled by a separate minister. As a MoF he got support from both Antall and Boross.

In part, his policies were characteristically "industrial policies." Szabó selected about a dozen large Hungarian firms to be bailed out by massive subsidies, and he finished the consolidation of the banking sector, which under the next government proved a factor in their rapid privatization. By 1994 Hungary had experienced economic recovery but with a dramatic worsening of the current-account balance. As the growth versus external balance debate resumed, Iván Szabó opted for growth even at the cost of temporary deterioration of external balance. He thought the

$3 billion deficit was not catastrophic, and he was against a sharp deval-
uation, partly for its inflationary effect and partly because he was
convinced that devaluation would not help the export sector.[15] Instead,
Szabó advocated supply-side incentives for restructuring, and most subsequent analysts blamed him for interventionist and expansionary policies that delayed vital adjustment measures.

Horn, the Party Boss of His Government

Following the MSZP's landslide electoral victory in 1994, Horn did not
have the same freedom in choosing his policy makers that Antall did.
His choice of László Békesi, his rival in the MSZP and the author of the
party's economic program, was a reflection of the tensions both in the
MSZP and the coalition.[16] The fact that both Horn and Békesi had to
govern with someone whom they mistrusted explains the remarkable
absence of learning from the experience of the Antall period, and the
close repetition of familiar patterns of interaction at the top, with predictable consequences.

Horn against Békesi

Békesi's program combined measures for short-term macroeconomic
crisis management, such as substantial devaluation and budget cuts, with
longer-term structural adjustment policies, including the outlines of the
reform of public finances and the acceleration of privatization. In his
public rhetoric, Békesi appeared as a pessimist, and could not convincingly articulate how and when his program would result in sustainable
growth. But Békesi did not fail primarily because he was a poor com-
municator, or his program was not appropriate to the economic situation; it was well received by economists. His ultimate defeat was the
result of conflicts with the prime minister. Békesi openly "went for the
whole" as far as his administrative strategies and personal decision-
making power was concerned. Horn, in turn, did everything to limit his

---

[15] By 1993–94, however, most Hungarian economists (excluding Bod, then the president
of the National Bank of Hungary) had shared the view that a substantial devaluation
was needed.

[16] Horn also had to face the control of the SZDSZ over the choice of his top policy makers.
Especially in the beginning, the coalition agreement and the Coalition Council for
Reconciliation of Interests provided the junior partner with the means of partisan influence over a wide range of issues (Pető 1995: 184; interview). No matter how stubbornly
Horn tried to get rid of this constraint, he ran up against it whenever he attempted
to restructure state administration or search for allies outside the coalition (Szekeres
1996: 96).

power, encourage rivals, and push him onto the sidelines. The result closely resembled 1990 and 1992: intensive rivalry, government inaction amid accumulating economic tension and imbalance, and policy paralysis on almost all fronts.

Békesi felt that the prime minister and important groups in the MSZP were unwilling to fully back his program. The first visible sign of the prime minister's mistrust was his attempt to set up an advisory body just after Békesi entered office. Békesi (interview) said that, "Horn wanted to bypass me by setting up an advisory body headed by Péter Medgyessy. Although it was a short-lived body, it was meant to prepare an alternative to the MoF's strategy. After one month it turned out that it neither could nor wanted to formulate a rival plan, so Horn quickly dissolved it."

Békesi also wanted the Economic Cabinet to handle all the details; only strategic issues would be decided in the government. However, Horn soon allied with most other MSZP ministers against Békesi and the SZDSZ ministers, and subordinated the cabinet to the government. As Békesi (interview) recalls, "whenever the ministers opposing one or another decision of the MoF could not win against him in the cabinet, they could ally with the prime minister and the rest of the ministers, and defeat him in the government."

In the field of privatization, Békesi tried, and initially succeeded, to expand his control over the legal framework, strategy, government agencies, and receipts (Sárközy 1996). Like Kupa, Békesi argued that the MoF was the only top official not to be bound by particularistic interests and thus was committed to competitive bids and maximizing cash receipts, which were crucial in Hungary's critical financial situation. But he also knew that

being in charge of privatization implies much more than just influence over economic policy. It implies controlling the most important means for redistributing property and acquiring power in the economy and society. In this sense, it is a preeminent political question. This is why privatization has been a primary target for the lobbies, interest groups, and the broader or narrower constituencies in the backyard of political parties any time. (interview)

Békesi's time-consuming efforts to control privatization could be one of the reasons why privatization was practically brought to a halt in 1994 (Sárközy 1996); at least this was turned against him later. However, Békesi's defeat became obvious in late 1994. Around this time, Horn personally nullified one large privatization contract and fired Ferenc Barta, Békesi's man responsible for privatization. Like Antall, he nominated his political and personal intimate, Tamás Suchman, as minister of privatization without portfolio.

There was one more, political, arena, where Békesi tried and failed: Hungary's major tripartite corporatist forum, the Interest Reconciliation Council. In accordance with the coalition's electoral promises, extensive negotiations with the major trade unions and business associations started right after the new government was formed. The negotiations aimed at a socioeconomic agreement on the transformation strategy for the following three years. In early February 1995 negotiations over the pact failed. Most participants and observers attributed the breakdown to the absence of a long-term strategy, or the unwillingness of the trade unions to accept short-term losses in exchange for long-term gains (Héthy 1996).

But I believe that the pact was not signed in part because it would have increased the political capital of the prime minister's main rivals, Békesi and Sándor Nagy, chairman of the largest trade-union federation, the MSZOSZ. Békesi had invested a lot in the pact: he participated actively in the negotiations and was ready to make concessions in terms of both softening and delaying some of his adjustment measures. Similarly, Nagy, much more than other union bosses, was moderate; in principle, he was not against accepting real wage concessions in exchange for compensation on organizational and political issues (Békesi, Nagy, interviews). It is understandable that Horn did not really support the two of them to come to an agreement. Rather, the failure of the pact entailed *gains* for the prime minister in terms of his own relative political standing (Kőhegyi 1995). Békesi resigned in late January 1995, after the MSZP faction, to which he apparently was held accountable, did not support him against Horn in their debate over the desirable strategy.

The Bokros Package

When Békesi resigned, the prime minister turned to Lajos Bokros. The new MoF was also supported by the SZDSZ and had a good professional reputation both in Hungary and abroad. Other factors might have played a role as well. First, Bokros was not a rival to Horn in any sense. Although he was a member of the MSZP, he never seemed to have a realistic chance to build up a political career within the party. Second, in his original program Bokros advocated export-led growth based on domestic savings (Bokros 1996: 825), which allowed Horn to show that there was an alternative to "one-sided restrictive policies" advocated by Békesi (Szekeres 1996). Thus despite the fact that the actual Bokros package profited from Békesi's last stabilization plan, Bokros, like Kupa two years earlier, also succeeded in presenting it in a politically attractive form.

Finally, the Mexican crisis, the refusal of expected financial aid by the German government, the pressure of foreign actors, and intensifying capital flight – all paved the way for Horn's approval of the Bokros package.

The differences between the Békesi and Bokros programs were not purely rhetorical. While the latter included drastic stabilization measures such as a sharp devaluation, it also promised to maintain macroeconomic stability without recession and to facilitate growth through decreasing consumption, increasing investment, and expanding exports. In fact, this restructuring resulted in very large losses in wages and salaries and declining welfare transfers and investment in the public sector.

The Bokros package was prepared in secrecy by Bokros and five or six other economists, including György Surányi, László Antal, Tibor Draskovits, and Riecke Werner. As Antal recalls, "it was a coup. This is why there were only five or six persons involved in the preparation, and the bureaucratic apparatus had nothing to do with it. . . . Horn's support was crucial in putting it onto the parliamentary agenda, and in getting full approval" (Antal, interview).

In the administration, Bokros, like his predecessors, tried to strengthen his position by establishing the Economic Cabinet's veto right over economic issues, and by expanding his ministry's control to include privatization (Bokros, 1996). He failed in both matters; Tamás Suchman became minister of privatization just as Bokros became MoF. As far as Bokros's management style, he formulated proposals in a limited circle, while the rest of the bureaucracy was limited to performing technical assistance. In his dealings with other administrative agencies, he relied on pressure rather than persuasion. Although some observers stress his personal style as the explanation for his recurrent conflicts with other top bureaucrats, I believe that his policy style was linked to the underlying logic of his program. Bokros's original twenty-five points envisaged comprehensive rationalization of the public sector, an "ordered retreat" of the state. Those plans could not have been prepared through bargaining and coordination. Bokros opted instead for an offensive method of trial and error. László Antal attributed to Bokros the following philosophy:

For the time being we implement drastic fiscal austerity wherever we can, and then we shall see what to do next. There will be areas where the service infrastructure will be able to adjust, and where it will not. In the latter case the state will have to intervene again anyway. Because scenarios for a rational and ordered retreat could not be prepared, we had to rely on pressure and enforcement: for example there was no possibility for wage increases, except in exchange for downsizing employment. Here is how simple a logic this was. (Antal, interview)

133

Because the program resulted in an upsurge of inflation, there was a sharp drop in real wages. His strategy thus left Bokros with little support in the administration save for Central Bank manager György Surányi, with whom he institutionalized close coordination. Bokros remained just as isolated in politics as in the bureaucracy; he was entirely dependent upon the prime minister's backing. This also implied that in conflicts with others, he did not have the political means to convince Horn of his views. Instead, he used the ultimate weapon: the threat to resign.

Suchman: A Suspected Rival Who Turned Out to Be an Ally

Surprisingly, however, while Bokros did not have many allies, only opponents, he did not have strong rivals either. After his appointment as minister of privatization, Tamás Suchman was widely perceived as a potential obstacle to the Bokros reforms, and it was feared that he intended to slow down privatization. What actually happened was the opposite. Under Suchman, privatization increased dramatically in 1995–96, both in terms of the equity sold and the amount of cash receipts (Voszka 1998: 65). Interestingly enough, Suchman himself explained his commitment to fast methods and decisions in truly leftist ideological terms: "The reason why we have to privatize fast is not that the state is an inappropriate, or incapable owner in general, but because at the moment it lacks the financial resources to restructure its firms." He also said, "I shall do my best to avoid introducing a new austerity program by claiming that the receipts from privatization are missing" (cited by Kocsis 1996: 55–56).

Clearly, the privatization success depended heavily on Suchman's personal performance, although at the beginning no one believed he would meet his targets. In the field of privatization, Suchman used the same "Blitzkrieg" tactics as Bokros in the field of public finance, and with similar controversy. Suchmann was no less a "lonely hero" than Bokros. He did not regularly attend the meetings of the Economic Cabinet, nor did he closely supervise the privatization bureaucracy, a fact that contributed to the late 1996 corruption scandal. "His criterion for personal success was to sell public property, and he had full authority to do that. He was a typical entrepreneur who did not need more than a second to take a decision" (Antal, interview).

Thus, paradoxically, in 1995 the challenge to the MoF's stabilization policies originated not from direct opposition but in the unexpected inflow of large cash receipts from privatization. Bokros's view, which was supported by the SZDSZ and most economists, was that the extra receipts should be used for servicing the country's foreign debt. Horn, however, took the lead in arguing that at least part of the cash should finance infrastructure and other development projects. Surprisingly, sixty Socialist MPs allied with the SZDSZ and the opposition, and voted against Horn in favor of Bokros. On this crucial economic issue the MSZP was divided, but its division supported a proreform rather than an antireform decision.[17] One cannot exclude the possibility that Bokros himself played an indirect role in the coalition's partial revolt against Horn, for which Horn could not forgive him.

The Superministry of Economy: A Phantom Threat to the MoFs' Authority

Between 1990 and 1998, proposals have surfaced repeatedly to restructure the Hungarian economic decision-making system by creating a "Superministry" of Economy. The superministry would be responsible for strategic economic planning and was usually intended to be a strong institutional counterbalance to the Ministry of Finance, which would be downgraded to a Budget Office. The plan addressed the core issue of the distribution of decision-making power; this is precisely why it was never implemented. Because of the diversity of its advocates over time, however, the superministry concept provides an interesting window onto bureaucratic politics.[18]

In 1995 the person picked by Horn as a would-be superminister was union leader Sándor Nagy, the number-two candidate on the MSZP's national list in the 1994 election, second only to the prime minister, and seen as a potential successor. The prime minister's initial plan envisaged substantial power for Nagy, including responsibility for economic strategy, policy coordination, and European integration as well as the post of vice-prime minister.

This proposal gave rise to sustained political conflict between the MSZP and the SZDSZ, and almost resulted in the breakdown of the

---

[17] This could probably happen, because for spending the unexpected cash receipts from privatization there were no credible programs available (Antal, interview). Other explanations include that there were too many competing priorities, or that MSZP MPs still had been under the shock of Hungary's external imbalance (Békesi, interview).

[18] In 1989–90 the plan appeared in the economic program of the MDF, which envisaged a strong Ministry of Economy empowered with medium- and long-term strategy formulation. A similar plan had been present in the Smallholders' program as well. Between 1990 and 1998 the advocates of the idea included the SZDSZ in 1994, Gyula Horn both in 1994 and 1995, and the Smallholders and the Alliance of Young Democrats (FIDESZ) in 1995. After the election of 1998 the new coalition government led by the FIDESZ indeed set up a Ministry of Economy.

coalition. While Nagy accepted the nomination, the SZDSZ passionately opposed both the plan of administrative restructuring and, specifically, Nagy's vice premiership. The SZDSZ felt it was undesirable to counterbalance the MoF's authority, and thought the plan signaled nothing but Horn's intention to deviate from the reform course. During the three-month dispute, the plan underwent several metamorphoses, each resulting in less dramatic administrative changes and less power delegated to Nagy. In late September at the MSZP's presidium, Horn gave up the idea entirely (Bauer 1996: 76–77; Szekeres 1996: 90–101). In a leading SZDSZ politician's interpretation, what was ultimately at stake were the rules of the coalition: Horn wanted to bypass the coalition agreement, whereas the SZDSZ tried to enforce it (Bauer 1996: 77).

Yet, I cannot exclude the relevance of a more tactical factor: that the plan of the superministry formed part of the prime minister's broader strategy to neutralize his potential political rival, Nagy. If it was a power game, it was one that the prime minister essentially could not lose. If Nagy had become a member of the government it would have implied his resignation as a union leader, the most important base of his own political standing in the MSZP. If Horn failed against the SZDSZ's strong opposition, Nagy's revealed preference for the vice-premiership would have weakened his position in the MSZOSZ and, consequently, in the MSZP as well. This is what actually happened as the year went by. Nagy got more and more criticism because he could not choose between his political and union roles. Finally, he resigned from his chairmanship in the MSZOSZ.[19]

Horn and Medgyessy: Reconciliation at the Top

As in the trial years of the Antall government, the relationship between the prime minister and the MoF in the last two years of Horn's term was one of alliance rather than rivalry. The difference was that the economy was in substantially better shape in 1997–98 than in 1994. A number of important institutional reforms had taken place in the field of public finance, including the centralization and reorganization of extrabudgetary funds, and the reform of the pension system (Nelson, Chapter 8, in this volume; Haggard et al., Chapter 3, in this volume). The success, in

---

[19] Beyond this outcome there are two more arguments supporting my interpretation. First, the prime minister could predict SZDSZ's strong opposition to the plan. Second, one might wonder how seriously Horn meant to undertake a substantial administrative restructuring in his government's midterm.

part, could be attributed to the fact that during the political fights of 1994–95 the prime minister succeeded in neutralizing his most important rivals, and his leadership in the MSZP was secure. Nor could the coalition partners put serious constraints on the prime minister's power any longer.

With Péter Medgyessy, Horn got a top policy maker whom he personally knew and trusted,[20] and whom he was ready to empower. Medgyessy, on his part did not challenge the prime minister either by his own political plans or by overly ambitious bureaucratic strategies. He did not lobby for veto power over economic policy, nor did he want to control privatization. In the government, he successfully tried to secure Horn's backing for his decisions, while in the administration he used his remarkable tactical skills to soften the conflicts between contrasting views and to establish alliances by sharing the responsibility with other agencies. One example is his cooperation with the Ministry of Welfare in the elaboration and implementation of the pension reform (Nelson, Chapter 8, in this volume). However, Medgyessy's success also was facilitated by the fact that Bokros had done much of the "dirty work" and fundamentally changed the attitude and expectations of the bureaucracy and Hungarian society in general.

Although Horn was a successful prime minister in terms of economic reforms and foreign policy, his political profile contributed to his and his party's loss in the polls in 1998. In a way, Horn finished his term in 1998 just as he started in 1994: as a party boss prime minister. He was too shortsighted to realize that his struggle to improve MSZP's image at the cost of SZDSZ's reputation would ultimately undermine his own chances to form Hungary's next governing coalition.

Summary and Conclusions

In 1990 Antall's preferences were still unclear about how he wanted to transform Hungary's economy, although he ran on a moderate, gradualist platform. To keep his options open, and to gather information, the prime minister appointed persons with divergent views to key policy-making positions. This strategy, and Antall's own biases, reinforced his cautious approach and explains why his honeymoon period was not exploited to undertake broader and more radical reforms.

---

[20] Medgyessy was MoF and vice-prime minister responsible for the economy in the last years of the Kádár regime. In this capacity he also was a member of the Central Committee of the Communist Party.

Dissatisfaction with the policy stalemate during 1990 led Antall to replace the radical reformer Rabár with Kupa, a man who had a politically and administratively feasible program and who initially appeared to pose no threat to Antall's political position. Under Kupa's leadership, and with Antall's backing, the government took more decisive steps, which included the reduction of the external debt, the completion of trade liberalization, the implementation of a draconian bankruptcy law, and the beginning of the bank consolidation, a condition for the sector's successful privatization. These steps could be undertaken despite the fact that the governing coalition underwent a process of increasing fragmentation.

Irritated by Kupa's ever more open leadership ambitions, but also suffering from deteriorating health, Antall gradually lost his control and leadership capacity, and gave in to intensifying antireform pressures from a fragmented coalition. Reforms in crucial areas stalled again. Kupa was replaced by Iván Szabó, who harbored gradualist and social democratic ideas.

In 1994 the Horn government faced both the threat of a financial meltdown, and the consequences of delayed fiscal reform. But Premier Horn was reluctant to take action until his leadership was challenged by party rivals. Unlike Antall, Horn was both more willing, and under more constraint, to act as a broker among party factions. His tactics for responding to challengers shifted between attempts to co-opt them and to outmaneuver and marginalize them. Horn's attempt to co-opt his rival Békesi led to stalemate in policy despite the mounting crisis, intensifying external pressure, and a cohesive parliamentary coalition. Replacing Békesi with a politically less threatening policy maker, Bokros, permitted radical action. Finally, after outmaneuvering another rival, Nagy, and, after the policy "dirty work" had been done by Bokros, Horn replaced Bokros with an administratively more capable "brother-in-arms," Medgyessy. This led to a sustainable reform course over the longer run, and peace at the top.

Political leaders were important in Hungarian economic transformation. Just as leadership thus mattered, so did the ideas, ambitions, and strategies of the Hungarian policy makers selected to key decision-making positions. Of the three broad patterns of the top reformers' behavior and their implications for policy – the lonely reformer, the strategy of institutional centralization, and administrative or political alliance building – we saw that some policy makers can be characterized by one pattern throughout, whereas others tried to follow different strategies in different periods of their term.

Ferenc Rabár, György Matolcsy, Tamás Szabó, Lajos Bokros, and Tamás Suchman were all lonely reformers, and shared a few important

138

commonalties. Their policy-making style reflected an antiinstitutionalist bias: they were either not capable of, or not interested in, utilizing existing bureaucratic capacity and networks. Occasionally they saw the state bureaucracy as little more than an obstacle, to be overcome by informality, tricks, or force. They rarely created new institutions or durable networks to back their mission. Thus, although they were newcomers in state administration, their strategies implied that they remained alone. Lacking both a strong bureaucratic base and independent political standing, they had to rely exclusively on the prime minister's backing. Their precarious standing was also reflected in their desperate attempts to push through their policies in the face of strong opposition, criticism, or mistrust. If they lost the prime minister's trust, it was not because they challenged him, but because they could not convince him about the viability of their program, or because its implementation devoured their energy and credibility.

The opposite strategy of institutional centralization is best exemplified by Kupa's first period as a MoF and Békesi's ministership. This strategy implied the elimination of rival policy-making centers, upgrading the role of the Economic Cabinet vis-à-vis the government, and controlling other institutions, most importantly the privatization agencies. It was the strategy of experienced and capable top bureaucrats, and rested on comprehensive and bureaucratically viable programs, with substantial conceptual, organizational, and legal preparation. However, institutional expansionist MoFs ran the risk of being identified as rivals by the prime minister, when their bureaucratic ambitions were coupled with independent political standing.

In order to avoid isolation, several policy makers, including Kupa and Medgyessy, tried to build administrative or political alliances. This implied power sharing with other agencies in order to improve the viability of reforms through widening influence within the government. However, this strategy proved successful only if the alliance did not run counter to the prime minister's will. When this occurred, the prime minister typically stopped the effort and established alliances under his own control.

Although my aim was to show how political leadership and reform strategies interacted and influenced the outcome of the policy process, from time to time I hinted at the powerful presence of other explanatory variables – economic conditions, external pressures, political institutions, and social coalitions – which were not central to my own inquiry, but get sufficient attention in other contributions to this volume. Thus my story of individual leadership styles and strategies is part of the broader story of structures and institutions.

References

Bates, R. H., and A. O. Krueger, eds. 1993. *Political and Economic Interactions in Economic Policy Reform: Evidence from Eight Countries*. Oxford: Blackwell.

Bauer, Tamás. 1996. Válságoktól a konszolidációig: az MSZP-SZDSZ kormánytöbbség 1995-ben (From crises to consolidation: The MSZP-SZDSZ governing majority in 1995). In S. Kurtán, P. Sándor, and L. Vass, eds., *Magyarország Politikai Évkönyve 1996*, pp. 72–80. Budapest: Demokrácia Kutatások Magyar Központja Alapítvány.

Beke, Kata. 1993. *Jézusmária, győztünk!* (Jeeez, we won!). Budapest: Belvárosi Könyvkiadó.

Bokros, Lajos. 1996. A leendő pénzügyminiszter huszonöt pontja. Bokros Lajos szakmai cselekvési programjának alapvonalai (The twenty-five points of the would-be MoF: Outline of Lajos Bokros' Professional Program for Action). In S. Kurtán, P. Sándor, and L. Vass, eds., *Magyarország Politikai Évkönyve 1996*, pp. 825–29. Budapest: Demokrácia Kutatások Magyar Központja Alapítvány.

Domínguez, Jorge. 1997. *Technopols: Freeing Politics and Markets in Latin America in the 1990s*. University Park: Pennsylvania State University Press.

Haggard, S., and R. R. Kaufman, eds. 1992. *The Politics of Economic Adjustment: International Constraints, Distributive Conflicts, and the State*. Princeton: Princeton University Press.

——— 1995. *The Political Economy of Democratic Transitions*. Princeton: Princeton University Press.

Haggard, S., and S. B. Webb, eds. 1994. *Voting for Reform: Democracy, Political Liberalisation, and Economic Adjustment*. New York: Oxford University Press, published for the World Bank.

Héthy, Lajos. 1996. Negotiated Social Peace: An Attempt to Reach a Social and Economic Agreement in Hungary. In A. Ágh and G. Ilonszki, eds., *Parliaments and Organized Interests: The Second Step*, pp. 147–58. Budapest: Hungarian Centre for Democracy Studies.

Kocsis, Györgyi. 1996. És ha nyerünk? (And what if we win?). *Tallózó*, January 11, pp. 55–57.

Kőhegyi, Kálmán. 1995. "Több szerep keres egy szerzőt" (Several roles in search of an author). Budapest, March 1995. Unpublished manuscript.

Kornai, János. 1990. *The Road to a Free Economy. Shifting from a Socialist System: The Example of Hungary*. New York: W. W. Norton.

——— 1992. *The Socialist System: The Political Economy of Communism*. Princeton: Princeton University Press.

——— 1994. Transformational Recession: The Main Causes. *Journal of Comparative Economics* 19: 39–63.

——— 1997. Paying the Bill for Goulash Communism: Hungarian Development and Stabilization in a Political Economy Perspective. *Social Research* 63: 943–1040.

Lengyel, László. 1993. *Útfélen* (On half-way). Budapest: Századvég Kiadó.

Brothers-in-Arms or Rivals in Politics

Nelson, J. M., ed. 1989. *Fragile Coalitions: The Politics of Economic Adjustment.* New Brunswick, N.J.: Transaction Publishers.

ed. 1990. *Economic Crisis and Policy Choice: The Politics of Adjustment in the Third World.* Princeton: Princeton University Press.

Pető, Iván. 1995. Az MSZP-SZDSZ kormánykoalíció (The MSZP-SZDSZ government coalition). In S. Kurtán, P. Sándor, and L. Vass, eds., *Magyarország Politikai Évkönyve 1995*, pp. 168–86. Budapest: Demokrácia Kutatások Magyar Központja Alapítvány.

Petschnig, Mária Zita. 1994. *Örökségtől örökségig* (From legacy to legacy). Budapest: Századvég Kiadó.

Rabár, Ferenc. 1991. Nyílt levél Antall Józsefhez (Open letter to József Antall). In S. Kurtán, P. Sándor, and L. Vass, eds., *Magyarország Politikai Évkönyve 1991*, pp. 672–75. Budapest: Ökonómia Alapítvány és Economix Rt.

Révész, Sándor. 1995. *Antall József távolról 1932–1993* (József Antall, from a distance, 1932–1993). Budapest: Sík Kiadó.

Sárközy, Tamás. 1996. *A hatékonyabb kormányzásért* (For a more efficient governance). Budapest: Magvető.

Szekeres, Imre. 1996. A koalíció 1995. évi tapasztalata (The experiences of the coalition in 1995). In S. Kurtán, P. Sándor, and L. Vass, eds., *Magyarország Politikai Évkönyve 1996*, pp. 81–104. Budapest: Demokrácia Kutatások Magyar Központja Alapítvány.

Voszka, Éva. 1998. A sokcélú menetelés (A multipurpose march). *Heti Világgazdaság*, February 7, pp. 64–69.

Williamson, John, ed. 1994. *The Political Economy of Policy Reform.* Washington, D.C.: Institute for International Economics.

Interviews (conducted by the author in early 1998)

Antal, László, Advisor to MoFs László Békesi, Lajos Bokros, and Péter Medgyessy.

Békesi, László, MoF.

Kocsis, Károly, Advisor to MoF Mihály Kupa.

Kupa, Mihály, MoF.

László, Csaba, Deputy Secretary of State, Ministry of Finance.

Nagy, Sándor, Chairman of MSZOSZ.

Pető, Iván, Chairman, Alliance of Free Democrats.

Rabár, Ferenc, MoF.

Szabó, Iván, MoF.

Szapáry, György, Vice President of the National Bank of Hungary.

PART II

The Welfare Reform

CHAPTER 5

Lessons from Sweden for Post-Socialist Countries

ASSAR LINDBECK

When reforming their own countries, several observers, ideologues, and politicians in former socialist countries have pointed to Sweden as a blueprint.[1] It is believed that Sweden, or the "Swedish model," has combined the efficiency, dynamism, and flexibility of capitalist market economies with the economic security and egalitarianism so highly valued by many social liberals and socialists. So, an analysis of the Swedish experience, and its relevance to former socialist countries, may be of some general interest.

When addressing this issue, it is important to realize that basic features of the economic and social system in Sweden have changed considerably over time. Though attempts to divide history into periods are hazardous, in this chapter I will partition modern economic and social history in Sweden into three periods. The first, the century from about 1870 to 1970, may be called "the period of decentralization and small government." During this period, the economic system in Sweden did not differ much from the ones in other countries in Western Europe, although Sweden

Most of this chapter was written during my stay at the Collegium Budapest in the fall of 1997. I am grateful for discussions with János Kornai, as well as for his written comments on earlier drafts. András Nagy has not only contributed comments on earlier drafts; he has also helped me with statistics and references to the literature on socialist and post-socialist countries. I am also grateful for useful comments on an earlier draft of the chapter by Fabrizio Coricelli, John McHale, and Ulf Jakobsson, as well as from one of the editors, Stephan Haggard.

Facts, figures, and interpretations about Sweden in this chapter are based on my book *The Swedish Experiment* (Stockholm: SNS 1997), if not stated otherwise. (This book is a slightly expanded version of an article with the same title in the *Journal of Economic Literature* 35 [September 1997]: 1273–1320.)

[1] Examples are Augusztinovics 1997; Ferge 1989; Nyilas 1992, 1995; Szalai 1986; Tárkányi 1997.

was probably one of the least regulated economies in this part of the world. The second period, from 1970 to 1985–90, may be characterized as a "period of centralization and large government." In this time span, Sweden acquired idiosyncratic features, though still within the framework of a capitalist market economy. The third period, from 1985–90 onward, may be regarded as a "period of transition," due to the deregulation of the markets for capital and foreign exchange, the intensified importance of private saving and private supply of capital, comprehensive tax reforms (with lower rates, a broader base, and fewer asymmetries), a shift of the macroeconomic-policy regime toward greater emphasis on price stability, a stricter budget process in the public sector, and some albeit modest attempts to reform and rewind various welfare-state arrangements.

This chapter deals mainly with the last two periods. By way of introduction, I will make a few comments on the first, century-long period, as it was largely then that the foundations of today's affluence in Sweden were established. Some of the experience from that period is also highly relevant to post-socialist countries.

The Period of Decentralization and Small Government: 1870–1970

In this period, the Swedish economy may be characterized as a decentralized, capitalist market system, highly open to international trade and factor mobility (of capital as well as labor).[2] The government was anxious to provide stable rules of the game, appropriate for an efficient capitalist market economy. Indeed, this had already been brought about in the mid-nineteenth century (in particular, in 1846 and 1864) by a shift from mercantilist regulations to "freedom of entrepreneurship" (*näringsfrihet*). Government activity was concentrated on the "classic" functions of government – that is, providing collective goods and an adequate and well-functioning infrastructure, and encouraging investment in human capital by comprehensive elementary education and the establishment of a number of engineering schools at various educational levels.

During most of the period, government spending and taxes, as fractions of GDP, seem to have been only between half and two-thirds of the average of the other countries that are highly developed today (Tanzi 1995). Not until 1960 did total public-sector spending in Sweden reach the OECD average – about 31 percent of GDP at that time – as com-

---

[2] Accounts on the economic system during this period include Lundberg 1956; Lindbeck 1975: 1–10; Myhrman 1994.

pared with less than 10 percent at the turn of the century and 25 percent in 1950.

Growth performance in Sweden was strikingly successful during the period. Sweden had one of the fastest, perhaps *the* fastest, rate of labor-productivity growth, also in terms of GDP per capita, of all the countries for which records are available (except possibly Japan). So the Swedish experience during this period illustrates how a decentralized market economy, highly open to international transactions, may be quite conducive to sustained productivity growth if the government fulfills its classic functions well.

At the very end of the period, in the 1950s and 1960s, there was an early buildup of welfare-state arrangements with about the same degree of generosity as those in other Western European countries at that time. Serious disincentive problems do not seem to have materialized, even though total public-sector spending gradually increased from 31 to 40 percent of GDP between 1960 and 1970. It cannot be said for sure, of course, whether this means that the welfare-state arrangements and related taxes in the 1960s were "harmless" or even favorable to economic efficiency and growth, or that serious disincentive effects were simply delayed – perhaps by as much as a decade.

It is important for those who regard Sweden as a blueprint for former socialist countries to observe the sequence of events. *First* came a relatively rapid economic growth over a very long period of time, *then* gradually came more ambitious welfare-state spending. Sweden was already a rich country when it embarked on the road to generous welfare-state spending. It had also acquired what might be called "administrative maturity," with an apparent ability to handle both the classic functions of government and the emerging welfare-state arrangements, including the financing of them.

If we consider the welfare-state arrangements in today's post-socialist countries, the degree of generosity of these in the three richest countries in the group – Hungary, the Czech Republic, and Poland – would seem to be about as great as in Sweden. For instance, they display about the same "replacement rates" in income-protection systems as Sweden, and many of their social services are as highly subsidized as Sweden's. Indeed, they are often free. This is the case not only for education but for health care, child care, and care of the old, although the subsidies have diminished in recent years. As a result, the size of both "social" and total government spending today is about as high in some post-socialist countries, relative to GDP, as it is in Sweden (Kornai 1992b), even though their GDP per capita is currently no more than a fifth of Sweden's (UN 1996).

Observations such as these form the background to János Kornai's (1992b) description of some post-socialist countries as "premature welfare states." The highly ambitious income protection and social services in these countries are to some extent inherited from the socialist period, although both cash benefits and services in kind were often tied at that time to employment contracts, which meant that much of the costs showed up in firms' budgets rather than in the central government budget.[3] The welfare-state arrangements in other post-socialist countries are still rather fragmentary.

Another important experience in Sweden during the century from 1870 to 1965–70, relevant to today's post-socialist countries, is that public-sector administrators seem to have been relatively honest. This was certainly no gift from heaven. Corruption had flourished in Sweden during the mercantilist period in the second half of the eighteenth and early nineteenth centuries. One reasonable explanation for the relative absence of corruption in the second half of the nineteenth century and first half of the twentieth century is that public-sector administrators did not have much left to "sell" after mercantilist regulations had been lifted. A complementary explanation is that they were well paid, which may have reduced the temptation to accept bribes: they could afford to be honest. For instance, at the turn of the century, high-level administrators (*generaldirektörer*) earned twelve to fifteen times the salary of an average industrial worker.[4]

It is also likely that honesty evolved into a *social norm* among public-sector administrators during this century-long period. A high standing with colleagues and the general public probably required honest behavior, in the sense that others expected it. The emergence of such a norm was facilitated because it was highly consistent with the existing incentive structure for government officials. The social norm of honesty – an important aspect of the work ethic – was probably internalized by the public-sector administrators, who incorporated it into their system of values.

This experience of having relatively honest public-sector administrators in Sweden for a long period conveys an important message to former socialist countries. It is a commonplace that chronic shortages and reliance on administrative allocations of resources bred corruption during the socialist period. This probably helps to explain why the field

---

[3] For instance, firms often owned or financed kindergartens, workers' old-age homes, sport facilities, vacation centers, and cultural institutions. With the subsequent privatization many of these services were sold or dismantled.

[4] A main source for this information is *Sociala Meddelanden*, 1927, no. 5, pp. 401–2.

became wide open for new types of corruption during and immediately after the process of privatization – with lingering regulations, low relative salaries for civil servants, and policy-induced uncertainty about their job security.[5] Based on the Swedish experience, I imagine that a combination of four policies would mitigate these problems: a strong legal crackdown on corruption; relatively well paid civil servants; strict legislation that prevents monopolization and cartellization in the private and the public sector; and an acceleration of the process of deregulation and privatization, so as to shorten the period in which public-sector administrators have permits and other favors to "sell."

The Period of Centralization and Large Government: From 1965–70 to 1985–90

The Swedish experience in our second period also provides highly relevant, though rather different lessons. As a broad generalization it can be said that Sweden from the late 1960s and early 1970s onward became dominated by large, centralized institutions and highly interventionist policies. Important manifestations of these developments were a drastic rise in government spending (to the order of 60–70 percent of GDP); a huge increase in marginal tax wedges (to 65–75 percent for most full-time earners); an increasingly interventionist macroeconomic policy, particularly in the labor market; greater importance for the government in aggregate saving and the supply of capital (about half of each being provided by the government); increased centralization of decision making *within* the public sector; and highly centralized wage bargaining designed to squeeze wage differentials. In addition there was a strong concentration of the structure of firms in the private sector. One important element of the earlier, highly decentralized market system was retained, however, and even accentuated: free trade in goods and services (excluding financial transactions).

It is important to realize that most of these interventionist policies and the centralist organization of society are quite recent in origin. (See Lindbeck 1997: 12–19.) While government spending, as a share of GDP, was relatively low in Sweden until about 1960, it had become 8 percentage points higher than the OECD-Europe average by 1970, and about 17 percentage points higher by the mid-1990s (OECD data base).[6] Efforts

---

[5] For evidence on the importance of corruption in socialist and post-socialist countries, see Galasi and Kertesi 1987, 1990; Moody-Stuart 1997; Nagy 1993; Klemm 1991; Holmes 1993.

[6] The difference is smaller if allowance is made for the fact that certain benefits that are taxed in Sweden are free of tax in some other countries; see note 9.

to redistribute income through very high marginal tax rates increased only gradually, in particular in the late 1960s, with an upward leap in 1971. Moreover, while the *idea* of Keynesian-type full-employment policies had been promoted by the Swedish government as early as the 1930s, it had little or hardly any influence on the policies actually pursued until after World War II. A strongly interventionist (selective) stabilization policy and tight regulation of the labor market were not introduced until the early 1970s. An active labor-market policy was not pursued on a large scale until the late 1970s, although the *idea* of such a policy had been developed in the 1950s, in particular by some labor-union economists. The government saving and credit supply did not become important until the mid-1960s, partly with the buildup of "buffer funds" (so-called AP funds) for the state pension (ATP) system.

Centralization within the public sector increased gradually during the post–World War II period, through the forced merger of 2,000 municipalities into about 280 between the mid-1950s and mid-1970s. After the early 1970s, the municipalities were increasingly ordered to augment their provision of services in quantities and qualities that were determined by the central government. Stricter political control was also exerted on various central government agencies, which had previously been relatively independent of the cabinet. Moreover, although wage bargaining had become highly centralized by the late 1950s, it was hardly used to squeeze wage differentials until the late 1960s, by way of the so-called solidarity wage policy. Centralization within the private sector likewise emerged only gradually after World War II, often encouraged by government policies.

So even though the *visions* of a highly centralized society with strongly interventionist policies can be traced back to the 1930s, 1940s, and 1950s, not until the late 1960s and early 1970s did they materialize in actual institutions and policies.

Similar developments took place in some other Western countries in the 1960s and 1970s, but the changes were more far-reaching in Sweden in several respects. As a result, institutions and policies in Sweden have diverged from those in other Western countries since the mid-1960s and early 1970s, to such an extent that it is appropriate to talk, from around that time onward, of a special "Swedish model" of economic organization and policies. Hence I devote particular attention to this period. It is also instructive to deal with a subsequent period, after 1985–90, when there was a partial retreat from important elements in this model, with related transition problems. Indeed, Sweden in the late 1980s and early 1990s may be viewed as a "minitransition economy."

Although the centralization of decision making in socialist countries may be regarded as an intrinsic characteristic of such a system – a "system-specific" feature – centralization of the economic system in Sweden after the mid-1960s was not, of course, an inevitable character-istic of a capitalist market economy. This is plain from Swedish history and from comparisons with other countries. Moreover, the centralist and interventionist development in Sweden during this second period was not the result of a grand "master plan" designed to overhaul the organization of society. On the contrary, the change may be regarded as an ex post outcome of hundreds or thousands of separate decisions. However, behind many of these decisions can be detected a specific view of the world, such as a firm commitment to income security, full employ-ment and egalitarianism, and a strong confidence in economies of scale and the efficiency of large organizations (government as well as private). There was also a strong belief in the welfare-enhancing effects of cen-tralized political interventions in the economic lives of firms and fami-lies, and, as a mirror image of this, considerable suspicion of markets, economic incentives, and private entrepreneurship not embodied in large corporations.

However, it still has to be explained why the shift to a more central-ist and interventionist economic system did not occur until the late 1960s and early 1970s. Attempts to do so have to be rather speculative. After all, the Social Democrats dominated politics continuously from the mid-1930s. One conceivable explanation for the dramatic expansion of public-sector employment in Sweden from the early 1970s to the mid-1980s is that the government was acting as an "employer of last resort," in order to sustain full employment. The strong macroeconomic distur-bances of the 1970s and early 1980s, particularly the two oil-price shocks, induced the government to expand public-sector employment faster, simply to sustain its full-employment guarantee. This role of the Swedish public sector may be regarded as a weak version of the job guarantees in the socialist countries, although in their case the task was performed by firms rather than government.

It is also tempting to speculate that the rapid expansion of public-sector spending, the increasingly progressive tax system, and the more interventionist policies toward firms in the late 1960s and early 1970s had something to do with an international radicalization of political opinion. That then leaves the problem of explaining why these ideological de-velopments had a greater impact on Sweden than on other countries. One conceivable though rather speculative explanation is that the new Swedish constitution of 1970 allowed new political trends to influence

policies faster than before. Among the constitutional changes were abo-
lition of the upper chamber in parliament (with an eight-year term), a
shortening of the term for the remaining chamber to three years, and a
shift to strictly proportional representation, which made it more difficult
to obtain a parliamentary majority.

Personal factors may also have been important. A new generation of
ideologically oriented former student politicians rose to political pro-
minence in the 1970s. An example was Olof Palme, who became prime
minister in 1969. There can also be speculation about whether these individuals, who did not have a strong background in the labor movement,
had less authority than their predecessors to resist demands from organized interest groups such as labor unions.

Similar, though much stronger centralist visions were prevalent among
ideologues and politicians in the socialist countries during the 1950–90
period. The most obvious difference from Sweden, of course, was that
the dominant decision makers in the socialist countries rejected political
democracy and the market system – or were coerced into rejecting them.
Moreover, government interventionism in Sweden had built up gradually, by a steady ("gradualist") democratic process. By contrast, the centralized economic structure in Eastern Europe after World War II was
abruptly imposed by totalitarian one-party rule, to a considerable extent
on orders from the Soviet Union. This basically meant imposing a Soviet-
type blueprint.

It is useful to consolidate the characteristics of the Swedish model
during the centralist and interventionist period mentioned earlier under
two headings: welfare-state arrangements, that is, government interventions directly influencing the life of the family; and interventions in
firms and factor markets. After discussing these two issues, I attempt to
evaluate the performance of the Swedish economy, in terms of economic
growth, macroeconomic stability, and employment, and draw the lessons
from it for post-socialist countries.

The Welfare State and Its Financing

Driving Forces

A combination of generous welfare-state benefits and large public-sector
employment in Sweden has contributed to creating a society where those
living on tax-financed income far outnumber those who are market-
financed. Whereas there was about a 0.4 tax-financed person for every
market-financed person in 1960, the proportion was 1.8 in 1995. About
a third of the tax-financed are employed in the public sector, while the

remaining two-thirds basically live on transfers from the public sector (some of them only temporarily, for instance due to unemployment, sick leave, or parental leave). This, of course, is the background to the high tax rates in Sweden. Similarly high figures can be found in some transition economies in Eastern Europe, notably in Hungary, where the ratio of tax-financed to market-financed persons was 1.65 in 1993 according to Kornai (1996: 965), that is, about the same as in Sweden.

It is a challenge in political economy to understand why the expansion of welfare-state spending and other centralist government interventions were more far-reaching in Sweden than in other developed countries from the mid-1960s and early 1970s onward. Reference is often made to the fact that the aging of the population started earlier in Sweden than in most other countries, giving an increased need or "rationale" for higher aggregate spending on pensions, old-age care, and health care. The labor-force participation of women also rose faster than in other countries, which increased the demand not only for child care but also for old-age care, although in this case it is more reasonable to talk of mutual causation rather than direct, one-way causation.

How, then, were these rationales for increased government spending translated into political actions? It is hardly surprising that the political process in democracies should have been able to carry out this translation – voters made demands and political entrepreneurs offered to satisfy them. Similar mechanisms are also likely in totalitarian countries, as the leadership can be expected to strive for popularity and status there as well. This may apply in particular to semitotalitarian regimes. For instance, Kornai (1996) argued that the socialist governments in Poland and Hungary became more anxious to please their citizens by implementing generous benefits in the 1970s and 1980s, as the totalitarianism gradually softened.

It is often assumed that the "universality" of welfare-state arrangements in Sweden, covering all income classes, tends to generate broad political support for generous and continually expanding government spending, because those with a stake in the benefit systems or a job in the public sector make up a majority of the electorate. Comparative studies also suggest that the budget process was softer in Sweden than in most other developed countries, prior to a budget reform in the mid-1990s. The budget process in the public sector in Sweden showed similar characteristics to the production firms in socialist countries, which were characterized by a "soft budget constraint" (Kornai 1980).

A more profound question is *why* the budget process was allowed to be so soft. Part of the explanation may be that policies in Sweden, including economic policy, tend to rely on *discretion* rather than on fixed rules.

Ad hoc seems to be the basic principle of political intervention. Strict budget processes would certainly be an obstacle to such decision making. In other words, a partial, although perhaps not very profound explanation may be the "political culture" in Sweden. In particular, constitutional and other legal rules designed to constrain political decision making had not been an important element in politics after World War II. Nor had the notion of balance between different branches of authority: the government, parliament, and the judiciary. It can be said that this political philosophy of ad hoc – that is, of policy actions in response to current events – was institutionalized in the new constitution in 1970, which seems to have been inspired more by Rousseau than by Montesquieu.

Another conceivable explanation for the drastic increase in public-sector spending in Sweden in the 1970s and 1980s is that organized interest groups turned increasingly to the government for support and privileges. Indeed, although many interest groups in Sweden, as in other countries, had originally been established to serve their members professionally, for instance by directly bargaining with other groups in society, they tended to increase the energy they devoted to lobbying for various favors from the government. Metaphorically, the hypothesis may be that organized interest groups gradually transformed themselves from largely "Putnam-type" organizations, vitalizing civil society, to rent-seeking organizations, as described by Gordon Tullock, Anne Krueger, and Mancur Olson. This is probably a general phenomenon in pluralistic democracies, rather than a specifically Swedish phenomenon. The unique Swedish aspect is rather the strong political influence of one specific interest group, the labor unions. This applies, in particular, to the central organization of blue-collar workers, the LO, largely as a result of its alliance with the dominant political party in the country, the Social Democrats.

In fact, it is appropriate to say that economic and social policies in Sweden since World War II have been dominated by this alliance between the Social Democratic Party and the labor unions, often in conflict with the managers of firms and the employers' associations. It is therefore misleading to term Sweden a "tripartite" society with a strong consensus among unions, employers' associations, and the government, particularly since the mid-1970s. The LO has not confined itself to initiating new government policies in many fields, in confrontation with the employers' organizations. It has also exerted strong powers of veto against government policy proposals, particularly when the government has been Social Democratic.

The political influence of the central labor unions was less during periods of nonsocialist government in 1976–81 and 1991–94. But the modest retreats initiated by such governments from previous legislation that favored the unions were in many cases reversed by the ensuing Social Democratic government. The main exception was the "wage earners' funds," legislated for in 1982 and abolished in 1994 by a non-socialist government.

In principle, rent-seeking activities by various interest groups can be expected to promote corruption. The Swedish experience suggests, however, that open corruption in the form of cash payments to *individual* politicians or public-sector administrators in exchange for favors may be kept within reasonable bounds even in countries with big government. The social norm of honesty among public-sector administrators mentioned earlier seems to have survived both the expansion of government intervention and the fall in the relative wages of high-echelon public-sector employees, who today do not earn, after taxes, more than about twice the salary of an average industrial worker. This suggests that the "history dependence" of the social norm of honesty may be quite strong, once such a norm has been well established, even if it may not survive indefinitely.

Part of the explanation for the limited scale of corruption in Sweden may be that the expansion of government intervention has been directed more toward households than firms, where it may be that large-scale corruption can develop more easily. Moreover, government intervention in Sweden has rested more on incentives (taxes, benefits, and subsidies) than on physical regulations and permits (the main exception here being the financial markets). The latter type of intervention probably leaves society more vulnerable to corruption because it has a more discretionary, case-by-case nature.

All this does not mean that Sweden is free from exchanges of favors between private agents and political parties in control of the government. What it means is that the form it takes is less likely to be cash payments to individuals than mutual favors taking the form of job appointments in exchange for political loyalty – a practice that seems to flourish in all countries. My subjective impression is that politically motivated appointments, rather than those emphasizing competence, have played an increasingly important role in the public sector in Sweden in recent decades.

Another form of political exchange is legislated privileges and cash transfers to *organizations*, and hence indirectly to their representatives, in return for support for a political party in power. The unique feature

155

of Sweden in this respect is the importance of such exchanges between the government and various organizations connected with the Social Democratic Party. This extends to financing the salaries of representatives of these organizations. The participants include not only unions but tenants' associations, cooperative housing organizations, organizations of pensioners, party-affiliated study organizations, and youth and leisure organizations, and their officials, all in exchange for their support for the Social Democratic Party. There is no question that this exchange of favors is an important explanation for the power base of the Social Democratic Party in Sweden. Some observers would call this "rent seeking" rather than "corruption," but the distinction is rather subtle. If a corporation gets government contracts in exchange for gifts to a ruling political party, this is likely to be regarded as corruption in most democracies. It is not clear why an exchange of favors, largely in cash, between other types of organizations and the government should be looked upon differently.

It may take some time before strongly organized interest groups play the same role in former socialist countries as they do in Sweden and other parts of Western Europe, because much of civil society was destroyed during the socialist period. A corollary is that close connections between interest groups and the state have not, or not yet emerged. "Traditional" corruption, with cash payments to individuals rather than to interest-group organizations, seems to be more prevalent.

With Sweden, it is also tempting to hypothesize that increased competition between political parties in a world where party loyalties among the electorate are receding tends to result in an "overshooting" of the welfare state. By this I mean that voters would have opted for less expansion if they, and the politicians, had been able to take all the decisions simultaneously, and predict all the costs to society at large in advance, including delayed disincentives. This hypothesis is an application of the common notion that the political gains from providing additional *selective* benefits to various interest groups are higher than the political losses due to higher taxes, which are usually *general* and hence paid by most citizens.

Another likely part of the explanation for the magnitude and form of increased public-sector spending in Sweden is the political ideology of leading politicians. An example is the ambition among dominant Swedish politicians to "mobilize" female labor, by stimulating them to shift from work in the household sector to work outside the household, which tends to raise measured GDP.

Similar political ambitions were probably behind the encouragement after World War II of labor-force participation by women in socialist

156

countries. Indeed, in several of these countries, it reached rather high levels earlier than it did in Sweden.[7]

Another example of the role of ideology in Sweden is the ambition among politicians to standardize various welfare arrangements. All adults are supposed to work (or try to get jobs) in the open labor market, in many cases in the public sector. All children should ideally receive the same type of day care, organized by the municipalities, and subsequently the same type of schooling. Care of the aged is also supposed to be supplied by the public sector. Consequently, private initiatives have been discouraged in these fields. Standardized housing in huge municipal housing complexes has been provided. Behind these efforts may be detected the view that housing is a "social right," rather than a market good, and that access to it should be rationed by the authorities – an idea that was pushed much harder, of course, in the socialist countries (Dániel 1989; Enyedi, Lackó, and Szigeti 1994).

It is paradoxical that political efforts to enforce standardized solutions to the various problems became accentuated (in the 1970s) just before the population started to become more heterogeneous in various respects (professionally and ethnically), and individual preferences developed in more "individualistic" directions, according to available attitude studies (Pettersson 1992; Ziehe 1993).

Achievements

So, how successful were the centralist and interventionist policies in Sweden after about 1970? The ambitions to provide high income security and ample social services were certainly realized. Policies also seem to have contributed substantially to reducing poverty and to making the overall distribution of disposable income relatively compressed. In this sense, the welfare-state policies basically attained stated objectives.[8]

---

[7] For instance, it was not until around 1980 that the labor-force participation rates of women in Sweden reached the same level as in Hungary (ILO 1990).

[8] One indicator that welfare-state policies and related taxation were important in reducing the dispersion of disposable income is that the dispersion of the distribution of disposable income is only about two-thirds of the dispersion of factor income (with Gini coefficients of 0.2 for disposable household income and about 0.33 for factor income). Moreover, during the period when the wedges between the distribution of factor income and disposable income were widened, from the late 1960s to the early 1980s, the distribution of factor income for the fully employed did *not* become more dispersed, rather the opposite. Thus the Swedish experience does not provide much support for the common hypothesis that higher benefits and more progressive taxes will simply be "shifted" onto higher factor prices, so working against the attempts to equalize the distribution of disposable income.

Some welfare-state arrangements have also improved economic efficiency and economic growth. Various social-insurance arrangements
compensate for well-known imperfections in private capital and insurance markets. Positive external (interpersonal) effects of investment in
human capital mean that economic growth may be promoted by subsidies to education, and by prenatal care and child care outside the home
– at least for children from low-income families.

It is often argued also that various welfare-state arrangements, including social insurance, social assistance, and compression of the distribution of income, contribute to social and political stability. This point is
highly relevant to today's post-socialist countries as well. Electoral gains
by "reformed Communists" in the later 1990s are often interpreted as
dissatisfaction with deteriorating income security and widening dispersion of incomes during the transition period, by contrast with the rather
high economic security and low measured income inequality during the
socialist period.[9]

Interventions in Firms and Factor Markets

While socialist countries nationalized production firms, Sweden nationalized – or, more accurately, "communized" – the income and service production of households instead. This shows up in the national accounts,
where "public consumption" reached about 30 percent of GDP in
Sweden in the 1980s, as compared with 10–15 percent in most other countries in Western Europe. By contrast, the proportion of government ownership of production has been smaller in Sweden than in most other
Western European economies during the post–World War II period: 8–10
percent of value added in the business sector. This does not mean that
the government abstained from trying to influence the operations of
firms. Probably the most important tools for exerting such influence were
selective taxes and subsidies and capital-market regulations. An example
is tax incentives to induce firms to invest retained earnings rather than
pay dividends. Another important ambition was to make firms shift their
investment from booms to recessions, although in the 1970s and 1980s
these policies gradually turned into selective subsidies to branches of
industry and geographical regions regardless of the cyclical state of the
national economy.

It is important to emphasize that these attempts to influence the size,
composition, and timing of real investment were made under a regime
of detailed regulation on capital markets, including controls on interest

[9] See Adam 1984; Atkinson and Micklewright 1992; Flakierski 1981; Galasi 1995.

rates. By keeping interest rates low, indeed often negative in real terms, it was possible to squeeze profits without a collapse of investment incentives. Moreover, foreign-exchange controls limited the scope for firms and other holders of financial assets to shift their investments abroad.

One effect of these policies was that the government and the central bank were favoring low-cost capital flows to residential construction and a number of large corporations, and loans to the government itself. It is easy to understand that these policies created quite arbitrary allocations of investment, using rates of return as a bench mark for an efficient allocation of resources.

Another typical feature of policies in Sweden toward the business sector was the ambition to partition off the returns of firms from the earnings of their owners. Important tools for that purpose were double taxation of profits, and taxes on capital gains. This attempt by the government to prevent private owners from becoming rich while allowing firms to make handsome profits was one reason for the low level of private saving in Sweden, in particular household saving. The government tried to compensate for this low rate with high government saving and capital supply.

From an ideological point of view, these policies may be characterized as attempts to create "capitalism without capitalists" – hardly a viable economic system, in particular if the aim is to have a vital sector of small private firms, which in general cannot easily acquire equity capital from abroad.

The intellectual and political background to these ambitions cannot be understood without referring again to the labor unions, especially the central organization of blue-collar workers, the LO. Four, closely related policy ambitions of the unions were particularly influential in forming policies from the late 1960s to the early 1980s: to squeeze profits between rising wage costs and a fixed exchange rate; to compress the distribution of wages drastically (the "solidarity wage policy"); to enhance job security for those who already have a job ("insiders" in the labor market), and thereby increase union influence at the workplace; and to shift the ownership of firms to collective, tax-financed "wage earners' funds."

The unions argued that the first two types of policies would redistribute income to labor, in particular to unskilled workers, and also favor productivity growth, by forcing low-profit firms to contract or even close down. The potentially negative effects on aggregate employment and investment could, it was argued, be effectively counteracted by administrative devices, such as mobility-enhancing labor-market policies, public-sector employment, government provision of capital and selective investment subsidies, or tax concessions for firms that invest. This was an attempt to integrate union wage policy and interventionist government policies, and can be regarded as a distinct feature of the "Swedish model."

Although many low-productivity firms indeed contracted or disappeared as predicted, there was also a gradual fall in aggregate capital accumulation from the mid-1970s, connected with a falling rate of return on real investment. Moreover, the fact that profits were locked into firms with historically high profits tended to conserve the existing production structure. This thwarted the ambition of the unions and government to speed up the rate of structural change.

Naturally enough, aggregate private employment did not flourish in this environment. While the number of public-sector employees increased by about 700,000 between 1965 and 1990, private-sector employment contracted by about 200,000 employees.

The influence of the unions on government policies also shows up in the legislated changes in the property rights of firms. When the unions were not able to achieve their ambitions concerning job security and union power by bargaining with the employers, they often got what they wanted by way of legislation instead. Important examples were the laws that expanded union influence within firms, such as the legislation that gave the unions some powers over hiring and firing decisions. So, even though the formal ownership of firms was usually unchanged, the *content* of the property rights was certainly altered.

However, the idea of creating "capitalism without capitalists" was replaced in the mid-1970s and early 1980s by outright ambitions among union leaders to supplant private, capitalist ownership with collective ownership, under strong union control. The proposed tool was tax-financed "wage earners' funds," whose proponents argued that the funds would also prevent capital accumulation in firms from making private individuals richer.

Even if the proposed wage earners' funds were designed to make Sweden a socialist country, the proposal differed in two important respects from nationalization in the socialist economies in Eastern Europe. The most important difference was, of course, that the suggested transformation to socialism was to be gradual and conducted in the context of a democratic society. Another important difference was the "corporatist" nature of the proposal. The boards of the funds were to include representatives of the unions, the employers' associations, and the state, although it was assumed that the funds would pursue industrial policies that reflected the values and objectives of the unions.

160

The proposal was basically, though somewhat reluctantly, accepted by the leadership of the Social Democratic Party. A revised version of it was implemented in 1983, but in a diluted form, after heavy criticism from the political opposition, business leaders, and others (including some economists). A decade later, however, the funds were abolished by a nonsocialist government in 1994, by which time they had acquired shares corresponding to about 8 percent of the Swedish stock market. The adventure with wage earners' funds is as close as Sweden has ever been to becoming a socialist country, although representatives of the unions, rather than the state, would have been in control.

Economic Performance I: Economic Growth

Although the objectives of Sweden's social and redistributive policies seem to have been realized to a considerable extent, it is obviously also important to look at the consequences of the living standards of the population, including the poor. It is also necessary to consider the effects on aggregate economic growth.

By contrast with the century between 1870 and 1970, the period after 1970 brought rather slow economic growth relative to other developed countries. I choose to look at developments after 1970 simply because the economic system in Sweden changed considerably during the second half of the 1960s and the first half of the 1970s. While per capita GDP increased by altogether 52 percent in the OECD area as a whole during the period 1970–90 (weighted average), it increased by only 40 percent in Sweden. The difference is even greater during the period 1970–97: 62 percent for the OECD and 42 percent for Sweden.

In 1970 Sweden was fourth among the developed countries in terms of the *level* of GDP per capita, and 6 percent above the OECD average (excluding two developing countries, Mexico and Turkey). By 1990 Sweden had fallen to ninth place, 5 percent below the OECD average, and by 1997 to fifteenth, and 14 percent below the OECD average.

So, Sweden did not simply, like Switzerland and the United States, lose some of its previous lead in terms of GDP per capita due to the productivity of other countries catching up. About a dozen OECD countries actually overtook Sweden in the international income league. There is little to attract countries contemplating the Swedish model (from about 1970) as a blueprint for rapid economic growth.

How can the sluggish productivity growth in Sweden after about 1970 be explained? It is helpful to distinguish between "proximate" sources of economic growth, which exert a direct influence via the production function, and background factors, which influence the proximate sources.

According to conventional growth accounting of proximate sources, the slowdown of productivity growth in Sweden is associated with a retardation of the accumulation of real capital, a slowdown in reallocations of resources, and lagging improvements in technology (including the organization of production). According to a study of the business sector by Ragnar Bentzel (reported in Lindbeck 1997: appendix 3), retardation of the accumulation of real capital was responsible for a quarter of a percentage point in the fall in labor productivity growth, slower reallocation of resources for about three quarters of a percentage point, and slower technological (and organizational) development for about 1 percentage point, as reflected in the "residual" of the calculations. Slower accumulation of human capital is also likely to have played a part, although it has not been possible to quantify the importance of this factor, which in Bentzel's growth-accounting analysis of Sweden is incorporated in the "residual."

It is even more difficult to quantify the influence of the various *background forces* underlying these proximate sources. With investment in real capital assets, it is natural to refer to the fall in the return on such assets relative to capital costs from the late 1970s. As we have seen, this fall was a deliberate policy for a considerable period. The return on investment in human capital, including higher education and the acquisition of skills by workers, also fell due to the compression of wage differentials and the increased progressiveness of the tax system. Whereas the after-tax rate of return on a university education seems to have been about 10 percent in the late 1960s (according to conventional static calculations), it had fallen to about 2 percent by the early 1980s. This probably goes a long way to explaining the fall in the number acquiring university degrees in the 1980s and early 1990s. In fact, fewer of those born in the 1960s acquired university degrees than of those born in the later 1940s.

The slowdown in the reallocation of labor was probably related also to the drop in the reward for changing jobs. Furthermore, there was a shift in the 1970s from mobility-enhancing policies in the labor market to providing subsidies to declining sectors and regions. The deterioration of the incentive structure for individual employees had well-known substitution effects that acted against work intensity and striving for promotion, and substitution effects in favor of leisure, do-it-yourself work, barter, and work in the underground economy.

It is important to realize, however, that the disincentive effects of taxes and welfare-state benefits are not *uniquely* related to the size of aggregate government spending or taxes. Indeed, the disincentive effects may vary considerably between two countries with the same level of welfare

162

spending, depending on the "fine structure" of the benefit and taxation rules applied in them. For instance, strong actuarial elements in the social-insurance system may help to mitigate economic distortions even when government spending is high. Similarly, taxes that provide the same revenues to the government (as a percentage of GDP) may have distinctly different effects on economic incentives, depending on the relation between marginal and average tax rates, and on asymmetries in the taxation of different types of earnings and assets.[10] However, for a given structure of welfare-state arrangements and taxes, a further increase in public-sector spending (above a point that is difficult to determine exactly) will necessarily result in damage to economic efficiency and growth.

The fall in the rate of technological and organizational change, as measured by the "residual" in growth accounting exercises, is more difficult to explain. When comparing the development with other countries, one explanation is clearly that others caught up technologically and organizationally, although this cannot explain why Sweden was *overtaken* by many countries. It also seems that the expansion of sectors with high value added and rising terms-of-trade was rather sluggish. There may also have been a relatively slow rate of improvement in product quality during the 1970s and 1980s, as an additional element in the process of technological catch-up by other countries (Lindbeck 1997). Barriers to technological and organizational change are, of course, likely to have been much more pronounced in Soviet-type economies than in Western economies, including Sweden's.[11]

Economic Performance II: Macroeconomic Policy and Full Employment

Sweden has often been hailed for its successful full-employment policy. Indeed, it turned out to be possible to maintain approximately full employment until the early 1990s while unemployment had been increasing inexorably in most Western European countries since the mid-1970s.

---

[10] There are also *measurement problems* in connection with government spending. For instance, whereas benefits are taxed in some countries (including Sweden), they are untaxed in others. This tends to exaggerate the size of public-sector spending in countries with the former system relative to countries with the latter. While public-sector spending in Sweden in recent decades has been 20–25 percentage points higher than the average in the OECD countries (as a share of GDP), the figures shrink to 10–15 percentage points if benefits are measured net of tax.

[11] See, for instance, the discussion about such obstacles in Adam 1989; Gomulka 1986; Jeffries 1992; Kornai 1980, 1986; Lavigne 1994.

How was this accomplished? And why did full employment finally break down in Sweden in the early 1990s, when open unemployment rates reached the OECD average of over 10 percent according to internationally standardized statistics and, in addition, a sizable proportion of the work force (8 percent) took early retirement?

Contrary to widely held beliefs, especially among foreign observers, it cannot be argued that full employment in the 1970s and 1980s was the result of "responsible" (employment-enhancing), centralized wage bargaining and a successful incomes policy by the government. From about 1970 until the mid-1990s, nominal wage costs increased by a factor of seven, while after-tax real wages were basically constant. Such an increase in nominal wage costs seems to be a rather clumsy way of bringing about constant real wages after tax.

It is true that real wages in Sweden were "flexible" during this period, in the sense that they fell in connection with tendencies toward higher unemployment. This flexibility, however, was not brought about by nominal wage restraint but by recurring devaluations. Moreover, occasional attempts by the government to pursue an incomes policy were not very successful. For instance, when the government was particularly heavily involved in wage bargaining in the mid-1970s, nominal wage costs per hour actually increased by 65 percent over a three-year period.[12]

Nor is it possible to explain the low unemployment rates in the 1970s and 1980s *either* by the construction (and administration) of the unemployment benefit system *or* by the so-called active labor-market policy, both of which are likewise popular explanations among Swedish politicians and foreign observers. Neither type of policy could prevent a collapse of full employment when the economy was exposed to serious macroeconomic shocks, which dramatically reduced the number of job vacancies in the early 1990s. Without vacancies, it becomes hardly possible to implement strict work requirements in the unemployment benefit system. An active labor-market policy, designed to help individuals to "swim" from unemployment islands to vacancy islands, becomes powerless under such circumstances.

The only realistic explanations of why unemployment was low in Sweden during the 1970s and 1980s are that real wage costs, as mentioned before, were reduced from time to time by a series of devaluations, in connection with wage-cost crises; and that public-sector employment increased gradually until about 1985 (Lindbeck 1997:

---

[12] An exception was the government-appointed Rehnberg Commission in the early 1990s, which convinced labor unions to accept a dramatic reduction in the rate of nominal wage increases.

69–81). Once politicians, faced with a severe wage-cost crisis in the early 1990s, came to the conclusion that the "devaluation cycle" should be brought to an end, and no further increase in public-sector employment be allowed, full employment broke down. So, it would seem that full employment had been maintained in Sweden during the 1970s and 1980s by methods that were not sustainable in the long term – the devaluations and increases in public-sector employment could not go on forever.

The abrupt rise in unemployment in 1992 and 1993 was exacerbated by a number of exceptionally severe macroeconomic shocks, at that time, including high real international interest rates, a crisis among domestic financial institutions, and a collapse of construction activity (after the financial and construction bubbles in the 1980s). There was also a drastic fall in the household consumption rate, partly in response to higher after-tax real interest rates, to falling asset prices, and probably also to greater uncertainty about jobs and entitlements under the social-insurance system.

There are interesting lessons to be learned from the employment experience in Sweden. First of all, it is important for both domestic macroeconomic policy and the system of wage formation to be consistent with the exchange-rate regime that is chosen. Unless wage costs can be kept under strict control, a fixed-exchange regime is quite hazardous in a world in which there are huge and highly mobile supplies of international financial capital. As soon as international portfolio managers notice, or suspect, that a certain currency is overvalued, speculation on a future devaluation is bound to emerge, resulting in drastically raised interest rates and related damage to national economic activity. Second, cost accommodations through devaluations and increased government employment are not sustainable strategies for bringing about full employment. Third, though strict implementation of "work requirements" in the unemployment-benefit system and active labor-market policies are useful complements to other policies, they cannot act as replacements for them.

There were both similarities and differences in the employment policies of Sweden and of the socialist countries, before full employment broke down in the early 1990s in both cases. The Swedish government functioned to some extent as an employer of last resort, while the state-owned firms in socialist countries had a similar obligation, regardless of the financial consequences to them. Aggregate demand management and recurring devaluations in Sweden boosted labor demand and occasionally created an overheated labor market, while the socialist countries had a chronic excess demand for labor, which was a crucial element in the shortage economy (Kornai 1980). One important background factor was, of course, that prices were set below their potential equilibrium values. Another was a "soft budget constraint" with an unlimited (or almost unlimited) availability of credit, which made it possible to neglect profitability considerations and the financial structure of firms. One consequence was a relentless willingness to invest, a phenomenon that Kornai (1980; 1992a) baptized "investment hunger."[13] With hindsight it can be said that this was an even less sustainable situation than the full-employment policies in Sweden, in the sense that the whole system finally broke down.

Sweden as a Transition Economy: 1985–90 Onward

Reforms and Retreats

Discussion of the emerging economic problems, including slow productivity growth and rapid inflation, intensified in Sweden toward the late 1970s, but it was a long time before politicians tried to do much about them. One reason was simply that many of the contributing policies had strong support among the electorate, as they still do. Another was that adequate policy measures would have required considerable deviations from ideological beliefs widely held among politicians, especially in the Social Democratic Party.

The first sign of a retreat from the previous policies was a modest tax reform in 1983 (by a Social Democratic government). The top marginal rate of income tax was reduced from 85 to 72 percent and there was a reduction to 50 percent in the marginal rates against which deficits in capital income accounts could be deducted for tax purposes.

What made the 1983 tax reform politically feasible? Economists' criticisms of the tax system, based partly on systematic empirical studies, were probably influential, but everyday experience and casual observations, by economists, journalists, and the general public, were probably more important. For instance, in a widely read article about the Swedish tax system, Gunnar Myrdal argued (as early as 1978) based on casual observation that Sweden had become a "nation of cheats." Moreover, some influential politicians seem to have been convinced that the tax system was contributing to the country's long-term growth problems.

The 1983 reform of capital-income taxation was facilitated by the fact that the government was not receiving any *net* revenues from this type

---

[13] It is interesting to note that a similar weakness – neglect of rates of return and balance-sheet considerations – turned out to be harming a number of fast-growing countries in the Asian-Pacific region in the late 1990s.

166

of tax. On the contrary, it was losing revenue by it. This was because individuals were able to report deficits in their capital account, partly because of large loans on real estate and clever capital-market transactions, which could be set off against labor income when taxes were being assessed. A specific factor that helped make this reform politically feasible was probably that it dealt with rather technical issues, which made it difficult for the public to discern the distributive consequences.

The next major retreat from centralist government intervention was the deregulation of capital markets in the mid-1980s and subsequent removal of foreign-exchange controls in the late 1980s. Such reforms had been demanded by the business community for a long time. The banks and the Swedish multinational firms especially regarded such regulation as a curb on their international competitiveness. Also cited by those who favored deregulation were the examples of other countries and recommendations of international organizations such as the OECD. In any case, many firms by then had learned to avoid these regulations by exploiting the growth and internationalization of financial markets outside the strictly regulated banking sector within Sweden. Thus, the regulations looked more and more like a Swiss cheese, at least for some firms.

These bouts of deregulation did not create serious political complications for the Social Democratic government. Although previous advocates of strict regulation of the financial markets probably regarded its removal as ideologically unfortunate, they seem to have accepted it reluctantly, as necessary under existing world conditions. Part of the explanation for the feasibility of the deregulation was probably that there were hardly any interest groups arguing against the reforms. It is also tempting to hypothesize that, as with the reform of capital-income taxes in 1983, the general public was not very concerned by such relatively technical issues. Assessing the consequences must have been difficult, as the reforms were motivated by rather abstract principles about the efficiency of capital and foreign-exchange markets.

International examples were also significant in the case of the comprehensive tax reform in 1990–91. Indeed, the reform followed a common international pattern at the time: lower rates, a broader base, and removal of various asymmetries in the taxation of different types of earnings and assets. The reform resulted from an agreement between the Social Democratic government and a number of nonsocialist parties, which had been arguing for such reforms for some time. However, it was ideologically and politically much more difficult for the Social Democratic Party than both the 1983 tax reform and the deregulation of financial markets had been. One reason was that the distributive consequences were more apparent. More specifically, income-tax rates became less progressive, which gave rise to serious ideological concern among activists within the Social Democratic Party. It is likely that the reform was facilitated by an erosion of the legitimacy of the tax system in the eyes of the general public. Respected individuals, including prominent politicians and some labor-union leaders, declared that the existing tax system was "rotten'" and "perverse," echoing Gunnar Myrdal's assertions.

It is clear, however, that different individuals were alluding to quite different matters when they criticized the tax system in this way. Some (a number of economists and politicians at the center and on the right of the political spectrum) referred to the high marginal tax rates, and hence to the fact that most individuals were able to keep only a little (usually about 30 percent) of their additional earnings. Others, such as labor-union leaders, deplored the way the tax system allowed the rich to avoid taxes through smart capital-income transactions. So the political support for the 1990–91 tax reform was based on a somewhat unholy alliance of individuals with varying complaints about the tax system, but this alliance made the tax reform possible from a political point of view.

Worth noting is that all these reforms were decided upon *before* Sweden ran into its acute macroeconomic crisis and serious financial problems for the government sector in the early 1990s. These brought an accumulated GDP decline of 5 percent, a rise in "total" unemployment (open unemployment *plus* individuals covered by various labor-market programs) to 13 percent, and public-sector budget deficits reaching 12 percent of GDP. So the sequence of events shows that it may, occasionally, be possible to reform laws and regulations in a more market-oriented direction without first undergoing an *acute* macroeconomic crisis and financial problems for the government.

The reforms were probably facilitated by a stronger realization that Sweden's long-term growth performance was slipping, that the regulations of the capital and foreign-exchange markets were not functioning as their proponents had hoped, and that the legitimacy of the tax system was being eroded. Another, specific explanation for the political feasibility of the 1990–91 tax reform certainly was the devoted work put in by a small group of prominent politicians, in particular the two ministers at the Treasury Department in the Social Democratic government and the leader of the Liberal Party, along with senior officials at the Treasury Department.

All four reforms – the two deregulations of the financial markets and the two tax reforms – were initiated from above rather than below. Indeed, the Social Democratic government seems to have preferred to minimize its consultation with its members in these cases, perhaps to speed up the political process and prevent a buildup of grass-roots political resistance. Of course, the question remains of how sustainable reforms are when introduced in this way. International commitments make it unlikely that controls on the capital and foreign-exchange markets will be reintroduced unilaterally by Sweden. The fate of the tax system is less certain. Indeed, it was not long before the marginal tax rates were raised again, by between 4 and 8 percentage points. Moreover, as the tax reform in 1991 violated some long-held ideological principles, it is understandable that some of the Social Democratic politicians and administrators responsible for it had to pay a political price. Several of them subsequently disappeared from high political and administrative positions.

A number of problems with the welfare system had also been identified by the early 1990s. One type consisted of unwanted adjustments in individual behavior, another of changes in the external environment of the welfare state.

The former resulted not only from marginal tax distortions but from a huge increase in the number of beneficiaries, due to moral hazard and, to some extent, to cheating with benefits. In other words, the welfare state was generating its own "clients," so that the economic costs to society became much higher than had been expected when the reforms were introduced.

Obvious examples of the second problem – changes in the external environment of the welfare state – are demographic changes, in particular the aging of the population, the rise in labor-market participation by women, and the slowdown in the growth of productivity. All these factors also tended to increase welfare-state spending relative to the tax base. The problems were accentuated by the rise in unemployment in the 1990s. It is not completely true, however, that these changes were "exogenous" in relation to the welfare-state arrangements themselves. All these factors were a *result*, to some extent, of the accumulation of welfare-state provisions, and perhaps even the aging of the population. The slow rate of measured productivity growth in the public-service sector, as compared with manufacturing, also tended to raise public-sector spending as a proportion of GDP, even though the number of public-sector employees had remained constant – an application of the celebrated Baumol's Law.[14]

---

[14] A slow rate of measured productivity growth in the public-service sector is, of course, a general rather than a specifically Swedish phenomenon. In the national accounts, the productivity growth in the public sector is schematically set at zero in Sweden. Avail-

Even though these problems were identified a long time ago, in Sweden as in other developed countries, it turned out to be difficult to do anything about them, for several reasons. One is that cuts in previously promised benefits may create serious difficulties for individuals who have adjusted their lives to existing benefit systems. Many individuals may, for instance, have abstained from personal saving or voluntary insurance. It is also easier for the public to see the direct distributive consequences of welfare-state reforms than of complex tax codes being revised or of financial markets being deregulated. So changes in benefit systems are bound to generate more socioeconomic conflicts and political controversy.

In the case of Sweden, it is also important to note that 65 percent of the electorate today is tax-financed. It may therefore be difficult to convince a majority of voters that they should support policies designed to cut government spending (as a share of GDP), or even policies that avoid new rounds of increased spending. Many voters probably have to be convinced that such cuts are actually in their long-term interest, even if they lose by them in the short run.

There may also be complex *psychological* problems when welfare spending is reformed. For instance, voters are more likely to be upset by losing a benefit they already have than by never having received it in the first place. This hypothesis is consistent with Kahneman and Tverski's "prospect theory," which assumes that utility functions are steeper to the left than to the right of the initial position. In other words, individuals may have acquired subjectively experienced property rights in existing benefits.

Another difficulty when reforming welfare spending is that one can never be *sure* how great the problems with existing systems are. So there will always be politicians and observers, including some economists, who deny that existing taxes, regulations, and benefit systems actually create serious problems.

How can this issue of *genuine uncertainty* be tackled? I would suggest applying the same type of "safety principle" as in environmental policy, for instance. Environmental damage often fails to show up immediately after a rise in pollution. There will always be observers who deny that serious problems exist or even are likely to arise. On the other hand, strong negative effects may suddenly emerge after a time lag, when certain threshold values are reached. This is particularly likely if the eco-

able studies indicate, however, that productivity growth in most of the public sector was *negative* (minus 2–4 percent per year) during the 1980s. Thus statistical conventions seem to have overestimated, rather than underestimated, the GDP growth in Sweden.

logical system is suddenly exposed to some exogenous shock, such as extreme weather conditions. There may then be irreversible effects that impede chances of repairing the system. Nowadays, however, even vague suspicions of severe, or possibly also irreversible, damage are regarded as an argument for avoiding ecological disturbance, precisely because of these lags and irreversible effects.

Similar delays and irreversible effects may exist in economic and social systems, because economic behavior is often influenced only after a considerable time lag. For instance, habits and social norms inherited from the past may constrain various disincentive effects for a time, so that early warning signals may not reach the public or politicians. This is particularly serious if it subsequently takes a considerable time to restore the earlier habits and social norms, after they have adjusted to a new incentive structure.

These observations make out a strong case for being on the alert for early warning signals, and for trying to avoid "overshooting" of welfare-state spending in the first place. There are strong arguments for adhering to the same kind of safety principle as in environmental policy. This advice applies, of course, to the former socialist countries as they build up their welfare arrangements. Even though such advice may be too late for some of these countries, it is certainly relevant for those whose welfare systems are not yet comprehensive.

Against this background, it is easy to understand that cuts in welfare benefits turned out to be politically difficult in Sweden. They were initiated by the nonsocialist government of 1991–94 by reducing replacement rates to 80 percent in various social insurance systems, despite the protests of the unions and the Social Democratic opposition. Subsequently, however, the Social Democrats continued with the same policy, cutting replacement rates to 75 percent, when they regained power in the fall of 1994.

It is clear that these cuts were politically facilitated by the financial crisis of the government in the early 1990s, which allowed the government to say that it had "run out of cash." But heavy reliance on this argument raises the question of whether the reforms will be sustainable when the budget deficit disappears. There is some danger here of using the wrong argument for the right measure. Indeed, when the government budget moved closer to balance in 1997 and 1998, the Social Democratic government raised the replacement rates again in several social-insurance systems, in several cases to 80 percent.

The pension reform in 1998, based on an agreement in 1994 between a number of political parties, was probably also facilitated by the acute financial crisis of the government. In this case, however, politicians mainly referred to structural arguments, in particular to the risk that the old pension system would not be viable in the long run.

The old pension system, known as the ATP system, was initiated in 1960. It was basically a benefit-based pay-as-you-go system, with full pensions (after thirty years of payments into the system) amounting to about 60 percent of the income earned during an individual's fifteen best-paid years. A buffer fund (the so-called AP fund) was also established. The *new* system will create a stronger connection between contributions and benefits. Pensions will be based on accumulated contributions over the entire lifetime of the individual. This means that the implicit tax wedges in the system will be *somewhat* smaller than in the old system (except for low-income groups), although this was not a major official argument advanced by politicians. The future system will still be basically pay-as-you-go, but with a small funded portion (based on 2.5 percentage points of an individual's contributions of altogether about 18 percent). Individuals will be allowed to choose for themselves to which institution, private or public-sector, to assign the management of the funded portion of the contribution. The new pension system decided on in 1998 is also designed to make the distribution of income between retired and active citizens more resistant to variations in real wage growth and to changes in the remaining life expectancy of pensioners.

Clearly, the reform of the Swedish pension system is less radical than those recently introduced, or at least contemplated, in some other countries, including some post-socialist countries. One probable reason for the modesty of Sweden's pension reform is that the existing system is far from financially "broke" at present, although it would probably not remain viable in the long run. It is also tempting to speculate that the Swedish public is still less suspicious of future entitlements promised by the state than the public in several other countries, including former socialist countries. Moreover, the Social Democratic Party has long regarded the ATP system as one of its main achievements, almost as a fetish. The party therefore had great difficulty in admitting that the foundations of the system had to be reformed. It even found it difficult to accept the small funded portion of the new system, with the right of individuals to assign private institutions to administer their funds.

Efficiency problems and related high costs in day care, education, and health services have also generated heated discussions, but very little genuine reform has emerged so far. The financial crisis in the public sector during the 1990s has resulted in a reduction of about 10 percent in the number of employees in public-service production and probably considerable efficiency gains as well. The organizational changes have been modest, however, and reluctance to allow private and cooperative

172

alternatives is still strong. These areas have to be regarded as basically unreformed from an organizational point of view, though there is some growth in the number of private producers of these types of services.

The recent reforms in Sweden have not been confined to actual policy measures, such as taxes, financial regulations, and various social-insurance arrangements. A number of *constitutional changes* have also been implemented, largely to constrain the asserted tendencies by the public sector to "overspend." Examples are shifts to a longer parliamentary term (four years instead of three) and greater independence for the central bank, which has been assigned a strict inflation target (of 2 percent, plus or minus 1 percent). Another example is that the budget procedure has been stiffened considerably. The new budget procedure will start with formal decisions about the aggregate level of spending, which will subsequently be broken down into individual items, rather than the other way round, as in the existing procedure.

A more active anticartel policy, complying with European Union rules, may also be in the offing. (Anticartel policies have been very lax in Sweden, probably due to Swedish politicians' weak belief in the advantages of competition.) *Attitudes* among politicians and the mass media toward small firms also seem to have improved considerably in recent years. (Such attitudes were antagonistic in the 1970s and early 1980s.) Moreover, the shift to a floating exchange-rate regime in the autumn of 1992 and the fall in inflation have diminished the risk of new cost crises for tradables.

If my earlier diagnosis of Sweden's poor economic performance after about 1970 is correct, recent reforms of institutions, policies, and attitudes among politicians have increased the probability of more favorable economic development in the country in coming years, so long as these reforms turn out to be sustainable. Indeed, productivity growth has increased considerably in the 1990s, although it is still too early to say whether this is a temporary effect or reflects a new long-term trend.[15] Manufacturing output has also recovered and by 1999 has considerably exceeded the previous peak. Since the bottom of the recession in 1994, GDP has increased by 2.8 percent per year. Until the end of 1999, however, Sweden has only regained 3 percentage points of the country's lag since 1970 of 20 percent relative to the OECD average. Aggregate employment has also recovered, though only about a third of the loss in

---

[15] In the early 1990s, productivity growth was enhanced because some of the least-productive firms closed down in connection with a fall in manufacturing production of about 15 percent. After the cycle had reached its trough, in 1993–94, productivity growth was enhanced by higher-capacity utilization.

employment in the early 1990s has been restored so far.[16] Public-sector spending, which exceeded 70 percent of GDP in the early 1990s, had by the end of 1999 been brought down below 60 percent, and is soon likely to come down to 55 percent. Inflation has been brought down to about 2 percent, and the budget deficit for the public sector has been removed. Thus, there is no doubt that the Swedish economy has recovered considerably from the crisis in the early 1990s and that the long-term prospects have also improved.

Transition Problems and the Sustainability of Reforms

I have emphasized that the reforms and retreats from the centralist economic system in Sweden in the late 1980s and early 1990s were initiated by changes in the economic, demographic, international, and social "environment" of the Swedish model, and by undesired endogenous behavioral adjustments, largely induced by various types of disincentive effect. Other probable factors were an increased understanding of the functioning of economic and social systems, and negative experiences with central planning (also in socialist countries) and attempted "fine tuning" of macroeconomic policies. Moreover, deregulation of capital and foreign-exchange markets made it increasingly difficult for the government and unions to keep rates of return on capital lower domestically than in the outside world. This process of deregulation has undermined important aspects of the "Swedish model."

The policy shift toward a market orientation in the late 1980s and early 1990s created various short-term transition problems. The deregulation of domestic capital markets contributed to a rapid expansion of credit in the second half of the 1980s (by 18 percent per year), which contributed to overheating and inflating the national economy. These effects were accentuated by the fact that the Swedish tax system favored borrowing, as interest paid was deductible from high marginal tax rates, while the taxation of returns on important real assets, such as owner-occupied houses and durable consumer goods, were low or even zero.

Even if the central bank had *tried* to counteract these inflationary tendencies, it would not have succeeded well while the exchange rate remained fixed. (A shift to a floating exchange rate would have given greater national autonomy over monetary policy.) Moreover, by dereg-

---

[16] Employment in the economy as a whole fell from about 4.5 million in 1990 (4.3 million in 1988) to about 4.0 million in 1994, and has subsequently increased to about 4.15 million by the end of 1999.

ulating capital markets *before* the removal of foreign-exchange controls, the increased demand for real assets (including real estate) was bottled up within the country. This contributed to an enormous increase in asset prices in the second half of the 1980s and a related building boom.

These developments in the late 1980s also laid the foundations for a subsequent collapse of asset prices and construction activity in the early 1990s, and a related crisis in financial institutions that had lent extensively to the building sector. These were important background factors to the recession in Sweden at that time. Deregulation also made it apparent that the allocation of resources over several decades of regulated capital markets had deviated strongly from traditional profitability criteria. So one component of the economic crisis in the early 1990s was the need to make microeconomic adjustments during the transition to a more uniform tax system and an unregulated market for capital, including foreign exchange, with positive real interest rates.

The experience in Sweden from the mid-1980s to the mid-1990s also raises the issue of what constitutes the proper timing and sequencing of reforms. I refer in particular to the fact that some serious macroeconomic problems were accentuated by removing domestic capital-market regulations before the removal of foreign-exchange controls and before the enactment of a comprehensive tax reform. It is sometimes argued that such problems should be ignored. The argument is that politicians should seize on any "window of opportunity" that happens to open for politically difficult but important reforms. Sometimes it is even argued that the economic problems associated with the specific timing and sequencing of economic reforms are a blessing from a political point of view. If an isolated reform in one area creates new problems in other areas, this, it is asserted, makes it easier to continue the reform process – an idea similar to Hirshman's vision of the advantage of "unbalanced growth." An extreme version of this argument is that politicians have to heighten problems before they can solve them, and that they may even gain political credit for solving problems they have created themselves. However, Swedish experience in the late 1980s and early 1990s shows that tensions created by "poor" timing and sequencing of reforms may also create serious economic and social problems.

The Remaining Reform Tasks

In spite of partial retreats from centralist and interventionist economic and social policies in Sweden, there are still many potentially severe obstacles to successful performance by the Swedish economy. For instance, the marginal tax wedges remain very wide, which creates well-known efficiency losses, and also results in employment difficulties for low-productivity workers, whose wages cannot adjust downward in proportion to the tax wedges. This is a particularly important problem for the household service sector, as household production is a close substitute for purchases in the market in this case.

The benefit systems still subsidize nonwork relative to work, among low-productivity workers. For the time being, it is impossible to do much about this without reducing government spending. Public-service production has not yet been reformed much, although overstaffing was reduced during the financial crises of the government in the 1990s. Competition is not yet encouraged in this sector. Double taxation and a plethora of regulations still create serious problems for small firms and obstacles to the entry of new ones. The housing market remains in bad shape due to rent controls and the monopolistic rent policies pursued by public housing institutions (owned by municipalities). The labor market has not yet been reformed much either. I refer not only to legislation about hiring and firing, but also to the system of wage formation – that is, basically to wage bargaining. This is not just a question of aggregate nominal and wage costs. The rigid structure of *relative* wages is another problem, as it is in several other countries in Western Europe. There is not much awareness among unions and politicians of the role of relative wages, either for employment performance or for the efficiency of the allocation of labor.

The economic environment for small firms is still problematic because of taxes and regulations. This, however, has not prevented the emergence of dynamic entrepreneurship in the information technology (IT) sector. One reason is that knowledge and skills are relatively abundant in Sweden in this field, largely because of the activities of the telecom firm Ericsson. Swedes are also knowledgeable in the dominant IT language, English. Moreover, most firms in the IT sector are not much harmed yet by the Swedish tax system simply because they do not earn any profit. They have also been able to avoid rigid labor-market legislation because they use nonconventional labor contracts, including project work, options, and co-ownership. It is an open question if these firms, and their high-skilled employees and owners, will remain in the country in the long-term perspective, after they are exposed to the Swedish tax system.

Another problem that remains is that the rules of the game in the economic system, as determined by the government, are still unstable. For instance, tax rules tend to change all the time, even since the 1990–91 tax reform. Social-insurance rules have turned out to be even less stable, with more than two hundred changes since 1990. Such rule instability reflects a genuine dilemma, as the advantage of changing *bad* rules conflicts with the aim of having *stable* rules. The most reasonable compromise between these conflicting ambitions is to prepare the changes made in bad rules so well that the rules do not need to be changed yet again shortly afterward.

The problem of rule instability is, of course, much more serious in the post-socialist transition economies, at least until the system has "settled down" (Ékes 1997; Newbery 1991). In Hungary, twenty changes were introduced in the personal income-tax regulations and fifteen changes in the social-insurance regulations in early 1998 (*Heti Világgazdaság* 1997).

Another reason for unstable rules is a short-term horizon in politics, undoubtedly accentuated by the mass media. Politicians are tempted to intervene by bringing in new rules and regulations as soon as some specific problem in society has been highlighted by the media. As Harold Wilson once remarked, "In politics the long-run is three weeks." It is worth thinking about constitutional rules that might mitigate this short-sightedness in politics, which is a problem common to all countries.

Main Lessons

What are the main implications for post-socialist countries to be drawn from the Swedish case? Let me summarize them under six points.

1. Those in the post-socialist countries who suggest the adoption of Swedish-style welfare arrangements should bear in mind that Sweden was a far wealthier society when it instituted such arrangements. Moreover, Sweden had already developed a competent class of public-sector administrators, and social norms of honest behavior among them.

2. Strongly interventionist policies in Sweden, especially generous welfare-state arrangements, accomplished important social goals – high income security, considerable income equality and little poverty. But this has probably been at the expense of high costs in terms of productivity and economic growth. Moreover, the policies had become unsustainable by the 1990s, partly due to negative macroeconomic shocks. It is likely that these costs would be more serious in post-socialist countries, given the relatively low level of per capita income and the more competitive international economic environment of today.

3. Tripartite bargaining, which has been an important element of policy making in Hungary, Poland, and the Czech Republic, has been much less important, and much less successful in Sweden

than is generally believed by foreign observers. Real wages were not kept down, and full employment was not promoted, by concerted agreement on wage constraints reached between unions and firms in cooperation with the government. In fact, the main instruments were periodic devaluations and increased public-sector employment, mechanisms that turned out to be unsustainable by the early 1990s.

4. The Swedish experience suggests that people react more strongly when something is taken away than when some new benefit is not awarded, which is in keeping with the theorems of prospect theory. This has made attempts to reform and rewind the welfare state very difficult in Sweden, and perhaps in societies such as Hungary and Poland as well. In post-socialist societies that have not yet established extensive welfare systems, it implies a need for caution.

5. Eastern Europe, like Sweden, is likely to suffer from unstable rules of the game – probably more so than Sweden, given the uncertainties and depth of the transition. Sweden's experiences suggest that this is a serious problem.

6. Post-socialist countries should be aware that Sweden has experienced considerable macroeconomic disruption because of mistakes in the sequencing of reforms. The most important effects came from deregulating domestic capital markets prior to tax reform and the removal of foreign-exchange controls. This illustrates the importance of proper sequencing of reforms in the transition economies.

7. One encouraging experience in Sweden in the 1990s is that a democratic country may be able to reform itself in response to indications that previous policies have created serious economic problems. While some of these reforms started before the deep crisis in the early 1990s, major policy changes were not introduced until this crisis was apparent.

References

Adam, Jan. 1984. *Employment and Wage Policies in Poland, Czechoslovakia and Hungary since 1950*. London: Macmillan.

    1989. *Economic Reforms in the Soviet Union and Eastern Europe since 1960*. London: Macmillan.

Atkinson, Anthony B., and Micklewright, John. 1992. *Economic Transformation in Eastern Europe and the Distribution of Income*. Cambridge: Cambridge University Press.

Lessons from Sweden for Post-Socialist Countries

Augusztinovics, Mária. 1997. *Pension Systems and Reform: Britain, Hungary, Italy, Poland, Sweden. Executive Summary of the Final Report.* Institute of Economics Discussion Paper No. 49. Budapest: Institute of Economics of the Hungarian Academy of Sciences.

Dániel, Zsuzsa. 1989. Housing Demand in a Shortage Economy: Results of a Hungarian Survey. *Acta Oeconomica* 41: 157–79.

Ékes, Ildikó. 1997. Adózás, 1988–1996 (Taxation, 1988–1996). *Statisztikai Szemle* 75: 45–57.

Enyedi, György, László Lackó, and Endre Szigeti. 1994. *Urbanization and Housing Processes and Facts in East-Central Europe.* Budapest: Unch Habitat.

Ferge, Zsuzsa. 1989. *Van-e negyedik út? A társadalompolitika esélyei* (Is there a fourth road? The chances of social policy). Budapest: Közgazdasági és Jogi Könyvkiadó.

Flakierski, Henryk. 1981. Economic Reform and Income Distribution in Poland: The Negative Evidence. *Cambridge Journal of Economics* 5: 137–58.

Galasi, Péter. 1995. *A jövedelemegyenlőtlenség változása Magyarországon: 1987, 1992–1994.* (The change of income inequality in Hungary, 1987, 1992–1994). Budapest: Institute for World Economics.

Galasi, Péter, and Gábor Kertesi. 1987. The Spread of Bribery in a Centrally Planned Economy. *Acta Oeconomica* 39: 371–89.

1990. Korrupció és tulajdon (Corruption and property). *Közgazdasági Szemle* 37: 389–425.

Gomulka, Stanislaw. 1986. *Growth, Innovation and Reform in Eastern Europe.* Brighton: Wheatsheaf.

Heti Világgazdaság. 1997. December 22.

Holmes, Leslie. 1993. *The End of Communist Power: Anti-Corruption Campaigns and Legitimation Crisis.* New York: Oxford University Press.

ILO. 1990. *Yearbook of Labor Statistics*, 1945–1989. Geneva: ILO.

Jeffries, Ian. 1992. *Industrial Reform in Socialist Countries: From Restructuring to Revolution.* Aldershot: Edward Elgar.

Klemm, Volker. 1991. *Korruption und Amtsmißbrauch in der DDR.* Stuttgart: Dt. Verl. Anst.

Kornai, János. 1980. *Economics of Shortage.* Amsterdam: North-Holland.

1986. The Hungarian Reform Process: Visions, Hopes and Reality. *Journal of Economic Literature* 24: 1687–1737.

1992a. *The Socialist System. The Political Economy of Communism.* Princeton: Princeton University Press.

1992b. The Post-Socialist Transition and the State: Reflections in the Light of Hungarian Fiscal Problems. *American Economic Review, Papers and Procedings* 82: 1–21.

1996. Paying the Bill for Goulash Communism. Hungarian Development and Macro Stabilization in Political Economy Perspective. *Social Research* 63: 943–1040.

Lavigne, Marie. 1994. *A Comparative View on Economic Reform in Poland, Hungary and Czechoslovakia.* Economic Commission for Europe Discussion Papers No. 2. New York: United Nations.

ASSAR LINDBECK

Lindbeck, Assar. 1975. *Swedish Economic Policy*. London: Macmillan.
1997. *The Swedish Experiment*. Stockholm: SNS.
Lundberg, Erik. 1956. *Business Cycles and Economic Policy*. London: Macmillan.
Moody-Stuart, George. 1997. Mibe kerül a makroszintű korrupció?" (What is the price of corruption on the macro level?). *Vezetéstudomány* 28: 43–48.
Myhrman, Johan. 1994. *Hur Sverige blev rikt* (How Sweden became rich). Stockholm: SNS.
Nagy, András. 1993. Plus ça change – Changes in Establishment Attitudes under Socialism. *Hungarian Quarterly* 34 (Winter): 77–92.
Newbery, David. 1991. *An Analysis of the Hungarian Tax Reform*. CEPR Discussion Paper No. 558. London: CEPR.
Nyilas, Mihály. 1992. A svéd nyugdíjrendszer példája" (The example of the Swedish pension system). *Esély*, no. 5, pp. 20–33.
1995. Mi történt a svéd modellel? (What happened to the Swedish model?). *Esély*, no. 6, pp. 63–83.
Pettersson, Thorleif. 1992. Välfärd, värderingssförändring och folkrörelseengagemang (Welfare, changing values and civil society). In S. Axelson and T. Pettersson, eds., *Mot denna framtid*. Stockholm: Carlssons Förlag.
Sociala Meddelanden. 1927. No. 5.
Szalai, Júlia. 1986. *Az egészségügy betegségei* (The diseases of the public health system). Budapest: Közgazdasági és Jogi Könyvkiadó.
Tanzi, Vito. 1995. *The Growth of Government and the Reform of the State in Industrial Countries*. IMF Working Paper No. 130. Washington, D.C.: International Monetary Fund.
Tárkányi, Ákos. 1997. Európai családpolitikák: Összehasonlítások, következtetések svéd, francia és amerikai példák alapján (European family policies: Comparisons and conclusions on the basis of Swedish, French and American examples). *Demográfia* 40: 195–203.
UN. 1996. *Statistical Yearbook*. New York: United Nations.
Ziehe, Thomas. 1993. *Kulturanalyser. Ungdom, utbildning, modernitet* (Youth, education and modernity). Stockholm: Stehag B. Östling Bokförlag. Symposion.

CHAPTER 6

The Borderline between the Spheres of Authority of the Citizen and the State: Recommendations for the Hungarian Health Reform

JÁNOS KORNAI

The Problem

The answer given to a question depends, of course, to a large extent on how the question itself has been phrased. In this study, and the book on which it is based,[1] I am far more concerned to persuade readers I have formulated the question correctly than to gain assent to the answers I give. I regard argument about the answers as inevitable, but let there at least be agreement about the questions.

Scarcity – in which human wants outstrip the ability to satisfy them with the resources available – is the central subject of examinations in economics. Nowhere, at present, does the general problem of scarcity appear more acutely – one might say more brutally and mercilessly – than in the health sector. Human knowledge, science, and technology offer many more opportunities for avoiding and curing disease, relieving suffering, and prolonging life than the health sector can apply in practice. *That is the fundamental problem of health care.* There are patients who might be treated, as far as human knowledge is concerned, yet they are not treated, or not treated enough. This applies even to the richest

The chapter was written while I was a member of the Focus Group at Collegium Budapest in 1997–98. I am indebted for the invaluable help I got from the members of the group in the course of our stimulating discussions. I am also grateful to Nicholas Barr, David Cutler, Zsuzsa Dániel, Guy Ellena, Joseph Newhouse, and Andràs Simonovits for their advice and for the comments made in the discussions after my lectures at Collegium Budapest, Harvard University, and the World Bank. I express my special thanks to Mária Barát, Ágnes Benedict, Karen Eggleston, Béla Janky, Virág Molnár, and Julianna Parti for their valuable help with the research and the editorial work, and to Brian McLean for his excellent translation.

[1] Kornai 1998. The book is a product of a longer research about the reform of the welfare sector. My research is going on under the auspices of the Collegium Budapest, supported by the National Scientific Research Foundation (OTKA 018280) and the Hungarian Ministry of Finance.

countries, and, within them, not just to the poorest members of society, but to richer people as well. Not even there is the provision taken to the limit where the marginal health-enhancing effect of an increment in health-care expenditure would become zero; they stop far short of that. The same holds true a fortiori for a country at a medium level of development, such as Hungary. If it spent several times the present amount on health, it would still not exhaust the opportunities provided by science and technology. This gulf between scientific potential and health-care practice causes all the more bitterness because Hungarian doctors, and many patients, possess a great deal of information about what medicine is capable of in more developed countries.

It is a ghastly thought: here is a patient suffering who might be helped, but assistance is not forthcoming because the resources are going to something else. If the argument is followed to its conclusion, there is clearly no satisfactory solution to this cruel dilemma. Any decision reached implies not just help for some patients but *exclusion* for others: partial or total denial of care. Thinking about health-care reform means addressing the frightful dilemma of "inclusion" versus "exclusion." Recognition of this leads to a constructive rewording of the question:

- Who is authorized to decide "inclusion–exclusion" matters?
- What are the principles on which the decision is made?
- What procedures and institutions should provide the decision-making framework?
- What ownership relations and incentives should develop to motivate the participants in the process in the desired direction?

These questions have to be answered first. Only then can there be cogent discussion of the foremost subject of debate today: is the Hungarian health-care system "underfinanced," and if so, by what percentage should the sums available for health care be increased?

This study takes a position on all the constructive questions just listed. However, the discussion does not follow the same order as the questions. Its structure reflects the inner logic of how the tasks of reform present themselves. After presenting the initial principles, I cover the demand for the health sector's output, the supply, and the interaction between supply and demand. The economic and legal institutions, procedures, ownership relations, and incentives so far applied and recommended for the reform are analyzed first on the demand side and then on the supply side.[2] Finally, I consider the reception the reform is likely to receive.

---

[2] There is an extensive literature on reform of the health sector. Two works that I would single out for examining comprehensively the reforms taking place in the post-socialist

The Principles

Advocates of the reforms usually start out from the economic problems of the welfare sector or some subsector of it. They show there are troubles with financing the subsector (for instance, the pension or health system); these have already appeared, or if not, are due to appear. Expressly or implicitly, they consider it the reform's main task to raise the efficiency of the subsector in question and create the conditions for sustainable financial equilibrium. I also consider these to be very important assignments. Nonetheless, I place other criteria to the fore. My starting point is not financial sustainability or a value-free call for efficiency, but two ethical postulates.[3]

Principle 1 (sovereignty of the individual): The transformation must increase the scope for the individual and reduce the scope for the state to decide on welfare services. Respect must be shown for the autonomy of the individual. Let individuals have a greater right to choose, but let them be responsible for their choices, and if they have decided badly, let them take the consequences.

Post-socialist society would still have to reform the paternalist, excessively centralized welfare sector it inherited from state socialism if the sector's financial equilibrium and efficient operation were assured. The reform's main mission is to widen the scope for consumer sovereignty, free individuals from the patronizing care of the state, and tighten the connection between individuals' decisions and the provisions they and their families receive.

Principle 2 (solidarity): Help the suffering, the troubled, and the disadvantaged. Everyone as an individual and all citizens as a community have an obligation to help their fellow human beings when they have need of it.

I recommend that these postulates be the starting point for examining what sort of institutional system and incentive mechanism to apply to handling the health sector's fundamental problem of scarcity. The history of society belies the notion that it suffices to ground institutions on efficiency criteria, and then superimpose some kind of redistributive scheme to correct their unfairness. Economic institutions almost inevitably have distributive consequences. These need to be calculated in beforehand when institutional reforms are being devised.

---

countries of Eastern Europe are Precker and Feachem 1995 and Saltman and Figueras 1997.

[3] The book on which this study is based (Kornai 1998) deals in detail with other initial principles for the reform as well. I confine myself here to the ethical postulates among them.

Suppose we were to apply principle 1 by itself, with no concern for principle 2. Even then, a "pure" application of the mechanisms of market coordination could not be allowed. The economic literature on health care clearly demonstrates that the state has to intervene. The welfare sector exemplifies strongly shortcomings of the market mechanism known in other sectors: asymmetric information, adverse selection and moral hazard in insurance transactions, various beneficial and damaging external effects, and so on.[4]

Even if state intervention went no further than relieving these irregularities and averting the dangers of market failure, the distributive problem would remain: poorer people might be unable to pay for medical treatment. The very people coping with compound problems of poverty and of sickness would be denied the medical assistance they need.

Principle 2 calls for redistributive intervention. The question is how far to curb the application of principle 1 in favor of applying principle 2.[5] Where should the compromise be struck between the two postulates, which conflict with each other to a large extent?

In this study I often make use of the first-person singular. I openly admit that the position I advance rests on my personal choice of values, not on "objective" circumstances. Having said that, I would firmly reject any extreme egalitarian solution that gave everyone *strictly equal* access to health provisions.[6] Consistently egalitarian health care gravely breaches the first ethical principle by ignoring individual sovereignty, which in my view makes it unacceptable.

On the other hand there is a *specific egalitarian* principle that I find acceptable.[7] I express the principle in a general form and cite health care simply as an illustration of it. The requirement of equal access is specific in the following sense:

---

[4] On these questions, see the classic work by Arrow 1963, and also the writings by Besley and Gouveia 1994; Feldstein 1973; Pauly 1986, 1992.

[5] Due to limitations of space, the next two sections of the chapter concentrate on this question. In other words, I do not explore the albeit very important question of what kind of state intervention the health sector requires, irrespective of the redistributive problem.

[6] Here and elsewhere in the study I draw a distinction between two kinds of transaction: insurance, which shares risk, and redistribution, which lessens income differences. Suppose that A and B take out medical insurance with the same private insurer, sign policies on the same terms, and pay the same premiums. Later it turns out that A has been healthy all along, whereas B has fallen ill several times, needing frequent medical treatment. In effect, A has paid some of B's medical costs. However, it might have been the other way round, if A's health had been worse than B's.

The situation differs if A is richer and B poorer, and their insurance is not commercial, but A pays a higher contribution than B. In this case there is a redistribution in B's favor irrespective of their state of health.

[7] This expression was coined by Tobin 1970.

- Equal access has to be targeted: not applicable to every good and service, just to those that meet basic needs. The scope of these is arguable, but they certainly include health care.
- It cannot be comprehensive; it cannot encompass the whole volume of the service concerned, only a specific part of it. In health care, for instance, there needs to be equal access to a respectable minimum package of care – to *basic* health provision – and acknowledgment that individuals' access to *auxiliary* provision will not be equal.
- The state has to *guarantee* the equal access to basic provision. This awards an appreciable role to the state, but a much more restricted one than it received under the socialist system, when there was direct state control and financing in every sector, including health care.

With some of the dilemmas of choice, principles 1 and 2 can be applied so that they augment and reinforce one another. In other cases they stand in conflict, and there is a need to compromise. But what should the compromise be? No economist or other outside analyst could give a well-founded answer, and it is not from *them* that the answer should be awaited. The answer has to come from the persons actually concerned, within institutional frames and by procedures capable of promoting viable compromises in such situations of conflict. This idea accords with some of the more recent theories of social choice.[8] Often there is no way of establishing what the "socially optimal" decision is, but society can still manage to agree in a constructive way on a procedure for making the decision.

Operation of the health sector is a "game" in which a variety of organizations and individuals join: Parliament, the government, the central social-insurance organization and private insurers, doctors, other medical staff, health-care institutions, and the state health-care bureaucracy. Last but not least, there are the individuals: the patients and their relatives, and individuals as taxpayers and voters in parliamentary elections.[9] This game has been conducted so far under a specific set of rules. The reform entails introducing a new set of rules, which change the decision-making provinces and relative powers of the players, and thereby the dynamics

---

[8] See first of all the pioneering works of Buchanan 1954a, 1954b. Sen 1995 gives an excellent summary of the present state of the theory of social choice.

[9] The ideas about institutions and procedures I advance in this study refer mainly to Hungary, although they can be applied to other post-socialist countries with requisite caution and adjustments, so long as political democracy prevails there. I do not extend what I have to say to countries where the political regime remains a dictatorial one, even though there have been radical economic reforms.

of the health-related policy-making process. The new rules will mark an advance above all if they apply the principle of legitimacy more strongly, if the new distribution of decision-making spheres is more compatible with the operating principles of democracy.

Reform on the Demand Side: Alternative Mechanisms for Financing Basic Provisions

Let us return to the distinction between basic and auxiliary care. According to principle 1, the domain of optional, auxiliary care should be as wide as possible, whereas principle 2 requires a widening of basic care. Where can the dividing line that represents the compromise be drawn? This cannot be deduced from the value judgments themselves, but it is possible, from what has been said, to devise a *procedure* for arriving at a distinction between basic and auxiliary care. This distinction ties in with the question of how to finance the demand for health provisions. There are various possible institutional mechanisms for performing this function. I take two of them here to illustrate the dilemma of choice. They differ in the way they finance basic care, but coincide on auxiliary care.

In the case of *compulsory individual insurance*, the law obliges every citizen to have compulsory, minimum medical insurance coverage, in his or her own right, or as a family member. This has to meet the costs of basic provision. Those whom the letter of the law does not induce to take out this insurance must be forced to do so by legal means.[10] The compulsory minimum insurance may be obtained from the state system or a private insurer – any member of a decentralized insurance system, chosen voluntarily by the insured.

The solidarity principle applies when the state undertakes to pay the compulsory insurance premium for those who are in need of that assistance. In this way the state guarantees that all citizens have access to basic health care.

In the case of a *basic health service financed out of public funds*, citizens pay the compulsory contribution to a designated institution that

---

[10] Legislators, in enforcing minimum insurance cover, are not motivated only by the paternalist aim of saving citizens from their own mistakes. Suppose a citizen, through his or her own fault, has no insurance cover and is therefore not entitled to medical treatment, even if seriously ill. No morally upright society will leave that patient to suffer. Treatment will ultimately be received. Relying on this, many people will develop a "free rider" attitude: "I will not insure myself because society will help me anyway." Society, in its own interest, is defending itself from such "free riding" when it makes minimum insurance cover compulsory. On this, see the study by Lindbeck and Weibull 1987.

186

covers the costs of their basic provision. The contribution is not uniform, but redistributive in nature. The service, on the other hand, is uniform; all citizens have the same basic provision *available* to them. (Obviously they will not have *recourse* to the provision to the same extent, which will depend on their state of 'health.) Under mechanism B the state guarantee manifests itself in a universal entitlement, whereas under mechanism A it applies through targeted assistance to those in need.

Mechanism A and mechanism B both offer the public broad opportunities to buy auxiliary health provision, openly and legally, either paying out of one's own pocket or taking out private, voluntary insurance.

Neither mechanism has a laissez-faire character, but they differ in the *degree* to which individual sovereignty is curtailed by state intervention and income redistribution. The procedural and institutional choice made by citizens will certainly be influenced by what general attitude they take to limiting individual sovereignty, state intervention, and income re-distribution. The administrative costs of financing the health sector out of public funds are considerably less, and it eliminates the danger of a decentralized insurance institution becoming insolvent. Another danger with decentralized insurance is that the insurer may avoid high-risk clients, although this tendency can be countered to some extent with regulation and high-risk-adjustment schemes. On the other hand, the usual drawbacks of monopolies appear: defenselessness of clients, enfeeblement of service, and loss of the incentives provided by competition. However, let us lay aside for now the debate about the advantages and drawbacks of mechanisms A and B. Another criterion must be considered: the question of what is *feasible*, institutionally and politically. Here the initial state is decisively important.

There are debates going on about health-care reform in many developed market economies that have an extensive and sophisticated decentralized insurance sector. In the United States, for instance, most people are familiar with the decentralized system and attached to it. They would not be prepared to abandon it in favor of a nationalized, redistributive system of health-care financing paid for by taxation.[11] With that as the initial position, the feasible institutional means of applying principle 2, the solidarity principle, is mechanism A – provided the democratic political process is prepared to accept it.

---

[11] This was confirmed when President Clinton's plan for reforming the health service suffered a political defeat. Most people recoiled in alarm from the idea of a comprehensive state (federal) insurance system.

The situation is different in post-socialist Central and Eastern Europe, including Hungary. Here the initial position is a system of comprehensive state financing of the health system, in an extreme paternalist form. There is hardly a trace of any system of decentralized, private medical insurance. A jump to mechanism A from an initial position like that would certainly cause serious disturbance in the system of provision. The old institutions would cease to work before the new had begun, causing an institutional vacuum. A vacuum of that kind sometimes occurred in the narrowly defined business sphere during the first phase of the post-socialist transition. That vacuum was among the main reasons why there was a dramatic drop in production and the transformational recession. Although the slump in the business sphere caused grave hardship, it remained endurable. It would be unbearable in the health sector. The public cannot be left without an appropriate system of financing basic health provision, irrespective of where the dividing lines are drawn. The changes must take place smoothly, without any upheavals.

So my recommendation is to have two phases of reform. The first introduces mechanism B. This substantial alteration in the state financing of the health-care system includes a significant strengthening of individual sovereignty but retains many aspects of the previous mechanism. The development of decentralized private insurance is already beginning in the first phase.

The beginning of phase two is conditional. One condition concerns the *institutions*. Let us assume that this condition is met, that is, a system of sound, reliable medical insurance providers has developed, as the advocates of mechanism A hope, and satisfactory legal regulation and state supervision of their financial situation is in place. This development has occurred in an evolutionary way. The decentralized insurance industry has shown it is viable and has increasingly gained the confidence of the public. That confidence will be shown not by declarations but by a mass move to take voluntary medical insurance cover. Decentralized medical insurance needs to reach a critical, threshold level of development before the introduction of mechanism A can gain the requisite political support. Achievement of this critical level constitutes the second, *political* condition for the beginning of the second phase. There is no way to predict what preferences the public will show on this question. It would not be right to thrust mechanism A upon them. It can only be introduced generally by law if the majority of the public, in possession of the requisite information and experience, agrees with that course of action.

Having looked at the dilemma over the institutional mechanism, let us return to the question put earlier. Where should the dividing line between basic and auxiliary provision be drawn? When I seek an answer to this question, I assume that the framework just described pertains – that the first phase of the reform I recommend has begun. In other words, people have decided that basic health provision will still be provided mainly out of public funds.

Reform on the Demand Side: Distinguishing Basic from Auxiliary Provision

One idea often heard during the debates on the health-care system is that the doctors should decide where to draw the line between basic and auxiliary provision. I think this statement is untenable in this simplified form. It is a cheap piece of evasion to replace this dilemma with other problems of choice, for instance by considering instead the dividing line between interventions absolutely necessary from the health point of view and operations of a purely cosmetic character. The latter are obviously a "luxury service" for those who want to pay for it. This distinction can be drawn without any great crisis of conscience; that is not the dilemma that I tried to point out in the opening section. The truly hard decision occurs when medically justified health-care expenditures cannot be placed within the scope of basic provision to be guaranteed and financed by the state.

Deciding the total expenditure on basic provision – placing an upper limit on the aggregate, macroeconomic-level volume of these items of spending – is *not* a medical decision, in my view. It has to be realized that wherever the line is drawn, there will always be some medically justified course of treatment for some patients that cannot be squeezed into the macroeconomic budget.

The dividing line depends on two interdependent factors. One is how developed the country is – how much the public can afford to spend on health care. The line drawn in Belgium will differ from the one drawn in Pakistan, although Belgians and Pakistanis may need the same total amount of treatment from a purely medical point of view.[12] International experience suggests not only a strong relation between economic development and total health-care spending, but that the proportion of GDP spent on health care rises as a function of the level of development (see Figure 6.1).[13] Looking at the longer-term averages for countries, this

---

[12] Disregarding the geographical and climatic factors.
[13] Too much significance should not be attached to the exact position of the regression line in the figure, because there is a high degree of uncertainty about the data behind it. Different statistical definitions and approaches result in differing estimates, which would, for instance for 1996, move between 6.7 and 7.5 percent. However, it seems that the point representing Hungary is *above* the line. So the calculation suggests that Hungary spends no less – indeed, it spends more – on health care than its level of development would warrant.

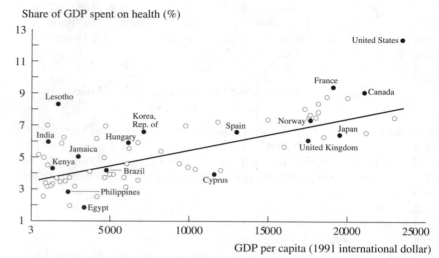

Figure 6.1. Income and health spending in seventy countries, 1990.
Note: The data for Hungary are 6 percent and 6,080
international dollars respectively (World Bank 1993: 297).
Source: World Bank 1993: 110. From *World Development Report* 1993 by World
Bank. Copyright © 1993 by The International Bank for Reconstruction and
Development/The World Bank. Used by permission of Oxford University Press, Inc.

means their total health-care spending rises more steeply than GDP.
Furthermore, if this relation pertains, it clearly allows a more developed
country to provide a greater total volume of state-guaranteed basic
provision than a less developed country.

The other factor on which the position of the dividing line depends is
the amount of tax a country's citizens are willing to pay to finance the
basic health provision. This is not a question of commercial insurance
but of redistribution, in line with the requirements of specific egalitarianism, so that households cannot decide about it individually. This has
to be a collective choice made by the community of citizens through the
democratic process.

Once the upper limit on the amount to be spent on basic provision has
been set at the macroeconomic level, the medical profession takes the
leading role in deciding how to use the macroeconomic amount that can
be spent on basic provision.[14] In practice this includes drawing up a

---

[14] I say the leading role, not exclusive responsibility. Committees deciding about microeconomic allocation should also include experts conversant with the economic, legal,
and ethical aspects of the health system. It is also worth considering the idea enabling
voluntary associations of various groups of patients to have a say.

190

schedule of the items that can be financed as basic provision, allotting the funds, and taking other allocation decisions on the microeconomic level.

More will be said later about microeconomic allocation of the macroeconomic sum available. For the moment, let us return to setting the macroeconomic limit and the democratic political process this entails. I have no naive expectations in this respect. I realize that this process does not reflect the "popular will" perfectly. There are several factors that affect the development of voters' preferences, including some that are undesirable according to my system of values. Furthermore, once these preferences have formed, there are frictions and distortions in the way they find expression in the political process. Nonetheless, I am certain there cannot be any substitute for the democratic political process, once the premise is accepted that the *state* will guarantee equal access to basic health provision.

The aim must be to reduce the distortions and frictions appearing in the political decision-making process that governs state financing of health care. Most such problems arise because the financing of the sphere is opaque. The average citizen is uncertain what is going on. Many people are misled by lies and half-truths into misjudging the situation. These lies and half-truths must be swept aside, so that the state financing gains *transparency*. The following rules would help greatly to achieve this:

1. Let us abolish the misleading term "social-insurance contribution." To call a spade a spade, this is not an insurance contribution but a specific kind of redistributive tax (which has an insurance premium component). The term applied is not immaterial for two reasons. On the one hand, it has a psychological effect on tax-paying, voting citizens. On the other, it has implications in constitutional law. There is no direct connection here between what citizens *individually* pay to the state and what they *individually* receive from the state. By contrast, an insurance transaction can be expected to provide greater compensation (if there is a claim) to those who pay a higher premium.[15]

2. Let us abolish the misleading distinction whereby employers pay part of the health-care contribution and employees the rest. In fact the employer views the whole contribution, which is mandatory and uniform, as a component of wage costs and effectively subtracts it from the total

---

[15] This criterion came up when the Constitutional Court was examining Hungary's 1995 package of economic stabilization and adjustment measures. The Constitutional Court called for the kind of "proportionality" between the social-insurance contributions and the services provided that can be expected of an *insurance* transaction. This proportionality cannot be required of a tax, although there are, of course, constitutional limits on taxation as well.

compensation paid to the employee. Because the whole social-insurance contribution is reckoned against the employee's total gross wage, it is the employee who really pays it. So wages have to be "grossed up" when the reform is introduced, and the health-care contribution then deducted from them. Employers have to be made responsible for withholding and transferring the contributions.[16]

3. In the light of points 1 and 2, a new kind of "earmarked" *health tax* needs to be introduced. Basically, this will be a levy of an income-tax nature. At the moment of introduction, it will not raise by a penny the fiscal load on any employee who has previously paid social-insurance contributions (along with his or her employer). It will simply express openly and make it transparently plain who is paying for the state-financed health care and how much they are paying. Taxation experts disagree about whether the advantages deriving from the transparency of earmarked taxes outweigh their disadvantages, above all their inflexibility, the way they tie the administration's hands by preventing reallocation. Without wishing to commit myself in the general debate, I would maintain my proposal for an earmarked tax in the health sector. The clear correspondence between the health tax and basic health care could be an effective weapon against the still prevalent fiscal illusion inherited from the socialist system, the false notion that health care is "free."

4. There must be legal regulation of all the compulsory, direct copayments to be paid by patients under the state-financed system of basic provision.

5. It must be emphatically declared that the "earmarked" health tax and the compulsory direct copayments are to be used exclusively for financing the basic health provision. Conversely, the same declaration must state that the health tax and the copayments are the sole source from which basic health provision can be financed. Other items of budget revenue may not be used for that purpose. There must be a one-to-one correspondence between the compulsory payments for basic health provision and the macroeconomic sums of the payments made with them.[17]

By these means it will become clear that the community of citizens has to decide, within the frames of legislation, how much the total compulsory payment for basic health provision should be and, thereby, what

---

[16] A different situation arises if the employer goes beyond the legally required, compulsory, and uniform insurance contribution and makes a *further*, voluntary, freely determined contribution to the employee's health insurance. That extra can be interpreted as an employer's contribution.

[17] A reserve fund will have to be built up, to bridge any short-term gap between receipts and expenditure. The budget can be allowed to cover such deficits only temporarily, until the reserve fund has accumulated.

should be the macroeconomic limit on expenditure for basic provision. That will end the intangible specter of "underfinancing." Basic health provision will be underfinanced only if the public, through its political representatives, has voted for a certain health tax and compulsory copayments, but these have not been collected, through negligence by the authorities charged with doing so. If the sum has been collected, that must be taken to be the macroeconomic volume of financing desired and endorsed by the community of citizens.[18]

If some members of the medical profession think this sum is too small, they can lobby to have it raised. They can try to persuade citizens to vote, through their representatives, for a higher rate of health tax and higher direct, compulsory copayments. If they succeed, they will have a larger macroeconomic volume available for basic provision. If they fail, the limit is *determined*, and further argument can only be about the allocation of it.

6. Institutional forms and procedures for microeconomic allocation of the macroeconomic budget have to be devised. I think some of this task could be performed by expert committees; there could be a territorial decentralization of this process. A health council would have to be formed, to give direction in principle to the allocation. The members should be doctors and other professionals whose expertise and personal integrity would guarantee that objective and humane decisions were taken. What is needed is a respected body free of political influence, analogous, for instance, to the Federal Reserve Board that runs monetary policy in the United States.

Allocative decisions of two kinds are required. On the one hand, guidelines, criteria, and perhaps itemized lists need to be compiled, to show what activities can and cannot be covered by basic care, at the prevailing level of macroeconomic funding. This highly difficult and intricate task has to be tackled, to prevent a mass of arbitrary, ad hoc decisions being taken.[19] The starting point can be present practice: basic

---

[18] Dr. Attila Kiss, head of a large Hungarian hospital, interviewed in the country's largest-circulation daily (Tanács 1998), expressed a view widespread among doctors when he spoke, and I quote, of the "chronic underfinancing" of the health-care system. Compared with what? Did he mean by comparison with the level of financing that doctors working in the hospital could spend to the marginal positive utility of the patients? That is certainly the case, but the same could be said of every hospital in the world.

[19] Although there is no one case that can be clearly taken as a pattern, there is experience available of setting guidelines of this kind. Much attention has been aroused in the United States by the list compiled in the state of Oregon, containing the health provisions available free to the elderly. Rather than the list itself, the political and professional procedure for compiling it and the principles that lie behind it are what merit careful study. (Among the works setting out the principles for establishing priorities among treatments and international experiences with these, including the Oregon project, see Ho 1998.)

care consists of the what patients in Hungary generally receive at present. Subsequently, initial state will have to undergo corrections. As time goes by and the macroeconomic budget increases, further activities can be included in the sphere of basic care.

On the other hand, the total must be divided among various groups of costs (e.g., wages or equipment), or among various medical treatments and branches (e.g., preventive spending versus treatment of the sick, or internal medicine versus surgery). The simple arithmetic of this kind of allocative decision making has to be acknowledged: more for one purpose means less for another. The institutions entrusted with the microeconomic allocation have to establish the desirable proportions and priorities. There will be no evading this by demanding a higher macroeconomic limit.

7. Patients must receive a detailed bill from the hospital or outpatients' clinic, showing as accurately and exhaustively as possible what tests and items of treatment were received and how much they cost. The bill should also show how much of the expenditure is financed out of public funds and how much out of copayments. If the auxiliary care is later financed by a private insurer, let the insurer's contribution appear on the bill as well.

Naturally this proposal cannot be applied from one day to the next. First of all, the accounting bases for it have to be established. Presenting a bill would encourage financial discipline and more efficient operation. Most important of all, it would help to dispel the fiscal illusions by increasing patients' tax and cost awareness.

Implementation of these seven practical institutional and procedural proposals could promote acceptance of the reform among those concerned, above all among the general public. It could have a cleansing effect on political debates surrounding health care. The more transparent the connection between public revenue and public expenditure in the health-care system becomes, the easier it will be to counter the cheap demagogic arguments in favor of less tax but more spending.

It is desirable to reduce the rate of health tax, which will be quite high at the initial state from which the recommended reform begins.[20] However, if the conditions just described are respected, this reduction can be achieved only in the following way:

---

[20] The first, rough calculation was based on the following assumptions: the tax will be levied only on income previously liable to social-insurance contributions; the direct, compulsory copayments will not increase; and the total expenditure on basic health care will not fall. Under these circumstances the rate of health tax would make up almost 20 percent of grossed-up wages.

- Most importantly, let GDP grow, and the country's national health expenditure can rise accordingly. However, it should happen in a way that changes the ratio between "basic provision" and "auxiliary provision" in the latter's favor. The macroeconomic limit to what can be spent on basic provision may rise, but only at a rate lower than the growth of GDP. This will allow the rate of health tax to fall.
- Widen the tax base. The health tax has to be levied also on income that has legally escaped from the social-insurance contribution so far.
- Within the macroeconomic limit on financing, raise the proportion of the direct, compulsory copayments – in other words, reduce the part to be financed by the health tax.[21]

By combining these methods, the rate of tax can be gradually reduced, and to a significant extent, while raising, not lowering the macroeconomic limit prescribed for basic health provision.

Now let us turn to auxiliary provision. The total macroeconomic-level volume depends solely on the combined effect of decentralized individual decisions: how much of their money individuals want to spend, directly or through voluntary insurance, on health care for themselves and their families. I am sure this sum would be sizable right from the start and steadily increase thereafter. It is not only the rich who are prepared to reach into their pockets for the health of themselves and their families, but many people in the middle- and lower-income brackets as well.

One grave shortcoming of the present system is that it leaves very little scope for citizens to finance their own health costs if they insist on doing so under legal, transparent institutional conditions. The law allows people to spend their money for all kinds of extravagant purposes. Yet it leaves no way, under openly recognized institutional forms, for people to pay themselves for more tests than would be paid for out of public funds, or openly to pay more for the doctor of their choice, who charges a higher fee on the basis of his or her authority, expertise, and reputation. This is a serious breach of principle 1, the autonomy of the individual. One of the main tasks of the reform is to overcome these shortcomings and ensure that consumer sovereignty applies to this field, at least in part.

When this change has occurred, along with the reform of public finance described earlier, it will emerge what total health-care demand

---

[21] It should be noted that although the principle of supporting the needy can apply to direct copayments, they are far less redistributive in character. Although patients pay only some of the cost, their expenditure is a function of the service received.

is generated by the two main kinds of financing: public and private. With some distortion and friction, this will express how much the country is willing and able to spend on the sector.[22] This is the level of health-care financing that the community of citizens accepts, through the mediation of the political process and the health-care market. In my view, financing the demand in this way constitutes the complex procedure whereby a democratically arranged market economy, under present Hungarian conditions, can address the fundamental problem of scarcity of health-care funding.

To conclude the sections on the financing of demand, it becomes possible to sum up the answer to the first question presented in the introduction. Who is authorized to decide on inclusion–exclusion matters? The procedures and institutions recommended in this study break this overall decision down into several partial decisions and divide the spheres of authority as follows:

1. All citizens have a right of access to basic provision, guaranteed by the state.
2. The community of citizens, by way of the democratically elected parliament that represents it, alone has the right to establish the macroeconomic budget for the basic, publicly financed provision accessible equally to all. This is where the main dividing line runs between the competence of the state and the competence of the individual.
3. The bodies of doctors and other professionals have primary responsibility for deciding the specific microeconomic allocation of the macroeconomic budget voted for basic provision.
4. In addition to that, all citizens may decide in a sovereign fashion what auxiliary provision to buy with the intermediation of the market.

Reform on the Supply Side

The two previous sections examined the financing of the demand for health care. Let us now turn to the supply side, the provision of health care. I had a curious feeling of déjà vu as I studied the present state of Hungarian health care. What I found was reminiscent in many respects of the reforms conceived in the final stages of Hungary's Kádár period,

---

[22] Mention has not been made so far of the curious "gray economy" in the health sector – financing in the form of gratuities to staff. This is considered later, in the next section. So long as gratuities continue, they augment the financial resources of total demand, of course.

in a spirit of "market socialism." The situation then was described as "neither plan nor market" (Bauer 1983) but a mixture of the two that tended to combine the drawbacks rather than the advantages of each. Whereas the "business segment" of the present-day economy operates according to the rules of a real market economy, most of the health sector is a whole chapter behind, still immersed in market socialism.[23]

State ownership continues to dominate the secondary and tertiary levels of health provision: specialist outpatients' clinics and hospitals. The assignment of real property rights, however, is muddled and opaque. According to the letter of the law, the owner of such facilities is the local government. The local government appoints the responsible head of a hospital or a clinic, but in practice it has no say in its financial matters, not least because it has no resources for the purpose. Again according to the letter of the law, the head of a hospital or clinic has wide powers and responsibilities. In actual fact his or her hands are tied in sundry ways, and there is frequent intervention from above, just as there was under the ambiguous system of market socialism. On the other hand, the head of a hospital or clinic can take advantage of the fact that the budget constraint is a soft one. Although there is a budget that has been passed, exceeding it does not have dangerous consequences; eventually the unpaid bills will be met and the debts written off. If the financial authorities should try to impose some financial discipline, a protest movement immediately springs up, outraged that patients may be left without treatment on inhumane, fiscal grounds. In cases like these, no attempt is made to tackle the fundamental problem of scarcity in health provision in a constructive, cooperative way. It is approached in a destructive fashion, with "every man for himself," which creates anarchic conditions. The money goes to those who shout longest and loudest. The outcome is that budgets are regularly exceeded and costs soar unrestrained.

In some ways the situation is worse than it was under market socialism. The allocation of investment, meager in any case, is almost totally centralized, and depreciation procedures are unsettled. The system of wage control is more centralized and rigid than it ever was during the market-socialist reforms, and even under the extreme, classic command economy that preceded them. Doctors and other health workers count as public employees, which constrains their pay within a rigid, narrow scale.

---

[23] What I term the business sphere is the sum of the sectors of the economy that operate outside the welfare sector (or social sector in American parlance). This is commonly called the "competitive sphere" in Hungarian economic jargon, which characterizes well the public belief that competition is admissible in the business world but not in the welfare sector.

Table 6.1. *Share of Private and Public Health Providers in Public Financing in Hungary in 1998[a]*

| Type of Care | Owner of Health-Care Providers | | | |
	State	Local Authority	Private	Other
Primary	0.03	18.63	81.21	0.13
Dental	7.03	55.35	37.18	0.43
Outpatient	17.81	79.62	1.46	1.11
Hospital	26.60	72.05	0.33	1.03

[a] As a percentage of total financing by the National Health Insurance Office (OEP) of the different service sectors.

Source: The table was compiled by Cecilia Hornok from data supplied by the OEP.

Conditions incompatible with a market economy are also conserved by the fact that the social-insurance system is the sole buyer from a hospital or a clinic. Although the social-insurance system has no administrative authority over the providers, its dominant, monopsonistic position allows it to dictate its own terms.

As with the business sphere under market socialism, one of the main achievements of the post-socialist health system is that a legal private sector has appeared, operating in a narrow sphere in various forms:

- The most important reform so far has been privatization of the primary level of provision. As Table 6.1 shows, more than 80 percent of primary-care physicians have ceased to be public employees since the reform and have contract relations with the social-insurance system. Although the privatization has not been consistent, so that there are still many strands tying primary-care doctors to local government, it has been a great step forward toward creating a health-care market.

- Many doctors and some other health-service employees (physiotherapists, masseurs, and so on) whose main job is in a state hospital or outpatients' clinic run a private practice as a sideline. However, individual private practice accounts for only a tiny fraction of all medical provision.

- There already exists a very small number of privately run hospitals, clinics, laboratories, and other health-care institutions employing a larger number of staff (see Table 6.2), but as it turns out from Table 6.1 the share of private hospital care in public health-care financing accounts for a mere 0.3 percent of the total.

198

Table 6.2. *Share of Private Specialist Providers in Budapest*

Specialties	Number of Licenses Issued in 1999[a]		Share of Private Providers[b] (%)
	Total	Private	
Internal medicine	1,892	1,217	64
Surgery	726	166	23
Obstetrics/gynecology	485	289	60
Pediatrics	478	324	68
Lung	155	38	25
Ear, nose, and throat	188	107	57
Ophthalmology	228	131	57
Dermatology and venereology	176	132	75
Psychiatry[c]	278	69	15
Urology	131	59	45
Primary-care dentistry and stomatology	1,974	1,877	95
Remedial gymnastics and massage	129	82	64

[a] Licenses were issued under several categories: physician in private practice; health-care entrepreneur; private clinic; unit of a public or private, nonprofit or for-profit hospital.

[b] Calculated as the percentage of column 2 to column 1. Following from the licensing mechanism, this ratio does not reflect the number of patients treated in the private sector, or the number of doctors working there.

[c] Neurology excluded.

Source: Personal communication by István Felmérai of the National Public Health and Medical Officers' Service of Hungary, 2000.

Alongside this legal, restricted private sector there is a flourishing and widespread "gray economy." It is a widespread practice for patients to give gratuities to the doctor or other medical staff who treat them.[24] The main recipient is the doctor in direct contact with the patient, although with hospital treatment, a gratuity is often given to that doctor's superior, the chief physician of the department. It is customary to give gratuities to nurses, masseurs, physiotherapists, and others who administer diagnostic tests. Patients feel they are not only expressing thanks but paying for the special attention or even privileges they have received – for instance, not having to queue for a test or an operation, or simply for admission to hospital. Patients give gratuities so that they will be placed

---

[24] The Hungarian euphemism is "gratitude money."

in a smaller ward or even a private room. There is no transparent scale of tariffs, of course. Patients are unsure of themselves and ask each other how much to give, often trying to outbid each other to make sure they receive the extra attention they are buying.

The doctors and other health staff have ambivalent feelings about this practice. A relatively small number of them profit greatly by it. Some hospital heads of department are almost feudally possessive about the beds in their wards, waiting for a rake-off from all who occupy them. Undoubtedly, the range of some kinds of provision available is not unconnected with whether the patient pays a gratuity, and if so, how much. Nonetheless, most doctors and other health staff feel that gratuities are an unreliable, unpleasant, and often demeaning way of being compensated for their work. They do not let their relations with patients depend on how much gratuity they pay. However, that does not mean that for many of them this is not an accustomed and indispensable component of their family income.

What direction should the reform take?

I think it is desirable for the private sector to expand. Foreign experience, not just in Europe but also in the United States, shows that even in a developed market economy, there remains a high proportion of hospitals and clinics that are publicly owned, or run by nonstate, nonprofit organizations. Nonetheless, looking at the proportions in Hungary today, there is still room for the private sector to grow very substantially.

There is no need for any uniformly conducted privatization campaign that follows centrally devised patterns and has a completion date by which the publicly owned organizations have to be transferred to private hands.[25] Institutions based on private ownership, or various combinations of private and public ownership, should be allowed to develop in many different forms, through initiatives from below.[26] Equipment, premises, or provisions in public hospitals and clinics could be leased to private health-care businesses. So long as the buyers are professionally and commercially reliable, state-owned organizations could be sold outright to private firms or nonprofit institutions. Much wider scope needs to be given for professional groups of doctors or other health staff to establish private firms that provide specific services. It must also become

---

[25] My recommendation for the business sphere was always to avoid privatization campaigns and the imposition of uniform, schematic solutions. Instead I advised a more varied, evolutionary approach to the transformation of ownership relations.

[26] Combination of private and public ownership did appear already in Hungary. See Orosz 1995.

possible for decentralized, independent, for-profit or nonprofit insurance institutions to arise, integrating the functions of insurance and primary-care medicine.[27]

It would be desirable for the unfortunate gratuity system to end eventually, which would benefit both patients and staff. There is no need for strong administrative bans on gratuities or for efforts to enforce bans by imposing penalties. Interventions of that kind have been tried in the past, but they have never succeeded. Gratuities need to die out naturally. They will become superfluous once there is organized, institutional auxiliary provision, a fair system of financial rewards for doctors and other health staff, and legal differentiation of earnings.

The Interaction of Supply and Demand

It is essential for the expansion of the legal private sector and for the atrophy of gratuities to have essential changes in the system of financing, beyond the ones discussed earlier. One of the keys to success for the reform is to apply the principle of *sector neutrality*, which, in Hungarian economic parlance, can be described as follows.

Buyers, even if they are buying with state funds, should not make their purchases dependent on whether the seller belongs to the state sector or the private sector. The period of market socialism was remarkable for a failure to apply this principle. When a state-owned enterprise or a state authority bought inputs, it had to obtain them from state-owned enterprises wherever possible. This policy was either laid down as a rule or, if not, it was imposed on senior state-sector officers by the official climate of opinion. A private firm or a self-employed supplier could be considered only if there was no state supply available. This pampered and gave privileges to the state sector and held back the development of the private sector. Remember that the input requirements of state-owned firms formed the overwhelming majority of aggregate demand at that time. This situation has remained to this day, not in the economy as a whole but in the health sector. The publicly funded social-insurance system is not impartial about whether to buy from the state or the private sector. It discriminates against the latter. To some extent it is forced to do so by the current regulations, and to some extent it shows bias voluntarily, so to speak, because its managers know this is what is expected of them. So the public spirit of the socialist period (priority for state ownership) lives on in the health sector.

---

[27] These could resemble in their operational sphere and regulations the HMO or other "managed health care" organizations found in the United States. See Feldstein 1994.

Let us take dentistry as an example. The social-insurance system pays fees to the dentists in state clinics for their work according to a set price schedule. Patients entitled to it according to the regulations receive the treatment free or against a copayment. Let us suppose that a private dentist charges a higher fee for some treatment than the social-insurance system is paying for the compensation of a doctor employed by the state. At present, if patients covered by social insurance go to a more expensive, private dentist instead, the social-insurance system does not even pay the part of the bill it would have paid if treatment had taken place in a state clinic. This is a typical infringement of the principle of sector neutrality. It gives patients a strong financial incentive not to go to a private dentist, which restricts the latter's potential earnings.

Nonetheless, many patients go to private dentists, because they hope for better treatment and they can still afford the cost. On the other hand, most patients would not have a stomach operation in a private hospital and pay the full price of it if the social-insurance system would pay for the operation in a state hospital.[28] So without demand generated by the social-insurance system, the supply offered by private hospitals does not extend to treatment that the social-insurance system finances in the state sector (and only in the state sector). This prevents the development of the private sector, which would be incapable of surviving if all its income came *only* from the patients' pocket (directly or through private medical insurance).

Applying the principle of sector neutrality will mean that treatment is financed out of public funds, according to a clear price schedule, regardless of the ownership form of the provider. That will be the minimum compensation, a fair price for giving the treatment in a reliable, professionally correct way, to an *average* standard. The reform will allow provider and patient to agree, within legal bounds, that the latter pays an *extra fee* for treatment, if the provider calls for it and the patient feels it is worthwhile. That will not deprive either side of the sum financed from public funds.

It will give an enormous boost to expansion of the private sector if sector neutrality becomes general. Healthy competition will develop between organizations offering the same types of provision, irrespective of their ownership form. Such competition will leave patients less defenseless and encourage higher quality and greater efficiency.

At the same time, the changes proposed will drive out gratuities. On the one hand, patients will feel they now have a real chance to buy above-average treatment for extra money. On the other, the pay of doctors and

---

[28] It is another matter that the patient receiving the "free" operation in the state hospital gives a gratuity to the surgeon as a precaution.

nursing staff will become legally differentiated. Pay differences will emerge, not only between public and private health care, but within publicly owned organizations as well, which will contribute to the simultaneous assertion of principle 2 (public funding of basic care to an average standard) and principle 1 (the sovereign right for individuals to buy treatment they judge to be better than average).

One of the foundations of economics is that supply creates demand and demand supply. The present situation – one in which both private supply and private demand are very limited – reciprocally restricts their expansion. Sector neutrality will allow this vicious circle to be broken. If demand expands rapidly, it will become worthwhile creating private supply for treatment that has hitherto been a monopoly of state organizations. This wider supply will provide an attractive field for private medical insurers as well. So far there has been nothing to finance with private insurance. In this way there can develop a "virtuous circle," in which extra demand promotes extra supply, which further enhances private demand, and so on.

Based on what has been said, it is possible to refine the four-point statement at the end of the section on the demand side. Sector-neutral financing makes it all the more possible for the country's total health expenditure to reflect the sovereign choices of the community of citizens, not the preferences of politicians in charge of central planning. Not only will the community of citizens decide, through the political process, how much health care to finance out of their taxes, apart from the sums covered by private sources; citizens can also choose how much of this tax-derived public money earmarked for health care to spend in the state sector and how much in the private sector. This enhanced opportunity to choose may induce the community of citizens, through the political process, to express changes in their preferences and devote more (or less) to financing health care through the tax system.

To conclude the discussion of demand and supply, let me return to the first question in the introduction, about who is authorized to take the decisions relating to health care. Transforming the ownership relations on the supply side, placing financial incentives on a sound basis, and stimulating market forces will all help to give both to patients and to doctors and other health staff a more active, effective role in making specific health-care decisions.

Other essential aspects of the reform, which restrictions of space prevent me from discussing in this chapter, include the following:

- What changes should be made in the province and responsibilities of central and local government in financing health care, in exercising financial and professional supervision over it, and in the distribution of property rights?

- How should the settlement between the health-care provider and the financing institution take place? To what extent should there be a "fee-for-service" proportionate to the treatment given or a "capitation" calculation proportionate to the number of patients treated? To what extent should it be possible to tie down a certain provider's capacity in advance by contract, and so on?[29] The various methods of calculation produce quite different sets of favorable and unfavorable incentive effects.

These questions need clarifying, whatever the outcome with the financing institutions (tax, private insurance) and the property relations discussed in detail in this chapter.

Concluding Remarks: What Support and What Resistance to Expect

The reform, which my book explores in more detail and of which this chapter presents a few of the main ideas, does not entail radical financial restriction or spending cuts at the expense of patients. It does not promise rapid results, but it can bring a lasting improvement in the medium and long term. It can distribute the tax burden more equitably. It may also reduce the tax rates, improve incentives, and develop competition within the health sector that encourages more efficient provision. There is no obvious reason why the reform should attract appreciable resistance. It could count on broad, mass support.

In reality, however, the reception for the future reform is unlikely to be so enthusiastic. For one thing, some will become temporary or permanent losers because of the transformation. For another, many who will not lose, or may actually gain, will be afraid of the change because they judge their interests mistakenly, or because they fear change as such.

The medical profession will presumably be divided in its reactions. There will be a direct loss to only two, partly overlapping groups. One consists of those whose position gains them more in gratuities than they would obtain by legal means through professional competition among doctors. The other consists of those who owe their present position of authority mainly to the bureaucracy and would find themselves relegated in a more market-oriented health sector. In fact the majority of doctors

[29] A comprehensive review of this sphere of problems can be found in Newhouse 1996.

Table 6.3. *Physicians' Income in Germany*

	Average Income of Physicians Compared with Average Income of Other Groups of Earners (%)	
Basis for Comparison	1989 (Federal Germany)	1992 (United Germany)
All earners	313	404
Civil servants	296	382
Architects	214	163
Lawyers	140	144

Source: The table was compiled by Roland Habich (German Institute of Economic Research, Berlin) on the basis of official German income-tax statistics.

would gain by the changes. The greater the extent to which market forces apply in a country, the higher the medical profession rises on the earnings list. (See Tables 6.3 and 6.4.) The reform will mean that doctors who have hitherto received humiliatingly low wages can receive higher earnings by open, honest means. Their independence and opportunities for initiative and enterprise will increase.

The general public will be affected by the changes in two capacities. As *patients*, the one real change for the worse will be that they have to make a greater copayment for many treatments and medicines that come within the sphere of basic provision. Political wisdom would suggest that this extra load be placed on the shoulders of the public gradually, in line with the general rise in real earnings and the improvement of health-care services. On the other hand, patients will experience several favorable changes: greater freedom of choice, a more open and transparent payment system, a lessening of their defenselessness, and, eventually, an improvement in quality.

The changes will also affect citizens as *taxpayers*. If the situation becomes more transparent, this will give citizens a clearer sense of how much they pay personally for health-care purposes and how much they receive in provision.[30] There will be some people who achieve a positive

---

[30] From this point of view alone it is worth ensuring that patients know, over as wide a field as possible, how much their treatment costs. For instance, on leaving hospital, a patient could receive a detailed invoice showing how much had been spent directly on the various treatments and how much of the hospital's general costs can be attributed to the patient. It should also emerge how much of this is paid out of public sources and, if applicable, how much the patient has to pay directly. Apart from that, the invoice system would allow patients to check whether they had actually received the treatment for which the hospital was charging.

Table 6.4. *Physicians' Income by Selected Specialties in the United States in Comparison with Average Incomes, 1993*

Average income	100
Average income of physicians	496
Primary care	350
General surgery	716
Anesthesiology	701
Radiology	763
Average income of those with university degree	100
Average income of physicians	286

Note: Those included in the table hold university degrees not higher than Bachelor's degrees.

Sources: The data on average incomes used as the basis for comparison come from the U.S. Bureau of the Census (1996: 462), and on medical specialties from the Physician Payment Review Commission (1996: 307–20), and were collected by Karen Eggleston.

balance, because they have paid relatively little but much has been spent on them and their dependents. There will be some who feel they are on the losing side, as insured persons (because luckily they are healthy) and/or as taxpayers (because they pay tax on a high income).

Up to now, the main cost of financing basic health provision has been borne by wage and salary earners (see Table 6.5). The greater the success in altering the proportions of the tax load and widening the tax base – one of the reform's tasks – the more today's free riders' can be drawn in as taxpayers. This brings up one of the well-known problems of political economy: the relation between the distribution of the tax burden and the political voting preferences of citizens. Today, the load of health-care expenditure is unfairly distributed. Altering that distribution and imposing tax on hitherto untaxed income will gain the reform friends and enemies in Parliament. The resistance is likely to be lessened because many of those who oppose redistributive taxation in general are more prepared to accept a specific egalitarianism in health care. They will endorse this more easily if it can be guaranteed that the extra tax they pay will be used exclusively for ensuring that everyone has equal access to minimum, basic health-care provision.

But how are these proposals likely to be received in the political sphere? Transparency will be attractive to those advancing a clear, open health-care and taxation program, and repellent to those wanting to

Table 6.5. *Distribution of Health-Care Provision in Kind Financed by Social Insurance and Social-Insurance Contributions, 1995*

Categories of Insured	Average per Capita Expenditure (HUF)	Proportion of (%)		
		Population	Provisioning	Financing
Old-age pensioners[a]	51,350	23.2	44.8	21.3
Employed	20,708	31.1	24.3	68.0
Self-employed	20,708	7.5	5.9	3.3
Unemployed	18,474	2.2	1.6	1.7
Other[b]	17,300	36.0	23.4	5.7

Notes: HUF = Hungarian forint.
[a] Contributions of pensioners were not deducted from pensions, but paid by the pension insurance system out of its budget, in proportion to the pensions. As the study relates, this arrangement ended in 1997.
[b] All those insured as dependents of the insured, whose contributions are paid by the budget.
Source: World Bank 1997.

avoid taking a clear position and continue to sidestep the sensitive questions of taxation and spending. The constitutional solutions proposed will be attractive to those who want to set the main figures for public spending by parliamentary means. They will be repugnant to trade unions and employers' federations whose representatives have so far had special powers over decisions on health-care finances, which they would lose under the reform. Finally, the position taken by politicians will depend on the social groups on which they build their support and on the set of values they put before their voters. The more they identify with the postulates put plainly at the beginning of the study, the more prepared they will be to support the reform. If they profess principles strongly opposed to those postulates (for instance, an extreme individualist or, on the other hand, an extreme collectivist position), they will also reject strongly the practical proposals as well.

The reform outlined here should certainly be introduced gradually. As I mentioned earlier, there has to be time for the new institutions required to develop. There has to be time for people to adapt. A further argument for a gradual approach could be added here. There has to be time for the people concerned to comprehend the changes and how they affect their interests. Having said that, I would risk the following statement. Once the misgivings and anxieties have been dissolved and the effects of the changes have been presented objectively, the majority of the public will come out in support of the reforms.

References

Arrow, Kenneth J. 1963. Uncertainty and the Welfare Economics of Medical Care. *American Economic Review* 63: 941–73.

Bauer, Tamás. 1983. The Hungarian Alternative to Soviet-Type Planning. *Journal of Comparative Economics* 7: 304–16.

Besley, Timothy, and Miguel Gouveia. 1994. Alternative Systems of Health-Care Provision. In G. de Menil and R. Portes, eds., *Economic Policy: A European Forum*, pp. 200–57. Cambridge: Cambridge University Press.

Buchanan, James M. 1954a. Social Choice, Democracy, and Free Market. *Journal of Political Economy* 62: 114–23.

————. 1954b. Individual Choice in Voting and the Market. *Journal of Political Economy*, 62: 334–43.

Feldstein, Martin S. 1973. The Welfare Loss of Excess Health Insurance. *Journal of Political Economy* 81: 251–80.

Feldstein, Paul J. 1994. *Health Policy Issues: An Economic Perspective on Health Reform.* Ann Arbor, Mich.: Health Administration Press.

Ho, Teresa J. 1998. Priority setting in practice – A tour d' horizon. Unpublished manuscript.

Kornai, János. 1998. *Az egészségügy reformjáról* (On the reform of the health-care system). Budapest: Közgazdasági és Jogi Könyvkiadó.

Lindbeck, Assar, and Jörgen W. Weibull. 1987. *Strategic Interaction with Altruism: The Economics of Fait Accompli.* Seminar Paper, No. 376. Stockholm: Institute for International Economic Studies, University of Stockholm.

Newhouse, Joseph P. 1996. Reimbursing Health and Health Providers: Selection versus Efficiency in Production. *Journal of Economic Literature* 34: 1236–63.

Orosz, Éva. 1995. Átalakulás az egészségügyben (Transformation of the health-care system). Budapest: Aktív Társadalom Alapítvány.

Pauly, Mark V. 1986. Taxation, Health Insurance, and Market Failure in the Medical Economy. *Journal of Economic Literature* 25: 629–75.

————. 1992. The Normative and Positive Economics of Minimum Health Benefits. In P. Zweifel and H. E. Frech III, eds., *Health Economics Worldwide*, pp. 63–78. Norwell, Mass., and Dordrecht: Kluwer Academic Publishers.

Physician Payment Review Commission. 1996. *1996 Annual Report to Congress.* Washington, D.C.

Precker, Alexander S., and Richard G. A. Feachem. 1995. *Market Mechanisms and the Health Sector in Central and Eastern Europe.* World Bank Technical Paper, No. 293. Washington, D.C.: World Bank.

Saltman, Richard S., and Joseph Figueras. 1997. *European Health Care Reform: Analysis of Current Strategies.* Copenhagen: World Health Organization, Regional Office for Europe.

Sen, Amartya. 1995. Rationality and Social Choice. *American Economic Review* 85: 1–24.

Tanács, István. 1998. Látlelet az egészségügyről. Interjú dr. Kiss Attilával (A Constat of the Hungarian health-care system: An interview with Dr. Attila Kiss). *Népszabadság*, January 24, p. 19.

Tobin, James. 1970. On Limiting the Domain of Inequality. *Journal of Law and Economics* 13: 263–77.

U.S. Bureau of the Census. 1996. *Statistical Abstract of the United States: 1996.* Washington, D.C.

World Bank. 1993. *World Development Report 1993: Investing in Health.* New York: Oxford University Press.

1997. *Public Finance Reform in an Economy in Transition: The Hungarian Experience. The Hungarian Health Care System in Transition: An Unfinished Agenda.* Budapest: Office of the World Bank. Internal publication.

CHAPTER 7

Security through Diversity: Conditions for Successful Reform of the Pension System in Poland

JERZY HAUSNER

The program for pension system reform launched at the beginning of 1997 in Poland was called by its authors "Security through Diversity" (*Security* 1997). This title emphasizes that pension reform – which is designed to ensure security for the insured – must combine a pay-as-you-go (PAYG) pillar, a second, fully funded pillar, and a third, voluntary component. The program was prepared in the second half of 1996 by a team of experts appointed by Andrzej Bączkowski, who at that time was minister of labor and social policy and also the government plenipotentiary for social security reform. In the course of ten months or so, the government prepared and passed through the Parliament a legislative package consisting of three Acts, which laid the foundations of the new pension system:

1. The Law of August 28, 1997, on the Organization and Operation of Pension Funds.
2. The Law of August 22, 1997, on Employee Pension Programs.
3. The Law of June 25, 1997, on Applying the Revenues from Privatization of a Portion of State Treasury Assets for Purposes Connected with Reforming the Social Insurance System.

I worked on this material during my fellowship at Collegium Budapest in the spring of 1998. I would like to convey my gratitude to Collegium Budapest for providing an excellent working environment, and I am deeply grateful to János Kornai for his critical comments and valuable advice.

I feel obliged to state that from June 1994 until the end of December 1996, when holding the post of director-general at the Council of Ministers' Office, I headed the team of advisors to Deputy Prime Minister and Minister of Finance Grzegorz Kołodko. Subsequently, from the beginning of February until the end of October 1997, when holding the post of under-secretary of state at the Prime Minister's Office, I was government plenipotentiary for social security reform. While I do my best to be objective and impartial as far as possible, my views might be influenced by my former actions and responsibilities.

This package specified how revenue from privatization would be used to bridge the financial gap that had appeared, and will continue to widen, in the present PAYG pension system. In addition, it initiated reform of this system and launched a second (mandatory) and developed a third (voluntary) funded pillar of pension insurance. It also fully regulated the organization and operation of second-pillar pension funds. Moreover, it laid down the rules determining how employee pension schemes – an entirely new and, in the future, dominant form of voluntary, fully funded insurance – were to be set up and run.

The adoption of this package by Parliament represented the first initiating phase of reform and gave an impetus and direction to future phases. Moreover, it represented the crowning achievement of efforts made by numerous experts and some politicians since the beginning of the 1990s to reform radically Poland's ineffective social insurance system.

This chapter does not provide a detailed presentation of this reform program but describes the circumstances in which it came to see the light of day. In particular, it presents the main lines of political and doctrinal division that stood in the way of the reform and shows how these differences were mitigated and overcome. I believe that this reform was largely made possible by the formulation of a clear and socially plausible conception of the reform ("Security through Diversity") and by the existence of an appropriate consultation mechanism for issues related to the program and the ensuing legislation.

Generally speaking, my analysis is restricted to the initial phase of the pension system reform, completed before the parliamentary election of September 1997. The second phase of the reform is entering a decisive phase as this text is being written (May 1998); it is thus too early for its evaluation at the moment. However, I supplement the present chapter with a brief epilogue on the work done since September 1997.

The Functioning of the Prereform Pension System

The beginnings of the pension system in Poland go back to the interwar period. It became a fully fledged universal PAYG system in the 1950s. Since that time, the way it operates has not fundamentally changed. Each new measure, especially those adopted between the 1960s and the 1980s, involved granting additional privileges to different occupational groups. In the 1980s, the system came to cover the rural population as well. Nonetheless, until the end of the 1980s the system operated in relative financial equilibrium, due in part to the gradual rise in the contribution rate. In the 1950s it amounted to 15 percent of gross earnings, but by the end of the 1980s it had reached a level of 38 percent.

Strain within the system only began to be fully felt in the 1990s, but, in retrospect, it is quite evident that the earlier modifications made to the PAYG system gradually led to its deterioration. Recalling Lindbeck's observations on the Swedish economy (Lindbeck, Chapter 5, in this volume), this was not the inevitable result of any master plan but the unintended consequence of many, isolated ad hoc decisions. The term "silent erosion," used in a similar context by Ferge (1997: 1), although with clearly different intentions, describes this process very well.

The financial insolvency of the PAYG pension system in Poland is attributable to three sets of factors: those typical of modern societies in general; those specific to socialist and post-socialist societies; and those specific to Poland.

With respect to the first set, an aging population, caused among other things by a fall in the birthrate and a rise in average life expectancy, increased pressure on the system. Demographic waves, caused by population losses in the Second World War and the postwar demographic boom, also created growing difficulties over time.

The ratio of pensioners to the working population, or the demographic dependency ratio (DDR), stood at 20.6 percent in 1985. Since that time it has increased and will continue to grow until around the year 2000, when it will reach approximately 23.8 percent. In the years 2000 to 2005, the situation will improve slightly as increasing numbers of children of parents born during the postwar demographic boom reach working age. The coefficient will fall as a result to 23.1 percent. Then, however, those born during the postwar baby boom will themselves reach retirement age, after which the DDR will rise sharply, reaching 33.9 percent in 2020. In 1990, for every one person of retirement age there were 2.2 working persons. In 2005 this figure will still be 2.1, but in 2020 it will fall to 1.8.

The main problem arising out of the socialist system is the pressure of branch interest groups characteristic of such economies. It is often said that a PAYG system is susceptible to political pressures and bargaining. In socialist systems, where certain occupational branch groups, mainly in mining and heavy industry, gain excessive influence, this problem is particularly acute. I call this phenomenon "socialist branch corporatism" (Hausner 1994).

In Poland, this pressure can be most clearly seen in the privileges granted to miners. Average retirement age for miners is 59.4 years, compared to 65.7 for the general population. The average retirement pension for them is more than double.

The powerful political pressure exerted by miners did not wane even after the beginning of the economy's transformation. Despite the fact that successive governments in the 1990s were aware of the financial difficulties facing the pension system, as late as June 1994 – during the Social Democratic–Peasant coalition government (SLD, the Democratic Left Alliance, and PSL, the Polish Peasants Party) – legislation on pensions for miners and their families was amended in their favor. The mining industry is the main debtor of the Social Insurance Fund (FUS), and some mines regularly fail to pay their insurance contributions, even though they have collected them (Czepulis-Rutkowska 1996: 198–99).

Among the factors specific to Poland are the protection of the purchasing power of pensions during the transformation-related recession, the policy of fighting unemployment by facilitating early retirement, and liberal legislation and entitlement regulations regarding disability status. The effect of all the causal factors discussed here has been to increase the total number of people receiving pension benefits in the 1990s. In 1996, their number was nearly 30 percent higher than at the end of the 1980s.

As a result, the system dependency ratio (SDR), the ratio of persons receiving social insurance benefits to persons paying insurance contributions, has increased steadily. In 1995 the value of the SDR exceeded the value of the DDR by close to 40 percent. As a consequence, Poland's pension system is under severe strain and contributions have been increased. At the beginning of the 1990s, the rate was raised to 45 percent (31 percent according to net calculation), which means that Poland has one of the highest contribution rates in the world – a fact that is undermining the competitiveness of the economy.

The general financial effect of the causal factors discussed here was a dramatic increase in expenditure on pension benefits as a share of GDP (Table 7.1). In the years 1989–95, it more than doubled. This increase, of course, prevents any significant rise in spending on other social services and investment in human capital – all the more so because, despite the rise in the contribution rate, the social-insurance system began to record a considerable deficit in the 1990s, which had to be financed from budget subsidies.

The data in Table 7.1 also indicate that while subsidies to the agricultural pension system were still growing, the deficit of the social-security funds declined in 1995–96. Three factors play a key role here: first, the favorable demographic trend connected with numerous age-groups reaching working age; second, falling unemployment; and third, a slight improvement in the collection of contributions.

These factors, however, did not represent a permanent improvement in the situation, for the favorable demographic trends were due to go into reverse after 2005. We can thus estimate very precisely that, ceteris paribus, expenditure on maintaining pension benefits would have

Table 7.1. *Expenditure on Disability and Retirement Pensions, 1990–95, and State Subsidies to the Social Insurance Funds (FUS, KRUS), as a Percentage of GDP*

Item	1990	1992	1993	1994	1991	1995	1996
Retirement and disability pensions	8.6	14.6	14.2	15.8	12.6	15.6	—
Social Insurance Fund (FUS) subsidy	—	4.3	4.2	3.9	2.9	2.1	1.9
Farmers' Social Insurance Fund (KRUS) subsidy	—	2.0	2.0	2.2	1.7	2.1	2.2

Sources: Author's own calculation on the basis of data in *Security* 1997: 25 and *National Report* 1997: 132.

increased rapidly after that date, reaching the alarming level of 22 percent of GDP[1] by around the year 2020.

The rapid growth in expenditure on pension benefits, as well as the need to heavily subsidize them, did put pressure on decision makers. The mechanism of backward-looking wage indexation for these benefits meant that periodically financial tension sharply increased. This tension was reflected, above all, in the inability to prepare a budget that would avoid the dramatic choice between a huge rise in the budget deficit and major cuts in expenditure on important social and economic goals. The successful defense of macroeconomic discipline by successive ministers of finance meant that it became necessary to weaken periodically the benefit indexation mechanism. With the help of so-called supplementary budget legislation, it was possible to limit the expected rise in retirement and disability pensions.

Such a course of action was opposed by pensioners and their representatives and became a major political problem, which helps explain the sharp fall in support for the post-Solidarity governments and their eventual collapse in 1993.

The post-Communist opposition (SLD and PSL), which won the 1993 elections and promised, among other things, a return to "fair" benefits, faced not only the same difficulties as before but also new ones. Public protests were accompanied by formal appeals to the Constitutional

---

[1] It is worth comparing this indicator with analogous projections for highly developed countries. The data concern the year 2010: United States: 4.2 percent; Japan: 7.5 percent; Germany: 11.0 percent; France: 12.6 percent; Italy: 15.2 percent; United Kingdom: 4.6 percent; Canada: 4.9 percent; Sweden: 8.1 percent (Chand and Jaeger 1996: 14).

Tribunal. On numerous occasions the tribunal ruled in favor of those who had questioned the amended regulations. The new parliamentary majority could have formally overruled the verdicts of the tribunal, but in most cases it did not, feeling bound by its election promises. The verdicts of the tribunal led to a further increase in the financial burden. The state's unpaid debts to pensioners rapidly grew and came to form a significant portion of public debt.

In its rulings, the Constitutional Tribunal consistently recognized as unconstitutional the practice of periodically and temporarily suspending a portion of the state's commitments to pensioners for fiscal reasons. At the same time, it clearly stressed that this did not preclude the possibility of a permanent systemic change in the regulations, provided that such a change was preceded by appropriate legislation. Thus, it was only when legal and political factors prevented ad hoc manipulation of the pension system that the warnings of experts and the idea of major reform came to be taken seriously.

The Reform of the Pension System

Competing Reform Projects and Basic Principles

In June 1994 the medium-term "Strategy for Poland" program, presented by the new deputy prime minister and minister of finance (Grzegorz Kołodko), first advanced the idea of radically reforming the PAYG system. Although the government and Parliament accepted this program, no specific measures followed. The delay was due to a dispute between the minister of finance and the minister of labor (Leszek Miller) over a proposed change in the rules for indexing pension benefits from the existing wage-related system to a price-related one. This stalemate lasted until October 1996, when Miller was replaced. The new minister (Andrzej Bączkowski) supported the idea of fundamental reform and the establishment of a multipillar system. He put a great deal of effort into getting the proposal for indexation passed by Parliament, which cleared the way for fundamental reform.

The heated debate between the minister of finance and the minister of labor, which lasted from mid-1994 to the beginning of 1996, did not simply concern the mechanism for valorizing benefits. Their visions of reform were also entirely different. The Ministry of Labor worked out a plan for rationalizing the PAYG system. In this plan, the role played by the funded pillar was marginalized.

These proposals – initially adopted by the government in May 1995 and then submitted to public consultation – were regarded by the minister of finance to be insufficient. Therefore, an alternative plan was prepared at the Ministry of Finance modeled on the Chilean reform. It envisioned the replacement of the PAYG system with a fully funded one and the introduction of a minimum state pension. However, this program was never submitted to the government and was presented only as a background study.

The intention was to generate a debate that might produce alternatives to a modified PAYG system. Extensive public opinion research showed that the Ministry of Labor's plan was perceived as conservative and that society expected more decisive reform. In the autumn of 1995, the government, summing up the results of social consultations, recommended the preparation of a version of the program that would give a greater role to the funded segment. The change in cabinet posts paved the way for a new program of pension system reform. Of key significance here was the attitude of the new minister of labor, Andrzej Bączkowski, who declared himself in favor of radical reform and began to cooperate closely with the minister of finance. Bączkowski held a unique position in the government. He was closely associated with the opposition, because he had originally been a member of Solidarity and in 1992, when still an activist, had been deputy minister of labor. He demonstrated his excellent skills as a negotiator and during the SLD–PSL coalition government was appointed chairman of the Tripartite Commission on Socioeconomic Affairs, a body that had been established at the beginning of 1994. He gained wide recognition for his work as chairman and established a reputation as an excellent civil servant.

Quarrels in the governing coalition caused some members of the SLD leadership, including the prime minister, to try to establish dialogue with the opposition. Awarding Andrzej Bączkowski a ministerial post was one way of winning the trust of the opposition. With the support of the prime minister and the minister of finance, as well as the encouragement of the opposition, he was thus able to commence work on the new pension reform program, "Security through Diversity."

Hence, the comprehensive program of fundamental pension system reform in Poland matured over the course of many years and was born during the impassioned debate with the advocates of rationalizing the PAYG system.

At this point, however, the advocates of the new multipillar system were mainly economists, whereas supporters of rationalizing the PAYG system were for the most part lawyers. This split resulted mainly from the fact that the legal doctrine of social insurance does not recognize funded pension insurance as being social in character. This was a serious problem, because if the Constitutional Tribunal were to adopt such a position, it could block radical reform.

In March 1997 the Legislative Council, an advisory body to the cabinet, examined the draft of the first legislative package of reforms in the context of the program as a whole. Most of the council's experts and members were critical of the program, especially with regard to the draft proposals on pension funds. Despite this opinion, the government accepted the draft acts, arguing that the "social character" of the pension system related to the whole system and not to its individual pillars.

As advocates of the multipillar system were gaining the initiative and preparing legislation, liberal-minded experts began to raise their own objections to the reform program. Their arguments, reinforced by the rapidly increasing number of foreign trust funds on the market, centered on limiting the PAYG pillar to a minimum, dropping the mandatory pension funds, and creating a large area for developing voluntary forms of insurance. This would also be achieved through generous tax relief. In a milder version, this plan involved rapidly reducing the mandatory contribution rate and giving a powerful stimulus to voluntary insurance, and only later introducing mandatory pension funds.

In the effort to counter such proposals, it was important to have a comprehensive program and to present it in the form of universally understandable and straightforward principles. These principles were formulated as follows (see also Kornai 1997):

1. *Full security.* The program must provide all age groups – pensioners (the grandparents' generation), longtime employees (the parents' generation), and new or prospective employees (the children's generation) – with a guarantee of economic security on termination of their working life or in case of inability to work.

2. *Protection of acquired rights.* Benefits acquired prior to the moment the appropriate new legislation takes effect must retain their real value – under the conditions of economic growth – for the rest of the holders' lifetime, and will be paid in accordance with previous principles. Thus, the reform does not apply to today's pensioners.

3. *Individual prudence.* One of the foundations of the system's security will be individual prudence, manifested through deliberate investment, in the form of appropriate social-insurance contributions, which will translate into one's future pension or disability benefits.

217

4. *A multisegment structure of the pension system.* High security of the system of pensions and disability benefits will result from its being based on three main pillars: PAYG, funded, and voluntary insurance.

5. *Maximum freedom of choice.* Payment of the insurance contribution will be mandatory, as it is now, but one will be able to choose the pension fund to entrust one's savings to, and it will also be relatively easy to transfer savings from one fund to another. In addition, one will be able to decide (within certain margins) about the date of one's retirement.

6. *Transparency.* Transparency will be ensured by the introduction of a universal system of individual social-insurance records and accounts. Besides, pension funds must be obliged by law to publish information about their financial results.

7. *Active (regulatory) role of the state.* By regulating the functioning of the capital market and, in particular, supervising the operation of pension funds, the state should guarantee full security of the pension system.

8. *Sustainable and balanced economic growth.* The new system of pensions will utilize mechanisms of secure investment of funds.

Breaking the Bureaucratic Deadlock

As noted, the dispute between the minister of labor (Miller) and the minister of finance (Kołodko) hampered the chances of carrying out reforms. Efforts at political mediation from the prime minister (Waldemar Pawlak, then Józef Oleksy) and the SLD leadership proved ineffective. The minister of labor blocked the initiative of the minister of finance (indexation), while the latter, unable to submit his own proposals officially, discredited the reform program prepared by the minister of labor.

As the stalemate continued into mid-1995, circles close to the minister of finance and deputy prime minister for economic affairs came up with the idea of appointing a special government plenipotentiary responsible for social insurance reform. This proposal was fiercely attacked by the minister of labor and was not seriously considered until Andrzej Bączkowski became the new minister of labor.

Bączkowski's idea was to concentrate all the work relating to social-insurance reform in the hands of one person, including health-insurance reform, which was the responsibility of the Ministry of Health and Social Security. There was a serious danger that these two segments of social insurance, considered in isolation from one another, would be incompatible. The minister of labor particularly feared that the earlier introduction of health insurance might so complicate state budget finances that pension reform would have to be set aside.

The appointment of a government plenipotentiary would considerably simplify complex interdepartmental coordination. The plans of the minister of labor/government plenipotentiary would be considered by a special interdepartmental team and bypass the standing committees of the Council of Ministers (economic and social). This would speed up legislative work. By appointing a plenipotentiary for reform and assigning this task to the new minister of labor, the Council of Ministers openly committed itself to supporting his reform-minded proposals. This strengthened the political position of the minister of labor and increased his prestige.

By becoming the government plenipotentiary, the minister of labor was also able to maintain that reform was entering a new phase and did not have to be entirely linked to the earlier reform program, which he had personally presented to Parliament on behalf of the government. He also could set up a separate office at the ministry which would be subject to his personal control, and which would make him independent from his deputies, whom he did not trust but could not dismiss.

The first of these assumptions – that health care and pension reform could be coordinated – proved completely incorrect; the government plenipotentiary gained no influence over health-insurance reform. Both reform programs have since taken separate paths, which may have serious consequences in the future. On the other hand, the other assumptions turned out to be correct. Setting up an Office of the Government Plenipotentiary allowed prominent experts to carry out work on reform independently of the ministry and allowed the preparation of a complex and innovative reform program in a couple of months.

The reform of the economic and administrative center of the government, which came into effect on January 1, 1997, added a new, important dimension to the situation. The adjustments made to the old system made it impossible to merge the post of minister with that of government plenipotentiary. Thus, the problem of the position and appointment of government plenipotentiary was once more placed on the political agenda. With the serious reservations of the new minister of labor (Tadeusz Zieliński), the government plenipotentiary (Jerzy Hausner) was placed in the office of the chairman of the Council of Ministers and directly subordinated to the prime minister. This gave him great freedom of action. Even with the highly unfavorable attitude of the new minister of labor, it was possible to perform essential tasks quickly.

During this period the plenipotentiary received yet another boost. Responsibility for the day-to-day running of the system was now to be separated from the task of long-term reform. The plenipotentiary and his colleagues could concentrate exclusively on reforming the system.

The appointment of a government plenipotentiary was not an antidote for organizational clashes and disputes. Yet in spite of many conflicts, the procedure for preparing draft legislation in the government functioned remarkably smoothly. An interministerial working group, presided over by the plenipotentiary and including representatives of all the ministries and central agencies concerned (mainly of the rank of deputy minister or departmental head), proved to be a very useful instrument.

The plenipotentiary, in his capacity as head of the working group, could impose a very intense pace of work. At group sessions the purely legislative aspects of draft projects could be corrected very quickly. Moreover, all disputes over content came to the surface during such sessions as well. Some of them could be settled through debate. Others required additional bilateral or, in extreme cases, trilateral settlements. Such decisions were immediately carried into effect by the plenipotentiary with the participation of the ministers concerned. When it was not possible to come to an agreement, which was rare, the plenipotentiary could quickly appeal to the prime minister for mediation. Thus, there were no surprises when a proposal finally got to the Council of Ministers for approval. Only rarely were alternative solutions submitted to the council for deliberation at its meetings.

During work on draft legislation, most reservations were aired by representatives of the Ministry of Labor and Social Policy. During meetings of the interministerial working group, they were made by the deputy minister responsible for problems related to social security. As a rule the minister of labor then submitted the same reservations in writing before sessions of the Council of Ministers and then repeated them orally, despite receiving written explanations. The minister of labor also systematically questioned the methods employed in preparing draft legislation. He demanded that such projects should be examined by the Sociopolitical Committee of the Council of Ministers, submitted to various consultative bodies for review, and discussed by the Tripartite Commission for Socioeconomic Affairs, which he himself chaired on behalf of the government.

The attitude of the minister of labor and his representatives was essentially obstructionist. The minister publicly declared his support for reform but clearly distanced himself from the reform project worked out by the Office of the Government Plenipotentiary. This was mainly due to doctrinal differences, but matters of prestige certainly played a role as well.

On the other hand, the minister of finance (Marek Belka after February 1997) was very supportive of the measures and projects proposed by the plenipotentiary. The minister's representatives made a number of criticisms and submitted many proposals of their own, but as a rule they went along with the plenipotentiary's plans. Most discussions concerned the plan to use revenue from privatization to finance future FUS deficits. The fears of the budgetary department at the Ministry of Finance mainly centered on the role to be played by convertible bonds, which would enable the Ministry of the State Treasury to obtain revenue from the privatization of the largest enterprises to support pension reform. The Ministry of Finance believed that this would lead to competition in the market between different government treasury bonds. As a result of tripartite settlements involving the minister of the state treasury, a solution was worked out that was finally accepted by the government and Parliament.[2] From this moment, the question of revenue from privatization ceased to be important for the reform process.

Cooperation with the management of the Social Insurance Institution (ZUS) also played a key role in the work of the plenipotentiary, for both substantive and personnel reasons. Under the reform program, the ZUS was to serve as a vitally important link in the entire pension system. First, it was to administer the PAYG pillar; second, it was to introduce and manage individual insurance records; and, third, it was to be responsible for the distribution of mandatory insurance contributions, which it would transfer to pension funds and other specialized insurance funds.

The Supervisory Board of the ZUS includes a number of important public representatives (from the trade unions, employers' organizations, professional associations) and experts. The president of the ZUS at that time was an SLD parliamentary deputy (Anna Bańkowska) who had a very influential voice in the SLD parliamentary caucus. In the plenipotentiary's relations with the ZUS, it was thus not simply a matter of gaining the latter's support for the reform program, but of this institution being willing to accept a new role, which would entail fundamental statutory, organizational, personnel, and technical changes. If appropriate and rapid changes are not made to the ZUS organization, the reform program will be unable to get off the ground, which is still one of the main dangers it faces. Cooperation with ZUS, however, proved effective,

---

[2] This essentially involved a change in how privatization revenue was to be classified. It ceased to be categorized as state budget income and became instead state budget revenue, which made it impossible to assign it for the purposes of current budget expenditure.

which was also an important factor limiting the ability of the Ministry of Labor to block the reform.

On the other hand, the plenipotentiary failed to defeat an amendment, prepared by the minister of justice, to the laws governing courts of first instance and the public prosecutor's office. The amendment excluded employees of both institutions from the universal pension system and created instead a separate system, financed in full by the state budget. The legal lobby had created a dangerous precedent. After a radical reform had been undertaken, a new privilege that limited the possibility of cutting back on existing privileges was introduced.

Financing the Reform

The question of the financing of pension system reform involves a number of factors: a comprehensive and accurate financial calculation of the costs of reform; the availability of resources that could be used to finance any interim deficit of the pension system during the transition period; and a commitment of these resources to finance such an interim deficit.

The Office of the Government Plenipotentiary calculated the financial costs of reform and presented its results in the "Security through Diversity" program. This calculation showed that if the changes proposed in the program were made with the aim of rationalizing the PAYG system, financing the interim deficit would require revenue from privatization equal to 2 percent of GDP annually for a period of approximately ten years from the beginning of the reform.

Limiting reform exclusively to rationalizing the PAYG system could yield the desired results. But the system would remain on the borderline of financial sustainability, which according to general consensus would require pension expenditure at a level of 10 percent of GDP. It would then be necessary, however, to introduce a rationalization program at once, and at the same time make the system foolproof against the introduction of future measures that might impair its functioning. Unfortunately, neither the first nor the second seems possible, as the introduction of privileges for judges and public prosecutors showed. Thus in Poland, the rationalization of the PAYG system must be seen as a necessary but insufficient feature of reform.

Using privatization resources to finance pension system reform has become a universally accepted canon in Poland. The link established between privatization and reform has benefited both. The idea of privatizing large enterprises (often referred to as Poland's "family silver") and using the revenue obtained for pension reform became socially acceptable, creating a very favorable climate for large-scale privatization.

At the beginning of 1997, and partly in conjunction with the work on pension system reform, the Ministry of the State Treasury calculated available privatization resources. Their net value was estimated – according to the situation at the end of 1996 – at PLN 141.8 billion, of which PLN 103.2 billion was concentrated in a relatively small number of state enterprises (284) and State Treasury joint-stock companies (162), which could be privatized without the need for restructuring. The ministry also estimated that the market value of these particular resources considerably exceeded their book value.[3] The country's privatization resources were thus sufficient to help carry out the program of pension system reform. The development of a capital market, the efficiency of the privatization process, and the level of preparedness of enterprises for privatization also justified such an assessment.

The problem then was not so much whether privatization resources were sufficient, but whether they would be used for other purposes. This discussion led to an argument in favor of beginning reform as soon as possible, for it would be difficult to imagine putting a check on privatization.

The main bone of contention concerned the method of using privatization revenue for pension reform purposes. Solidarity became the principal opponent of the government's plan. The union was committed to its plan of universal empropriation (as opposed to expropriation); particularly after losing in the 1993 elections it wanted to regain the political initiative. At the beginning of 1996, Solidarity managed to secure a referendum on this issue. Although the referendum was nonbinding because of the low turnout, a clear majority of those who actually voted supported the union's demand for empropriation.

At this juncture it is worth making a precise distinction between *empropriation* and *genuine privatization* (for more on this see Hausner 1997). Empropriation consists of transferring ownership rights to eligible persons or groups. In effect it is a formal act of ownership transfer to those who are seen as having the right to such ownership. It is motivated by a sense of social justice and basically concerns all adult citizens – that is, those who created state wealth in the past. The empropriated

---

[3] A second group of privatization assets was concentrated in approximately 640 large enterprises, which were not suited for capital privatization. Their book value was estimated at around PLN 31 billion. The remainder of the country's privatization assets were contained in a large number of small and medium-sized enterprises (approximately 2,700), many of which were in very poor financial condition.

do not buy their ownership rights with capital: they receive them on the basis of recognized eligibility. Thus, empropriation does not require financial restructuring or even a precise estimation of state assets.

In the case of privatization state assets are sold to those who are able and willing to meet the conditions determined by the seller. The specific characteristics of the buyer are not crucially important; what matters is whether the buyer can meet the economic conditions set by the agency responsible for privatizing state assets. A transaction such as this cannot take the form of a mass sale because it concerns specific buyers and a specific portion of state assets that have to be valued.

The economic consequences of these two types of ownership transformations are different. In the first case we are dealing with highly fragmented ownership rights, which do not lead to rapid changes in management and the structure of economic incentives. In the second case, the privatization process itself is longer, but it immediately leads to changes in management and economic behavior.

Solidarity's proposals for empropriation concerned all state assets that would be used for various social purposes, including pension reform. Privatized assets would first be transferred to specially established national trust funds which would administer them and try to raise their value. Only after a certain period of time would these assets be sold and the resources obtained as a result be transferred to citizens' individual accounts in pension funds.

The government was resolutely opposed to this proposal, arguing that its realization would postpone in reality the commencement of reform till a time when trust funds would be able to liquefy their assets. It also pointed out that such a solution, even if it yielded the hoped for economic benefits, would be costly.

The attraction of the Solidarity plan for society lay in the fact that it promised that people would receive "seed money" in their pension accounts. In other words, they would gain something specific from privatization. The government variant of reform did not include such a promise. Revenue from privatization was not to be transferred to pension funds, but rather to the budget instead, and would bridge the financial gap that would emerge when some contributions from the PAYG pillar were shifted to the funded pillar. The impersonal nature of this solution was less appealing. Taxpayers appeared to have gained nothing from it and assumed that others – for example, current or future pensioners – would profit in some way. At best they believed that the budget rather than citizens would profit from privatization.

In response to the Solidarity proposal, the plenipotentiary supported a bill on industrial funds that employed Solidarity's idea on a smaller

scale. These funds were to be involved in the privatization of large enterprises from "difficult" branches of the economy (e.g., the steel industry)
that were hard to sell. Entitled citizens would then receive share certificates. They (in the case of people under fifty years old) could then
pay them into pension funds, thereby gaining an additional financial
premium. In this way the plenipotentiary signaled that the dispute with
Solidarity was not over doctrine but was purely technical in nature, and
that the union's proposals had been accepted by the government as a
supplementary measure.

To some degree, this occasion provided the opportunity to address
other social aspects of the problem. Many experts believed, as did public
opinion in general, that the government's idea of a new system that
would be mandatory for all persons up to thirty years old and voluntary
for persons between thirty and fifty would leave fifty-year-olds in a relatively worse situation. Thus, in order to reduce the resulting tensions,
the bill on industrial funds included a provision on what it termed "generation preference": entitled persons over fifty years old had the right
to purchase (for a small payment) three share certificates of industrial
funds, whereas those under fifty could purchase only one.

Eventually, the government's position on how privatization revenue
should be used to finance pension reform was accepted by Parliament
and the most serious threat to the reform project was overcome. If the
Solidarity proposal had been accepted it would at the very least have
delayed reform. Nevertheless, the greatest danger lay in the fact that non-
renewable privatization assets, which are perfectly suited to financing
any reform-related liabilities, could not be used to create pension capital.
Permanent and productive (durable) resources must be generated to
support the pension system if it is to be financially effective (see Kornai
1997: 288; Nuti 1998: 6).

Building Public and Political Support for Reform

Securing the understanding and support of society is vitally important
if pension system reform is to succeed. Between the autumn of 1995
and the spring of 1997, a noticeable change took place in public opinion.
The percentage of respondents agreeing on the need for "fundamental
change" rose from 28.5 to 44.5 percent. By 1997, large majorities (62–85
percent) agreed that the present system does not provide security, is
based on unclear principles, fails to ensure adequate living conditions,
and is subject to political manipulation. Conversely, 68 percent agreed
that pensions should be based on employee contributions, and 73 percent
felt they should be closely related to the amount of the contributions and

the length of time they were paid. This change showed that the government's consultations and extensive surveys assessing the public's attitude toward the Ministry of Labor's plan had been a useful and profitable enterprise. Many respondents, who had earlier evaluated the pension system as rather bad, later saw it as in need of radical reform. In addition, the reasons for such critical views and expectations on the nature of future reform clearly corresponded with the arguments and proposals of the government plenipotentiary, especially with regard to the issue of individualizing insurance.

To some extent public opinion reflected general changes in the attitudes of society toward systemic and market transformation. The public became aware of the problems resulting from an unreformed social service sphere in the context of a marketized economy. More specific factors, however, also played a role in changing opinion on pension reform. We should emphasize here the enormously positive role played by journalists. The main newspapers as well as radio and television stations devoted a great deal of coverage to the problems of social insurance and, for the most part, presented the course of work on reform in a competent and fair manner. The Office of the Government Plenipotentiary did not run an aggressive media campaign but cooperated with a representative group of journalists, who received all up-to-date documents and information. Journalists also participated in study trips organized by the office to countries that had radically reformed their pension systems (Chile, Argentina) or had developed a funded pillar (United States, Denmark).

In order to consolidate a consensus on the use of privatization funds to finance the reform, the government made three basic commitments: the reform would not lead to an increase in taxes, to a rise in mandatory insurance contributions, or to a fall in the real level of existing benefits. These commitments eliminated any threats to existing pensioners, employers, or taxpayers and made it possible to adopt the "generation layer" as the main axis of social discourse. The intention was to avoid or marginalize other cleavages (e.g., employee–employer or poor–rich), which would complicate the discourse on reform and make it difficult to achieve broad-based social consensus.

The generation cleavage is very convenient because it can attract the support of younger and middle-aged generations. The latter have a stake in the introduction of a fully funded pillar and have turned against proposals that are confined mainly to rationalizing the PAYG system. Without the support of the middle-aged population, which has the most to lose if reform does not take place, it is difficult to carry out any type of reform whatsoever.

The adoption of the generation axis for public discourse raised the problem of how to calculate pensions for different age groups. Solving this problem entailed having to offer those thirty to fifty years old a choice between the old and the new system, which had not initially been anticipated. It also required introducing some generation preferences for the fifty-year-olds, who will bear the effects of rationalizing pillar 1 and will not be able to take advantage of pillar 2. This last problem could not be solved in full. One of the options considered was that of introducing tax relief measures – exclusively for this generation – linked to voluntary savings in pillar 3.

Two facts seem to demonstrate quite convincingly that Poland has achieved broad consensus in pension reform. First, the Tripartite Commission in April 1997 supported the idea of a three-pillar pension system and the bills from the first legislative package (Stanowisko 1997). Second, 90 percent of parliamentary deputies voted in favor of these bills (only a small group closely linked to Solidarity voted against them).

That Poland's main political parties could manage to come to such an understanding on this issue had seemed impossible to many observers, mainly because practical reform measures were undertaken in the period preceding the parliamentary elections that took place in September 1997. Apart from the elections themselves, other unfavorable political circumstances began to make their appearance:

- Constant political in-fighting in the governing coalition (SLD–PSL) finally led to the motion of PSL parliamentary deputies for a vote of no confidence in their own government (July 1997).
- Personal differences within SLD arose from attempts – even before the elections – to impose changes on the functions performed by its leader (Józef Oleksy), which made it difficult to establish a united position vis-à-vis its coalition partner.
- The election tactics were adopted by the leadership of the left-wing Labor Union (UP), in which they opposed all the planning initiatives of its rival, the SLD.
- Considerable popularity was achieved in the election opinion polls by the previously unknown pensioners' party, which was even given a chance of playing a role in the future government.

However, other circumstances were more favorable:

- The SLD–PSL coalition came under strong attack from the main forces of the opposition (Solidarity and the liberal Freedom Union,

UW) for resisting reform, including reforms of the social insurance system. The SLD leadership, in turn, seriously considered the possibility of an SLD–UW government after the elections. The prime minister was especially well disposed toward this idea. He was thus particularly anxious to convince public opinion that the SLD was a party of market reforms, which were associated with the UW.

- The main opposition parties had their own pension reform programs, which were very similar to the program drawn up by the Office of the Government Plenipotentiary. They also had at their disposal well-prepared experts.
- The Office of the Government Plenipotentiary also included individuals who had personal contacts with the UW leadership.

In these (favorable and unfavorable) circumstances, basic political agreement depended on the universal belief that reform was essential and could not be put off any longer. More specifically, Poland's major political forces recognized that if reform was to get off the ground by a suitable date (preferably in 1999, but no later than the year 2000), the present Parliament must pass measures that would initiate and condition the implementation of reform (e.g., legislation regulating the use of State Treasury assets) and that would require a relatively long period of implementation (e.g., legislation on pension funds and employee pension programs). In addition, consensus depended on recognizing that reform was not a political-party undertaking, but a public one, and thus should not be an issue during the election campaign.

Both these conditions were met due to the usage of the media as well as to purely political, official, and unofficial actions. The most important event in official channels was the setting up of a special working group of the Tripartite Commission for social-insurance reform. As this group was not an official negotiating forum, its work was not subject to political observation and supervision. In actual fact, however, this body, which comprised the main experts of the government and trade unions and involved the participation of the government plenipotentiary, made many substantive decisions on the reform program and draft legislation, several dozen of which were recorded in a joint document (Zmiany 1997). These changes failed to undermine either the concept of reform or the suggested pace of implementing it. Their acceptance added the final details to certain elements of the reform program and, at the same time, also created the belief that reform was a joint undertaking, a fact that the government plenipotentiary could systematically refer to. In this way, Poland's most important trade unions, together with its main political blocs (AWS, the Solidarity Electoral Alliance and SLD), jointly created reform, which made it more difficult for their allies to question the government's reform proposals.

This situation was particularly important in the case of Solidarity. In reality this movement performed a dual role as a political opposition bloc and as a trade union. The pension reform program was prepared by trade-union activists and experts. They also took part in the work of the Tripartite Commission and then in the work of the extraordinary parliamentary commission. They were exceptionally well prepared for work on the reform, and at the same time were not guided by any political motives.

On the other hand, the political leaders of Solidarity were not well versed in the substantive issues. For them only the political game and its consequences mattered, though they held the general conviction that reform was necessary. Thus, in cooperating with Solidarity, the most important thing was to maintain for trade-union experts maximum freedom in matters of content. In return, Solidarity's input in the work on the reform was highlighted in public.

The main unofficial mechanism for achieving consensus took the form of systematic consultations and the coordination of detailed solutions with parliamentary deputies, experts responsible in their respective parliamentary parties for legislation contained in the pension reform package. This arrangement was possible because all bills were examined by an extraordinary parliamentary commission, which was established following a government-sponsored motion presented in Parliament. The government argued that such a body was needed to direct work on urgent matters, although the projects in question were not officially of an urgent nature. As a result, the work of the extraordinary commission proceeded unusually smoothly and in an atmosphere of cooperation.

Finally, achieving political consensus in favor of reform during the preelection period clearly depended on excluding the most politically sensitive issues from the first legislative package. In particular, the first package of reform legislation was exclusively concerned with the employee system and thus bypassed those arrangements that dealt with farmers and agricultural laborers as well as the military sector. Moreover, it did not involve any further rationalization of the first pillar. Thus, it was mainly confined to changes made earlier to the mechanism for indexing benefits and disability qualification rules.

Such a solution was not simply a result of tactical and political calculations (if the PSL had been opposed to such legislation it would not even have reached Parliament), but was part of the general strategy adopted for implementing reform. For it was important to establish the legitimacy of the reform package and of the team reforming the system, which would enable the most politically sensitive problems to be tackled decisively and quickly at a later stage.

Positive trends in the party system, which were confirmed by the parliamentary elections in September 1997, represent an important component of the political conditions surrounding pension reform. Most of the parties that took part in the election were quick to react to the changing attitudes of voters. The most important of these trends included voting for parties that had a realistic chance of winning the elections or at least of entering a coalition government, the lower significance of purely ideological motivation, the greater importance attached by voters to political programs, and the rejection by voters of a sector-based understanding of politics. As a result, the parties that did worst were those which were perceived as class-based, ideological, aggressive, or unable to cooperate. Thus, voters rationally adjusted their preferences to the emerging rules of political practice, which, given the pluralization of the political scene and the proportional ballot (favorable to large parties), are making coalition governments more likely. The latter, in turn, are possible when parties are willing to cooperate, and effective when they are disciplined and accountable.

Another gradually emerging tendency in the evolution of the party system is the development of mechanisms of cooperation between governing parties and the opposition. At the formal level, the best example of this cooperation is the continuing practice of ensuring that opposition parties are represented in key parliamentary bodies and posts.

This balance of forces will undergo further transformation, mainly due to the expected changes within the AWS, the strongest parliamentary grouping. The latter emerged as an electoral coalition between a dozen or so right-wing political parties (including many small ones) and Solidarity. Thanks to the authority and the organizational structures of the union, this right-wing "people's movement" won the elections and was able to form a government. However, relations between the parties constituting the AWS, as well as relations between these parties and the union element, are so complicated and unclear that they may seriously undermine, or even paralyze, the AWS's ability to govern.[4]

Conclusions

This chapter is primarily concerned with the process – rather than the program – of the pension system reform in Poland. Yet this distinction, however useful it may be, represents an oversimplification. It is impossi-

[4] For more on the development of the Polish party system, see Hausner et al. 1998.

ble in practice to make a distinction between reform as a program and reform as an implementation process. This is not the case of a simple relationship between a product and its marketing campaign, but, rather, an extremely complex project in which the vision and the method of its implementation interact with and supplement one another. To be sure, no worthwhile achievement would be possible without a clear vision or program, but the implementation of such a vision requires an appropriate procedure for action. Without such a procedure, little could be done, even with the help of a good plan.

The Polish experience corroborates the observation that the awareness of an impending financial crisis cannot be relied upon as the decisive factor in the launching of a radical reform of the pension system. In an actuarial sense, the pension system in Poland had been bankrupt long before its reform could be launched. Reform occurred only when further short-term manipulation of the system's parameters aimed at deferring the crisis was no longer possible, either politically or legally. Such a state of affairs is a consequence of two factors: a restrictive fiscal policy and a system based on the rule of law. Any government that consistently adopts these two principles as the cornerstones of its policy (or is forced to respect them) has to take the path of radical reform, and this is precisely what happened. To put it differently, a reform such as the one in question becomes historically possible when (alas!) everything else has been tried and no other option is left open.

In Poland, other favorable circumstances include the large volume of assets eligible for privatization and the rapid development of the financial markets – which enjoy a high level of stability and security – including a dynamic growth of the private insurance market.

Success does not depend on the existence of a program and on favorable circumstances alone, but also on the adopted principle that the reform can be implemented only through consultation and negotiation (see Haggard, Kaufman, and Shugart, Chapter 3, in this volume). I am convinced that a radical reform of the pension system (involving the abandonment of the PAYG-system monopoly in favor of a multipillar system) could not have been implemented during the initial phase of the post-socialist transition, which was marked by the domination of an imperative (top-down, unilateral, "dialogueless") method of introducing system changes. The reform in question belongs to the second phase of system changes, which is more in the nature of transformation than transition (Hausner 1997). At this stage an interactive method is required, which combines strategic leadership with dialogue and social partnership. This juxtaposition involves no contradiction, as long as strategic leadership is understood as the capacity to form a strategic vision of the

231

development of the system and to win democratic legitimation for measures adopted for its implementation, a task facilitated by institutionalized partnership (Amin and Hausner 1997).

All this is particularly relevant to pension system reform, which is a project that takes many years from commencement to full implementation. Under a democratic system, ruling elites frequently change during the reform as the government and opposition alternate roles. It follows that the actual implementation of the reform calls for a majority far above that which is necessary to put through even the most difficult short-term projects. I call this kind of majority a strategic majority: a long-lived, nonopportunistic one, capable of effecting a profound structural change. It is hard to assess whether this kind of majority has been formed in Poland and thus whether the new coalition (AWS–UW) will pursue the reform while maintaining its previously adopted form and schedule.

To conclude, therefore, it may be worth reversing the reasoning behind this chapter and, rather than analyzing the favorable conditions for reform, look at the dangers instead. The six most important of these are:

1. The increasing resistance of interest groups toward any change that would limit privileges already awarded. Certain key sentences from the standpoint of the influential Federation of Trade Unions of Polish State Railway Employees on the draft bill on the social-insurance system[5] in October 1997 serve as a serious warning: "Railway workers are resolutely opposed to the current efforts to eliminate the separate status of the railway workers pension system."

2. The adoption by the Constitutional Tribunal of an interpretation of acquired rights that would make it impossible to include a new pension system for persons who began their working life before the new regulations came into force.

3. Delays in the reorganization of the ZUS and the nonintroduction, or faulty introduction, of a database system for individual insurance records.

4. A decision by the AWS–UW coalition to implement the empropriation ideas of Solidarity.

5. A slowing down in the work on reform, either as a consequence of the temporary improvement in the financial situation of the

---

[5] This was the most crucial reform bill – often called the mother bill – submitted by the government plenipotentiary for official consultation in September 1997.

FUS, or because of political fears, for example, those linked to local government elections (mid-1998).
6. A breakdown in political consensus over the reform program.

The emergence of these phenomena could hinder reform. Even a slackening in the pace of the program would have very negative consequences. For the temporary improvement in the demographic situation, the availability of privatization resources and favorable international agreements on Poland's debt create particularly favorable conditions for initiating reform in the year 2000. Any further delay would inevitably mean that the fiscal pressures resulting from it will reach their height just as the general budgetary situation begins to deteriorate.

Epilogue

The new center-right ruling coalition (AWS–UW) put an emphasis – both in the statements being made and in the coalition agreement – on pension system reform as one of its principal tasks. The document *Security through Diversity* (1997) remains the foundation of the reform program. In May 1998 the government initiated two bills of key importance, belonging to the so-called second package of reform legislation, one on the social-insurance system, another on pensions and benefits financed by FUS. The bills are generally consistent with the reform program adopted by the previous government and with the laws passed by the previous Parliament. Their main focus is on the transition path from the current to the new system and on the organization and streamlining of the "first pillar." There has been one instance of departure from the "Security through Diversity" program: the present government has abandoned solutions that were meant in practice to extend the retirement age for women to make it equal to the retirement age for men. But the government reaffirmed the introduction of the new arrangements as of January 1, 1999.

References

Amin, Ash, and Jerzy Hausner. 1997. *Beyond Market and Hierarchy: Interactive Governance and Social Complexity*. Cheltenham: Edward Elgar.

Chand, Sheetal K., and Albert Jaeger. 1996. *Aging Populations and Public Pension Schemes*. IMF Occasional Paper No. 147. Washington, D.C.: International Monetary Fund.

Czepulis-Rutkowska, Zofia. 1996. Zmiany w systemie emerytalno-rentowym (Changes in the pensions system). In S. Golinowska, ed., *Polityka społeczna w latach 1994–1996. Procesy regulacyjne i potencjalne skutki* (Social policy in 1994–1996: Regulation processes and their potential effects), Fascicle No. 11, pp. 192–207. Warsaw: IPiSS.

Ferge, Zsuzsa. 1997. The Actors of the Hungarian Pension Reform. Paper presented at the Fifth Central European Forum, The Politics of Welfare: Between Governmental Policy and Local Initiative. IWM, Vienna, October 24–26.

Hausner, Jerzy. 1994. Reprezentacja interesów w społeczeństwach socjalistycznych i postsocjalistycznych (Interest representation in socialist and postsocialist societies). In J. Hausner and P. Marciniak, eds., *Od socjalitycznego korporacjonizmu do . . . ?* (From socialist corporatism to . . . ?), pp. 11–25. Warsaw: Polska Praca Foundation.

——— 1997. Political Economy of Socialism's Transformation. Paper prepared for WIDER, Helsinki. Mimeographed.

Hausner, Jerzy, Mirosława Marody, Jerzy Wilkin, Andrzej Wojtyna, and Marek Zirk-Sadowski. 1998. *Accession or Integration? Poland's Road to the European Union. EU-monitoring II.* Warsaw: Friedrich Ebert Foundation.

Kornai, János. 1997. Reform of the Welfare Sector in the Post-Communist Countries: A Normative Approach. In J. M. Nelson, C. Tilly, and L. Walker, eds., *Transforming Post-Communist Political Economies*, pp. 272–98. Washington, D.C.: National Academy Press.

National Report. 1997. *National Report on Human Development. The Changing Role of the State: Poland '97.* Warsaw: UNDP.

Nuti, D. Mario. 1998. Alternative Pension Systems: Generalities and Reform Issues in Transition Economies. In S. Griffith-Jones, et al., eds., *Reforms of Pension System and National Savings.* Working Paper No. 84. Prague: Česka Narodni Banka, Institute Ekonomie.

Security. 1997. *Security through Diversity: Reform of the Pension System in Poland.* Warsaw: Office of the Government Plenipotentiary for Social Security Reform.

Stanowisko. 1997. Stanowisko Trójstronnej Komisji do Spraw Społeczno-Gospodarczych w sprawie programu reformy ubezpieczeń społecznych i przedłożonych projektów ustaw (The standpoint of the Tripartite Commission for Socio-Economic Affairs on the social insurance reform programme and submitted draft legislation). Internal government document.

Zmiany. 1997. Zmiany w programie reformy systemu ubezpieczeń społecznych, w ustawie o funduszach emerytalnych oraz w ustawie o wykorzystaniu części mienia Skarbu Państwa na rzecz reformy ubezpieczeń społecznych dokonane w związku z uwagami wniesionymi w trakcie prac Zespołu Robozego Komisji Trójstronnej do Spraw Reformy Ubezpieczeń Społecznych (Changes in the social-insurance system, in the act on pension funds and in the act on using part of State Treasury assets to support social-insurance reform in connection with proposals made by the Working Group of the Tripartite Commission for Matters Concerning Social Insurance Reform). Internal government document.

CHAPTER 8

The Politics of Pension and Health-Care Reforms in Hungary and Poland

JOAN M. NELSON

When the formerly Communist countries of Eastern Europe began their transformation into market-oriented economies, reforms in social programs and services were minor parts of the adjustment agenda. Government and public attention focused mainly on other issues: macro-economic stabilization, the opening of the economy, privatization of enterprises.

Half a dozen years into their economic transformations, however, those countries which had reasonably effectively addressed many of the initial economic challenges of adjustment began to focus attention much more squarely on pension and health-sector reforms. Hungary adopted radical changes in its pension system in mid-1997. Poland designed a similar set of reforms in two packages, one passed before the elections and change of government in autumn 1997, and the second approved in autumn 1998. Latvia had adopted partial pension reforms somewhat earlier and is now expanding its reforms, while similar measures are moving ahead in Croatia, Estonia, Macedonia, Romania, and Slovenia.

A great deal of analysis has focused on the substance of these reforms and the merits and drawbacks of specific design components. However, the context, the goals, and the character of these reforms combine to pose formidable political challenges. This chapter focuses not on design but on the politics of social-sector reforms.

I am indebted to Collegium Budapest for the invaluable opportunity to develop this topic, to members of the Focus Group of 1997–98 and very especially to János Kornai for guidance and comments on earlier versions, and to Nicholas Barr and other participants in the seminar of March 27–28, 1998. Viktória Danics provided valuble research assistance. My thanks also to all those interviewed (listed at the end of the References) for giving so generously of their time and insights. Particular thanks go to Jacek Kochanowicz and Irina Topińska for their guidance, support, and hospitality during my stay in Warsaw.

Social-sector reforms are usually "second (or third) generation" reforms in the broad structural adjustment agenda.[1] They are likely to unfold in a quite different political climate than initial macroeconomic measures. If early stabilization measures were reasonably successful, then widespread public perceptions of acute crisis will have faded. In other cases, poorly designed or irresolute stabilization measures may have had only limited effect, leaving most groups disillusioned with "reform programs." In either of these scenarios, what Leszek Balcerowicz (the architect of Poland's initial reforms) labeled the period of "extraordinary politics" will have passed.[2] Interest groups, legislatures, and the general public are likely to be much more resistant to autocratic styles of executive leadership imposing measures designed by technocrats with minimal consultation. Social-sector reforms will usually have to be designed, launched, and implemented in the context of "politics as usual," even if the impetus and rationale for reform comes from perception of a deep-rooted structural crisis.

The objectives of social-sector reforms are also more sharply disputed than are the goals of initial stabilization and liberalization measures. The first stages of transition were accompanied, in many cases, by a "negative consensus": the imperative need to stabilize the economy and the conviction that the old system had failed. But later stages require building a "positive consensus" regarding the emerging economy and society. That need is sharpened by unease in many quarters regarding the increased inequality and insecurity associated with market mechanisms. Education, health, and pension systems powerfully shape most citizens' opportunities and security. Public opinion demands reforms in these areas, but the precise design of the reforms is intensely controversial.

Beyond context and goals, the intrinsic character of social-sector reforms poses political obstacles. Early macroeconomic steps in the adjustment agenda rely on price changes such as devaluation and interest-rate adjustments and on cuts in government expenditures. Initial liberalization entails dismantling controls and subsidies. Such measures are politically controversial, but they are not complex administratively.

[1] Major systemic reforms in health, education, or pension systems are seldom part of the initial or early package of reforms in a sustained structural adjustment program. Structural adjustment is usually triggered by severe fiscal and external account imbalances. Social-sector reforms take considerable time to design and implement, and therefore cannot contribute to the initial dominant stabilization goal. Moreover, some social-sector reforms, especially pension reforms, virtually require that other institutional reforms, especially in the financial sector, be in place first.

[2] That period was much less marked in some countries, like the Czech Republic or Hungary, than others, like Poland, but nonetheless occurred in some degree in most post-Communist countries.

With the backing of top political leaders, they can be put into effect by a small number of senior economic officials. They take effect rapidly, sometimes overnight. They affect much of the population and can prompt widespread protest, but if the government can deflect or weather initial protests, the risks almost always subside.

Social-sector reforms, like most major institutional changes, are inherently slower and more complex. They demand the cooperation of far more agencies and groups within and outside of government, and they take months or years to put into effect. Multiple actors mean many potential veto players; lengthy implementation means multiple veto opportunities. Moreover, and in contrast to macroeconomic stabilization, institutional reforms are likely to mean permanent losses to specific groups, which may prompt tenacious resistance.

Some kinds of institutional reform seem to be more difficult than others. In broad comparative perspective, there has been considerably more progress in reforming financial systems or trade regimes than in restructuring social sectors or labor-market institutions. Among social sectors, in turn, pensions seem to be considerably easier than health and education. The contrasts almost surely reflect differences in the numbers, variety, and commitment of stakeholders and the length of time required to implement reforms. Further, this study argues that the presence or absence of a fairly clear blueprint for reform, or even of two clear contending visions, helps explain why some institutional reforms tend to move ahead more rapidly than others.

The chapter is organized around three questions or puzzles.

The first puzzle concerns timing. Social-security experts in Hungary and Poland recognized at least by the mid-1980s that their pension systems were inequitable and unsustainable in the long run. Both before and after the collapse of Communist governments, some modest steps were taken to reduce near-term pressures on the system. However, basic systemic reforms were not seriously pursued until 1996. *Why then, and not earlier?*

The second puzzle concerns political feasibility. In many of the world's wealthy, aging democracies, pension reforms are an urgent need. Yet in most of these countries, the issue provokes such intense political passion that even quite small changes are extremely difficult. *How, then, did Hungary and Poland manage to adopt radical revisions in their systems?* What were the interests and resources of the main actors? What were the channels and processes that permitted compromises?

The third puzzle focuses on the contrast between reforms in pension systems and in health-care delivery. In Eastern Europe and elsewhere, reforms in health care arguably are more urgent than pension reforms, on both welfare and fiscal grounds. Indeed, in Hungary and Poland the same groups that pressed successfully for pension reforms originally had hoped to introduce major health-sector reforms as well. But reforms in health-care delivery have proved far more difficult. *Why did pension reforms move so much more decisively than those in health?* This last question, in particular, may provide a partial test of the points sketched here regarding the reform of complex institutions.

The First Puzzle: Why Pension Reforms in 1997, Not Earlier?

In Hungary and Poland, severe problems with long-established pension systems had been deepening for more than a decade. As throughout Central Europe, the systems were state-managed, defined-benefit schemes financed on a pay-as-you-go (PAYG) basis. In such systems, today's work force (or, more precisely, that portion of the work force that pays social-security contributions) finances the costs of today's pensions. As populations age, however, there are fewer active workers relative to retirees. That demographic challenge confronts many of the countries of Eastern Europe, as well as most in Western Europe, North America, and Japan.

In Hungary and still more clearly in Poland, however, demographic changes were not the main source of difficulties in the 1990s.[3] At the beginning of the transition both countries deliberately encouraged early retirement and granted liberal disability pensions, in part to reduce anticipated unemployment. Therefore the number of pensioners and the costs of pensions surged. At the same time, workers paying into the social-security programs dwindled because of unemployment, a shrinking labor force, and widespread and growing evasion. Not only self-employed and informal-sector workers, but some major public employers – for instance, the Hungarian railways and some Polish mining companies – were chronically in deep arrears in their contributions (Orosz, Hausner, interviews).

As social-security revenues shrank, transfers from government budgets had to increase.[4] At the same time, high payroll taxes discour-

---

[3] In Hungary, the ratio of elderly to working-age population actually declined during the second half of the 1990s. In Poland, while the ratio increased somewhat during the 1990s, it is projected to fall slightly between 2000 and 2005 (Palacios and Rocha 1998: 187, table 7.5; Hausner, Chapter 7, in this volume).

[4] Hausner estimates that state subsidies to Poland's Social Insurance Fund reached 4.3 percent of GDP in 1992, and dwindled gradually in later years. Subsidies to the Farmers' Social Insurance Fund, a separate system with lower contributions, cost approximately an additional 2 percent of GDP in each year from 1992 through 1996 (Hausner, Chapter

aged investment and skewed it toward labor-saving patterns, while encouraging evasion.[5] Demographic projections made clear that current imbalances between costs and revenues would become much worse early in the next century. In addition, there were serious problems of complex and opaque formulas for calculating pensions and inequitable treatment across categories of workers. Public-opinion polls indicated widespread dissatisfaction with the systems.

In both Hungary and Poland, social-security specialists had recognized the inequities, complexity, and long-term unsustainability of the systems by the late 1970s or early 1980s. Poland's system was substantially revised in the early 1980s, but included politically motivated concessions to miners, teachers, and others. By the early 1990s, experts were again debating new reforms, including some very radical proposals, but mainline thinking focused on adjusting the existing system. In Hungary, meanwhile, the social-security system was removed from the general budget in the early 1990s. In 1993 two separate funds, each with its own elected governance board, were established to manage social-security contributions for health and pensions. Private voluntary pension and health-insurance funds were authorized in the same year, while changes in the design and administration of the PAYG system were under intensive study (Augusztinovics, Ferge, interviews).

In both countries, then, shortcomings of the pension systems had long prompted extensive analysis, proposals, and debate. However, the reforms of 1997 were broader in scope and more radical in design than any since the basic outlines of the systems had been established (in 1975 in Hungary, 1982 in Poland). What brought about the surge of reform action?

New Actors: The Ministry of Finance

New actors provide part of the answer to the question. Ministries of finance took an aggressive lead in promoting systemic reform. As guardians of the budget, they had always taken some interest in the

---

7, in this volume). In Hungary, payroll taxes funded pension and health care jointly and the deficits are hard to disentangle, but by 1993 and 1994 the two programs together required budget transfers of roughly 5 percent of GDP (Palacios and Rocha 1998: 179, fig. 7.1).

[5] In Hungary from April 1992 the total tax on gross wages for pensions was 30.5 percent, of which employers paid four-fifths. An additional contribution for the health fund brought the total tax to 54 percent (Palacios and Rocha 1998: 213, n. 4). In Poland, employers paid 45 percent of the gross payroll for pensions and health; employees did not contribute (Phare 1997: 116).

social-security systems. But until the mid-1990s, they focused mainly on short-run fiscal issues. After the pension systems were separated from the general budget, fiscal concerns focused on containing pension fund deficits and resulting demands on the general budget, generally by manipulating the formulas that linked the levels of pensions to changes in the levels of wages. Not until the mid-1990s did ministries of finance begin to spearhead radical changes in the long-term design of pension systems.

This new role was not driven by short-run fiscal concerns. Indeed, the kinds of reforms promoted by ministries of finance in both countries were known to increase rather than reduce fiscal burdens in the short and medium run. Rather than driving the neoliberal reforms, near-term fiscal considerations constrained them: in Hungary, fiscal burdens were a major and explicit reason for phasing in the new system very gradually. In Poland, certain revenues from the concurrent privatization program were earmarked to support the pension reforms, but as in Hungary, careful fiscal calculations were a major element shaping design.

Ministry of Finance emphasis on social-security reforms was driven mainly by the logic of the larger structural adjustment process. In Hungary, the macroeconomic austerity package introduced by Minister of Finance Lajos Bokros in March 1995 marked a turning point in Hungary's post-Communist economic policies (Kornai 1996). To consolidate the country's painfully reestablished economic stability, Bokros sought to reconfigure fiscal institutions. Pension reforms became part of this drive. In Poland, Grzegorz Kołodko, minister of finance from April 1994, described the pension system as "a veritable time bomb," and its reform as "an absolute precondition of sustaining – let alone improving – the country's fiscal integrity" (Kołodko 1996: 26). In both countries, the prospect of fairly rapid accession to the European Union reinforced a long-term perspective on public finance (Dethier, personal communication).

International Influences

By the mid-1990s, direct and indirect international influences also heightened pressure for radical pension reforms. In the wealthy industrialized nations, demographic shifts fueled intense interest in pension reforms. At the same time, the Chilean model for social-security reform challenged older ideas and exerted a powerful influence. In 1981 Chile had replaced its traditional system with a mandatory, fully funded, defined contributions system in which workers contributed over their working lives to individual accounts managed by private, competitive pension fund management firms. A means-tested social assistance program augments the incomes of those retired people who have only very low pensions. By the early 1990s, the system was attracting widespread praise (in good part for its impressive success in bolstering Chile's equity markets), as well as considerable criticism. Especially in Latin America, but increasingly in Eastern Europe as well, it also attracted partial imitators.[6]

International financial and development agencies sharply increased their attention to pension systems and reforms in the early 1990s, spurred by the need to consolidate hard-won fiscal gains, by mounting demographic pressures in much of Eastern Europe and the Southern Cone of Latin America, and by the possibilities suggested by the Chilean model and its variants. As early as 1990–91, both the International Monetary Fund (IMF) and the World Bank sent missions to Hungary analyzing social benefits including the pension system, but did not urge full or partial privatization (Kopits 1992; World Bank 1992). In 1994 the bank published a major study, *Averting the Old Age Crisis*, which strongly endorsed a multipillar approach to pension reforms. Since then, the bank has fairly consistently encouraged this broad approach, while supporting considerable variation in accord with specific country circumstances. Meanwhile other international and regional organizations, especially the International Labor Organization and the European Union (working mainly through its Phare Technical Assistance program) also increased attention to pension reform. While there is no neat one-to-one correspondence between specific agencies and particular outlooks (Deacon 1996), in general these latter organizations have emphasized improving PAYG.

In Eastern Europe, direct encouragement and advice from international agencies may have been supplemented by less direct influence from international capital markets. By the mid-1990s, ratings agencies and international markets had begun to include pension reforms in their lists of actions demonstrating serious commitment to reform. The need to attract foreign investment was particularly imperative in Poland and Hungary, which were burdened with large international debts. Both therefore had strong incentives to maintain external confidence in their economic management and growth potential, and to build their reputations as good places to invest.

---

[6] In the early or mid-1990s Argentina, Bolivia, Colombia, Mexico, Peru, and Uruguay adopted reforms that incorporated modified elements of the Chilean approach. Australia, Denmark, Sweden, Switzerland, and the United Kingdom also enacted major pension reforms.

The Second Puzzle: Why Were Pension Reforms
Politically Feasible?

Pension reforms involve complex and detailed projections and calculations, as well as difficult trade-offs regarding goals and values. Hungarian and Polish reformers had to address three levels or categories of
opposition. The ministries and agencies most directly concerned and specialists outside of government focused largely on technical issues, some
of which provoked bitter disputes. A different kind of opposition came
from vested interests: those groups and organizations that benefited from
the current systems and feared that reforms would reduce their benefits.
Still a third level or kind of opposition was rooted in principles and
values.

Competing Concepts of Pension Reform

Analysis, debate, and political maneuvering regarding pension reform in
both countries focused on two competing concepts of reform. The first
concept assumed that the public, PAYG system was both sustainable and
desirable, but required far-reaching reforms. Specialists agreed on the
need to raise the age of retirement, remove or reduce the special privileges of particular occupations or groups, cleanse the systems of the multiple irrationalities and inequities that had developed over time, tighten
the links between contributions paid into the system and benefits paid
out from it, and establish predictable and equitable methods for adjusting pensions to changes in prices and economic circumstances.

The second concept started from the assumption that mature PAYG
systems in aging societies could be sustained only by imposing ever-
higher costs on society as a whole. Those costs not only would cripple
post-Communist recovery and growth but also would induce such widespread evasion that the systems would gradually crumble. Many advocates of the second concept believed that PAYG (improved along the
lines listed earlier) could and should remain a component of a mixed
system for an extended period. But they focused on introducing a compulsory fully funded "second pillar," with benefits tightly linked to contributions. They argued that the second pillar would greatly reduce
problems of evasion. In order to generate returns high enough to provide
comfortable pensions, at least part of the funds should be invested in
equities and managed by competitive private firms. The flexibility and
sustainability of the system would be enhanced if there were also a
voluntary "third pillar" consisting of private individual supplementary
pension plans.

242

Advocates of the two concepts clearly disagreed over certain values. Most of those who favored fixing PAYG alone placed high priority on the intrinsic redistributive or solidaristic character of the established systems – that is, the principle that a basic (and not too minimal) pension is a right of all citizens, and that each successive generation has an obligation to help to support the preceding generation in its old age. Advocates of the second concept, in contrast, usually viewed the second pillar's emphasis on individual responsibility and self-reliance as a moral virtue, as well as a practical device for reducing evasion.

Some other major disagreements between the two groups turned less on values than on interpretations of facts and probabilities. Advocates of fixing PAYG were deeply skeptical about turning over management of compulsory individual second-pillar retirement accounts to private management firms. They argued that such arrangements imposed unnecessary and inappropriate risks on individuals and claimed that experience in Chile and elsewhere indicated serious problems. Proponents of mixed systems countered that only private-sector investments would generate adequate pensions in the face of the demographic pressures; they claimed the critics failed to grasp the workings of equity markets.[7] Mixed-system advocates often emphasized that once the contributions to the second-pillar accounts began to build up, they would provide a major deepening and broadening of equity markets. Critics responded that the redesign of the pension system should focus on fulfilling its own functions as well as possible. Building up capital markets was not an appropriate objective of pension system reform, especially if that goal jeopardized or diluted important pension functions.

The Struggle within the Governments

As the ministries of finance began to press for radical pension reforms in 1995–96, they met strong opposition within their own governments. In Hungary both the Pension Insurance Fund and the Ministry of Welfare initially opposed proposals for a strong mandatory fully funded component that would gradually replace PAYG. After several months of intense debate in winter 1996, the Ministry of Welfare agreed to cooperate with the Ministry of Finance to develop a modified multipillar plan, and the cabinet endorsed this approach on May 9, 1996. An interministerial committee prepared framework legislation outlining the proposed reforms; this was approved by the legislature in summer 1996. With this mandate,

---

[7] Hausner (Chapter 7, in this volume) suggests that in Poland lawyers tended to support PAYG whereas economists leaned toward more radical reforms.

the committee moved into a year of hectic technical projections and analysis, coupled with extensive discussions and negotiations with a wide range of interests. A set of bills was sent to Parliament in June 1997. The key bill establishing the second pillar and regulating the new privately managed funds was approved by 78 percent of those present and voting (or 56 percent of all MPs). Throughout this process, however, the Pension Insurance Fund continued to reject the multi-pillar approach bitterly, for reasons discussed shortly.

In Poland, the idea of radical, Chilean-style reform had been introduced as early as 1991 by the then chairman of the Social Insurance Institution (ZUS) Wojciech Topinski and Marion Winiewski, but was rejected as too radical at the time. By mid-1994, however, Minister of Finance and First Deputy Prime Minister Grzegorz Kołodko called for a basic shift in pension arrangements as an important element in his "Strategy for Poland" (Kołodko 1996: 52). As Jerzy Hausner describes more fully in this volume (Chapter 7), it was blocked for almost two years by adamant opposition from Minister of Labor and Social Policy Leszek Miller, whose stance reflected both his and his staff's commitment to PAYG principles and strong personal rivalry with Kołodko.[8]

The stalemate was broken in spring 1996, when Miller was replaced as minister of labor by Andrzej Bączkowski. By autumn, Bączkowski established a small task force, the Plenipotentiary for Social Security Reform, charged with drawing up detailed plans for pension (and initially for health) reform. Bączkowski himself took on the role of plenipotentiary. In November a heart attack tragically terminated his leadership. His replacement as minister of labor, Tadeusz Zieliński, was hostile to radical reforms. However, in the interim Jerzy Hausner, long a senior economic advisor of Kołodko, had been appointed to replace Bączkowski as plenipotentiary. As a condition for accepting the position, Hausner insisted that the task force be attached not to the Ministry of Labor but to the office of the prime minister. From early 1997, the office of the plenipotentiary spearheaded the reform effort, with the backing of the Ministry of Finance, the prime minister, and the president, but with mixed support and opposition from the remainder of the cabinet.

Like Hungary's interministerial committee, Poland's extraministerial plenipotentiary was under pressure to complete a reform package before

---

[8] During this long period of intragovernmental stalemate, the Ministry of Finance continued to work toward radical pension reform. It commissioned a detailed study based on Chile's experience, sponsored a series of professional opinion surveys, and consulted representatives of various economic and social groups (Hausner, Chapter 7, in this volume, and interview).

upcoming elections. The deadline in Poland was considerably tighter: with elections scheduled for September 1997, the reform team worked intensely to present a partial package of draft laws (including the crucial provisions establishing a second pillar) to the Parliament by summer. The laws won approval, but a second package needed to complete the system (including controversial changes in the ongoing PAYG component) was postponed until after the elections. The new government took some time to review the bills and submit them to the legislature. Once submitted, the bills' progress through the key legislative commission was also slow, but the pension package was approved in late September 1998, and the new system went into effect early in 1999.

The specific designs of the reforms were overwhelmingly results of domestic rather than international goals and pressures. The point is worth emphasizing, because both reform teams were directly and extensively supported by the World Bank, and to some extent by other external agencies and donors. In Hungary, the World Bank provided major financial support for the group's work. Perhaps as important, the Budapest office of the bank put the task force in touch with a large network of pension specialists all over the world and helped to provide two-way translation of documents and comments on specific issues. In Poland, the technical director of the plenipotentiary was a World Bank staff member seconded from Washington. Both he and the part of the bank from which he was drawn could provide extensive networking as well as technical support.

Predictably, such involvement provoked criticism in both countries. Yet there is little in either reform story to indicate that the World Bank dictated, or even strongly influenced, the specific choices and design details that emerged from the process of analysis and political negotiations. The international financial community (including but going well beyond the World Bank and the IMF) contributed powerfully to the evolution of thinking regarding pension reform options and to the political decision that early action was imperative. Both timing and the broad shape of reform were influenced by outside forces. But the more specific design details were outcomes of the analysis and political judgment of the reformers themselves, and of their negotiations and compromises within their governments and with interest groups, watchdog institutions, and legislatures.

Public Opinion and Major Vested Interests

In both Hungary and Poland, survey evidence shows that most of the public had lost confidence in the traditional pension systems by the mid-

1990s. Earlier proposals to reform those systems by specific measures such as increasing the age of retirement and equalizing it for men and women had prompted widespread opposition. The new, broader reform proposals bundled such measures with the introduction of the second, fully funded, privately managed pillar. The broader package apparently was more acceptable politically, in part because it appeared more credible. Moreover, a sizable part of the public – particularly the younger and better-educated – liked the idea of individual accounts and a strong link between contributions and benefits (Müller 1998).[9] But while public opinion was permissive, in neither country did it drive the reforms. Most people were confused by the technical details and skeptical about some aspects of the new proposals.

Pensioners might have been expected to dominate the politics of pension reforms. In both countries, the surge of early retirements after 1989 had swelled the number of pensioners beyond the already substantial fraction of the population at or above retirement age. And because older people (except the very elderly) tend to vote in greater numbers than the young, pensioners may account for 30 to 40 percent of voters (Slay and Vinton 1997). Moreover, many pensioners are affiliated with potentially influential organizations: unions (particularly the post-Communist ones) or specialized associations. In Poland, two separate pensioners' parties were formed before the 1997 national elections.

Yet in fact pensioners played little direct political role. In both countries, the reforms were designed to have minimal impact on current pensioners or on those expecting to become pensioners in the next few years. Concerns that the new fully funded pillar would siphon social security contributions from the ongoing first pillar were eased by introducing the new system gradually, while continuing to direct the bulk of funds into the PAYG component. Pensioners also were concerned with reforms in the indexing arrangements, and (in Poland) argued that they should share in the earmarked benefits from privatization of certain state assets. In Hungary, potential opposition was substantially deflected by an advi-

---

[9] A survey commissioned by the Polish plenipotentiary in April 1997 to help gauge the acceptability of a multipillar system found strong majorities in favor of a tighter link between contributions and benefits. Most respondents were not much concerned that such an approach would result in increased inequality (*Security* 1997: 179–83). This evidence was used in the intragovernment debate to counter Ministry of Labor assertions that Poles would not tolerate a reform that significantly increased inequality (Hausner, interview). In Hungary, the Ministry of Finance commissioned a series of five surveys beginning in October 1996. The surveys found a growing proportion of the public (60 percent initially, 80 percent later) were aware that pension reforms were being developed; younger and more educated Hungarians were most likely to favor a multipillar approach.

sory Council of Elder Affairs, created shortly after Prime Minister Horn took office, to discuss pensioners' concerns. They were also promised a 6 percent real increase in their pensions, effective at the beginning of 1998. In Poland during the electoral campaign of autumn 1997, it is striking that neither of the two pensioners' parties attacked the pension reforms, despite the fact that the second half of the package, which included controversial changes in the ongoing traditional component, would come before the legislature for approval during the next administration. Neither party attracted the minimum 4 percent of the vote required to win seats in the Sejm.

In both countries, labor unions were far more involved than pensioners in negotiations over pension reforms. But the unions did not speak with one voice. In Poland, some elements within both Solidarity and the post-Communist union confederation OPZZ were deeply skeptical about diluting the PAYG system, partly on the grounds that fully funded, individual accounts would destroy the redistributive and solidaristic character of the system. However, some leading Solidarity officials were more receptive to radical changes, had criticized earlier government proposals that lacked a fully funded component, and had submitted their own proposals for far-reaching reforms.

The plenipotentiary consulted extensively with representatives of the major unions. The formal channel of discussion and negotiation was the Tripartite Commission, established in February 1994 as part of an attempted social pact. The commission includes representatives of unions, private employers, and government. At the suggestion of the plenipotentiary, a smaller and less formal group was formed to screen proposals for the full council. This group took a number of specific substantive decisions, which modified but did not undermine the basic goals of the reform and contributed to the sense that the reform was a collaborative and nonpartisan undertaking (Hausner, Chapter 7, in this volume). Unionists also took part in study visits to Chile and elsewhere.

One of the most serious points of contention with Solidarity was the method of using revenues from privatization of certain state assets to support the pension reform. The plenipotentiary wanted to transfer sales proceeds directly to the budget, to cover costs associated with the creation of a second pillar. Solidarity urged "empropriation," a different and more complex approach to transforming ownership of state enterprises (see Hausner, Chapter 7, in this volume; Gesell, Müller, and Süß 1998). The Solidarity proposal was attractive because it promised "seed money" from privatization for individual pension accounts; however, it would severely delay the reforms and would entail other costs. An ingenious compromise, utilizing the empropriation idea on a small scale, succeeded in winning sufficient support to pass the legislature (Hausner, Chapter 7, in this volume).

In Hungary, solidaristic leanings probably contributed to opposition within the post-Communist union confederation MSZOSZ. In contrast, SZEF, the major union confederation representing public service workers, favored reforms. Beyond ideology and calculations of members' interests, however, unusual institutional arrangements created a powerful incentive for MSZOSZ to oppose reforms.

As mentioned earlier in this essay, in 1993 Hungary established separate autonomous institutions to manage the pension and health-care systems, both funded largely from the social security contributions paid by employers and workers. (For the origins of this system, see Haggard, Kaufman, and Shugart, Chapter 3, in this volume.) The Pension Insurance Fund and the Health Insurance Fund each had governance boards, composed in equal halves of representatives of union federations and employers. Among union representatives, MSZOSZ dominated, and because the employers' representatives were usually rather passive, the post-Communist union federation effectively controlled both boards. Until the government elected in 1998 eliminated the boards' autonomy, this control was a valuable asset for a union federation that, while probably still the largest in the country, has steadily lost members and influence. Despite legal safeguards, the board's control over large flows of money permitted financial maneuvering widely believed to have benefited the union as an institution, key leaders, and political parties.

Therefore, pension reforms that channeled a sizable and growing fraction of pension contributions away from the system managed by the Pension Insurance Fund and into individual, privately managed accounts clearly threatened MSZOSZ power and financial interests. The Pension Fund's governing body and especially its MSZOSZ members were intensely hostile to the proposed reforms. They were bolstered by some of the social-security analysts in the pension administration, who held strong solidaristic values and questioned the technical analyses of the interministerial reform commission.

However, rivalries and disagreements regarding strategy within MSZOSZ gave reformers some room for maneuver. Whereas MSZOSZ representatives on the Pension Fund governing board were unyielding in their opposition, those representing MSZOSZ on the Interest Reconciliation Council (Hungary's Tripartite Commission) were more moderate (or, according to varying interpretations, more opportunistic). When the proposed pension reforms were submitted to the council for approval in May 1997, MSZOSZ won a series of concessions, but did not attempt to block the measures entirely. Several of the concessions were temporary: for instance, it was agreed to postpone reforms of disability pensions and to delay by two years introduction of a revised formula for indexing pensions. This latter concession, however, locked in large real pension increases for 1998 and 1999, based on an expected decline in inflation. Widows' benefits were also increased (Ladó, interview, Palacios and Rochas 1998: 203).

Perhaps the key concession related less to the pension reform itself than to MSZOSZ political concerns. MSZOSZ wanted to change the method by which the governing boards of the pension and health funds were selected. Members of the first boards had been chosen in national elections in May 1993, for four-year terms. These terms were due to expire just as the pension reform bills were coming before the Interest Reconciliation Council (IRC), prior to submission to Parliament. Fresh elections might erode MSZOSZ dominance. The union sought a differ-ent formula for selecting the new boards, a formula that would preserve its control and the associated political power and financial opportunities. The IRC agreed to ask each of the "sides" in the pension and health fund boards (i.e., labor and management) to reach agreement among them-selves regarding how to allocate their seats. That formula was ratified in legislation passed in the summer of 1997. The unions then reached an agreement allocating seven of fifteen labor seats to MSZOSZ and divid-ing the balance among other major labor federations (Ladó, interview). MSZOSZ therefore maintained control over the pension and health insurance boards, in exchange for dropping opposition to the modified pension reforms.[10]

In both Hungary and Poland, the governments' capacity to manage union opposition to pension reforms was enhanced because the then current governments were controlled by post-Communist parties with strong ties to the post-Communist labor federations. In Poland, parlia-mentary deputies affiliated with the post-Communist union OPZZ held about a third of SLD seats (Surdej, interview). Similarly, in Hungary the Socialist Party contained a sizable MSZOSZ component. But both governing parties also included influential moderate and neoliberal fac-tions. In Hungary the Socialists' coalition partner, the Free Democrats, further counterbalanced the more hard-line union wing of the Socialists. In Poland, the SLD coalition partner, the Peasant Party, was not at all reformist in its leanings, but was largely indifferent to the pension issue because farmers' pensions were separate from the main system and excluded from the proposed reforms. While union officials were given

---

[10] This solution prompted bitter criticism from a range of politicians and others, including the Socialists' coalition partners, the Free Democrats.

their say, primarily in the Tripartite Commissions, the dominant parties were able to exert party discipline on crucial votes.

In addition to the major union federations, reformers also had to deal with a number of more specialized groups. In both countries, miners, teachers, railway workers, and some smaller occupational groups enjoyed early retirement or higher pension privileges. In Poland, miners received double the average pension and retired roughly nine years earlier (Hausner, Chapter 7, in this volume). These groups are politically powerful: for example, the Hungarian railway system has been permitted to accumulate massive arrears to the pension system over many years. In Hungary, potential opposition from these groups was avoided by postponing any attempt to alter their privileges. In Poland the first package of laws sent to the Sejm similarly evaded the issue. The second package, approved in late 1998, established a uniform system for all workers who have not already qualified for pension privileges. The government proposed and the unions have agreed that older workers in previously privileged sectors who have not yet worked the full number of years required to qualify under the old system will be compensated on terms to be negotiated within the Tripartite Commission (rather than through the legislature) after the new system has been adopted. Costs of compensation will be borne by the general budget rather than the pension system. An important feature of the Polish reform scheme is the creation of notional defined contribution accounts within the old PAYG component, linking individual workers' contributions more closely to the benefits they can expect on retiring. Among reasons why the reformers favored this feature (adapted from Swedish and Latvian experience) was the fact that it is inconsistent with, and therefore might ease the elimination of, privileges for particular groups (Hausner, interview).

Among major stakeholders one other category must be mentioned: private insurers and (in Hungary) firms already established to manage voluntary pension funds. In Poland, representatives of the association of insurance companies met a number of times with the plenipotentiary. They sought reforms based on capitalization, broad access for private insurance firms (including foreign firms) to second-pillar programs, and equal tax treatment for firms managing mandatory and voluntary pension funds. The group was disappointed with respect to several features of the semifinal design, and indeed reopened certain questions of tax treatment with the new government after the September 1997 elections. The process of consultation itself, however, was viewed as transparent and reasonable (Kostkiewicz, Myjak, interviews).

In Hungary, the process through which existing private insurance and pension firms had access to the reformers was less transparent. Private voluntary individual and group pension funds had expanded rapidly after they were authorized late in 1993. By late 1997 some 250 pension mutuals had been established, with about 600,000 members (over 15 percent of the labor force). Employers favored such plans because they did not have to pay taxes on the wages contributed to the pension accounts (Gál, interview). Whereas experts from the sector were invited to advise on technical aspects of the reforms, no channels were set up for more structured representation or negotiation. Perhaps because of concerns that too many firms would compete for the new opportunities created by the reforms, or perhaps in part because of political influence, the legislation governing the qualifications for managing mandatory second-pillar funds favors the largest already-established firms, many of which are linked to large, often foreign insurance or banking companies.[11]

Watchdog Institutions and Their Influence

In designing politically feasible reforms, the pension reform teams in Hungary and Poland had to consider not only stakeholders and public opinion, but also the probable reactions of oversight institutions. Constitutional courts in both countries, and the institution of the Ombudsman in Poland, can review and reverse the actions of government agencies. These institutions are independent of other governmental bodies, including the judicial system. The constitutional courts are responsible for protecting the integrity of the constitution and the values it embodies. They have the power to overturn specific features of laws judged to violate constitutional guarantees of individual rights; in Hungary this can be done even before a law is implemented.

The legal concept of acquired rights to benefits has proved an important constraint on changes in the design and financing of social benefits. In Hungary, Minister of Finance Bokros's 1995 austerity package included provisions to substitute targeted for universal family assistance and to modify sick pay and other provisions. The Constitutional Court promptly declared some of these measures invalid, because they failed to provide an "adequate adjustment period," or were more fundamentally in conflict with the constitution. The minister of finance stated that

---

[11] After obtaining a formation license, a firm had six months to recruit at least 2,000 members and to meet requirements regarding staff, procedures, and equipment. The requirements favored those third-pillar funds linked to insurance companies, with large numbers of agents to recruit members, and ready access to capital to finance start-up equipment and arrangements. Of 250 funds handling voluntary pension funds, about 50 applied for licenses when the reforms went into effect in January 1998, and only a handful had recruited 2,000 members as of March 1998 (Spat, interview).

the court's decisions wiped out half of the expected savings from the austerity package (Sajó 1996: 35; Dethier and Shapiro 1998: 458).

Anticipation of such rulings led the pension reform teams to certain decisions about design. For example, in Hungary the reformers initially planned to require all workers below a cutoff age (in the mid-thirties) to direct part of their social security contributions to individual second-pillar accounts. However, later they decided to make contributions compulsory only for new workers entering the labor force (who did not yet have acquired rights in the old system), while letting current workers of any age choose whether to do so, thereby avoiding possible adverse judicial rulings (Dethier and Shapiro 1998: 463).

In Poland, in addition to the Constitutional Court and ombudsman, a legislative council advises the prime minister regarding the constitutionality of proposed legislation. Composed of established, mainly older lawyers, the council was familiar with Communist and traditional Western European social-security arrangements. Most of its members opposed the mandatory fully funded second pillar, which they regarded as contrary to the basic principles of solidarity and to state guarantees underlying a pension system. Some of their concerns were met by adding a state guarantee underwriting any deficits in the mandatory pension funds. Doubts that the new system even qualified as "social security" within the meaning of the constitution were resolved by noting that the PAYG pillar would continue to receive more than half of the mandatory contributions to the system.

Outcomes

Concessions to pressures from oversight institutions and varied interest groups substantially reshaped both Polish and Hungarian pension reforms from the ideas originally put forward by ministries of finance. But in both countries multipillar systems have replaced the single traditional PAYG approach. Hungary now has, in essence, a four-pillar system: "a 'zero' pillar consisting of a means-tested income guarantee for the old, financed from general taxes; a first pillar, consisting of an earnings-related PAYG, financed entirely from contributions; a second pillar, mandatory, private, and fully funded; and a voluntary pillar" (Palacios and Rocha 1998: 211). As a result of compromises regarding the allocation of workers' contributions between the first and second pillars, the new second pillar initially will receive only a quarter of pension contribution funds, while the first, PAYG pillar will continue to constitute the bulk of the system for many years into the future. The reforms also substantially modify the PAYG component, including a gradual increase in the normal retirement age to sixty-two (from sixty for men and fifty-five for women), an increase in minimum years of service for early retirement, and a slightly delayed change in the formula for indexing benefits (linking pensions to wages and prices equally, rather than solely to net wages).

In Poland, legislation approved in June and August 1997 creates a mandatory fully funded second pillar, authorizes and regulates a voluntary pension insurance system, and earmarks revenue from privatizations to help finance the costs of the transition to the new system. The second package of bills, approved in September 1998, creates notional individual accounts within a reformed PAYG first pillar and reduces or eliminates special privileges within that system for specific occupations. As in Hungary, the system offers workers in the middle generation (in Poland's case, between thirty and fifty) a choice between the old and new system. The parliamentary commission that reviewed the legislation rejected government proposals to change the age of retirement from sixty for women and sixty-five for men to sixty-two for all workers, but accepted the rest of the proposed legislation.

In both countries, critics from both sides – those opposing the concept of a multipillar system and those who would have preferred more rapid and thoroughgoing shifts to a fully funded system – were left dissatisfied with the outcomes. In Hungary the former group in particular felt marginalized by what it viewed as a steamroller process (Ferge 1997). But most major stakeholders felt that they had been consulted and had had an impact on the outcome. In short, the democratic process substantially molded but did not block major systemic reforms.

The Third Puzzle: Why Pensions but Not Health?

In both Hungary and Poland in 1998, it is often claimed that "health reform has not begun." That is an exaggerated view, especially in Hungary. There have, in fact, been major changes in health-care delivery. But in contrast to the stories of pension reform, to date there has not been a focused drive to establish a new model or vision for the sector. Therefore there is no compact "reform story" to be told.

Problems of the Sector and Attempts at Reform

Hungary and Poland inherited from the Communist era health-care delivery systems that provided universal coverage and some high-quality services but were also burdened with major inefficiencies. These included excessive emphasis on hospital care and excessive hospital capacity, a lack of long-term care facilities like nursing homes (adding to the pressure on hospitals), neglect of public health and healthy life-style programs, and too great reliance on medication, among many other problems. In both countries, as almost everywhere in the post-Communist world, patient copayments were virtually unknown but under-the-table "gratitude money" was ubiquitous, both to reduce waiting time and to obtain better service. Historical allocations and political jockeying largely determined the distribution of investment funds, and maintenance was widely underfunded and neglected.

In Hungary, a series of reforms considerably altered the health-care delivery system after 1989. But most of the changes proved to have severe flaws (Orosz, Ellena, and Jakab 1998: 227, box 8.2). Funding was switched from general taxes to compulsory insurance in 1990, collected jointly with pension contributions from workers and employers. As mentioned earlier, in 1992 the Social Insurance Fund was split into a Health Insurance Fund and a Pension Fund. The responsibilities and powers of the Health Insurance Fund were not entirely clear, and there were constant power struggles with the Ministry of Welfare and the Ministry of Finance. The fund also had chronic deficits. After the 1998 elections the Health Insurance Fund was placed under the authority of the prime minister's office.

Private practice was legalized in 1989. Many physicians with private patients free-ride on the public system, for instance, using the laboratory services and diagnostic facilities of public clinics or hospitals where they are also employed. The pharmaceuticals market was also liberalized. While products became much more available, their prices also soared, contributing to high public spending on health care. Ownership of public hospitals and clinics was transferred to local governments in 1990, but little control over financing and operations went with the legal titles. Primary care was reformed in 1992, converting district doctors to "family physicians," introducing capitation payment, and offering greater scope for patient choice, but primary doctors continue to offer mainly prescription and referral services. An attempt in 1995 to cut back on excess hospital capacity accomplished little but generated tremendous opposition among health workers and the public.

János Kornai (Chapter 6, in this volume) suggests that by the mid-1990s the health-care sector in Hungary displayed many of the characteristics of "market socialism" in the larger economy a decade earlier. Opaque and muddled property rights for facilities, tight wage controls, fixed service prices, the limited autonomy of the directors of operating units and frequent intervention from above, and soft budget constraints create an array of perverse incentives. A small private sector provides

254

choice and better-quality services for the wealthy and near wealthy; most of the population grumbles.

When the Hungarian Ministry of Finance began to press for pension reforms, in late 1995, it intended to tackle health-care delivery reforms as well. Indeed, health was viewed as the more important of the two, because the system provided greater scope for manipulation, was more opaque, and was subject to pressure from many lobbies. The double program proved too ambitious politically, and health reform was quietly dropped as a near-term goal. Indeed, it was a dispute between the reformist minister of finance Lajos Bokros and the remainder of the cabinet over the deficits of the Health Insurance Fund that triggered Bokros's resignation, although the underlying causes for his resignation were broader. By autumn 1997, however, with pension reform legislation safely passed, the Ministry of Finance appointed a new deputy state secretary whose primary responsibility was to plan and coordinate health-sector reforms if the government won reelection in May 1998. However, the elections put in power a new coalition, which promptly eliminated the autonomy of the pension and health insurance funds and split the former Ministry of Welfare.

In Poland, planned reforms in health-care delivery have been less extensive, although there has been considerable change in the actual system "by default" (Kochanowicz 1997: 5). Private practice and private hospitals were authorized in August 1991. By 1997 roughly half of Poland's 70,000 doctors split their time between public and private practice, while the remainder worked solely within the public system. Particularly in Warsaw, not only the wealthy but the middle classes increasingly turned to private practitioners. An estimated 40 percent of all resources spent on health care comes from out-of-pocket payments; that sum includes sizable copayments for medications and widespread illegal gratuities within the public system (Koronkiewicz, interview).

Most public health care is provided through the vovoidships or provinces, and by local integrated health-care management units. From 1992 on, health funds from the national budget bypassed the Ministry of Health and went directly to the vovoidships. A number of limited but important programs have been introduced to improve health-care provision, including measures to strengthen the role of primary-care physicians, encourage use of contracting, and experiment with integrated services that include prevention and public-education components.

Despite planned and unplanned changes, basic problems persist, and new ones have been introduced by the changes themselves. Health-care providers and the public are both deeply dissatisfied. Proposals for more far-reaching and integrated reforms have been debated since the beginning of the decade. In 1995 the Ministry of Health and Social Welfare prepared and the government approved legislation that would shift health-care funding largely to an insurance basis and restructure aspects of health-care administration. Meanwhile a small commission associated with the Solidarity opposition prepared a less detailed alternative approach reflecting the views of the physicians' union. This competing sketch was also submitted to the Sejm, through President Wałesa (Tymowska, interview). The Parliament established a special commission to develop an integrated proposal. In February 1997, after eighteen months of work including extensive consultations with many foreign experts, a bill establishing the broad outlines of a new national health-insurance system was approved by the legislature (Bossert and Wlodarczyk 2000: 13–15).

Yet even as the legislation was nearing completion, some within the government sought different changes. The mandate of the Government Plenipotentiary for Social Security Reform, established late in 1996, originally included health-sector reforms as well as pensions. The Ministry of Health strongly objected to what it viewed as an intrusion on its responsibilities. After the death of Minister of Labor and Plenipotentiary Bączkowski, the new plenipotentiary made clear that he would address health reforms only if the primary responsibility were assigned clearly to him and not to the minister of health. That was not politically feasible,[12] and the plenipotentiary therefore focused on pensions alone (Kornatowski, Rutkowski, interviews).

The new government that took office in autumn 1997 drafted legislation needed to implement the broad health-insurance reforms designed by the previous government. But it was critical of aspects of the earlier legislation. The coalition members also disagreed with each other, especially regarding the role of local governments in the new system (Tymowska, Kornatowski, interviews). Indeed, for years proposals for reorganizing the health care system were entangled with the broader issue of restructuring subnational governments and their relations with the center, and neither reform was able to move forward. In July 1998, however, a bill restructuring local government was finally passed. Legislation establishing independent public health-insurance funds and a new system of contracting for health services followed. But the Amended Health Insurance Act was partly inconsistent with the Public Administration Act on subnational government, and left important issues to be

---

[12] Among other factors, the minister of health was seriously ill at the time, and the prime minister was most reluctant to undercut his authority (Hausner, interview).

determined by future regulations (Bossert and Wlodarczyk 2000: 15–17). Dispute over specifics continues, and implementation has been extremely difficult.

In short, in both Hungary and Poland the need and demand for health-sector reforms have been strong, but decisive action has been difficult or impossible. What accounts for the contrasting histories of pension and health-care delivery reform efforts?

Political Obstacles to Reform: Multiple Powerful Interests

Proposals for health-care reforms affect a broad and varied array of vested interests. Given the widespread dissatisfaction with the systems, most of these groups seek not to block but to control change.

In both countries, the ministries of health tended to reflect the interests of specific groups of doctors, rather than a broader spectrum of health-care providers. In Poland under the SLD government, for instance, the ministry was strongly influenced by the medical elite associated with teaching hospitals (directly linked to the ministry). This influence was reflected in ministry proposals for revised administrative structure, carving the country into regions that corresponded with medical academy locations but not with other administrative units (Tymowska, interview). In Hungary, control over most aspects of health-care administration shifted from the Ministry of Welfare to the Health Insurance Fund when the latter was created in 1993. The division of responsibilities and power between the fund and the ministry became a chronic source of tension. In neither country was the ministry particularly powerful within the government.

Health care providers in both countries are fragmented, in part as a result of highly segmented and specialized Communist health-care systems (Ellena, interview). Doctors are divided along many lines: by primary care versus specialized services; by specific specialties; by engagement in private practice versus full-time public-sector employment. Doctors' interests also diverge from those of other medical workers. In Poland there are often ten or more unions represented in a single hospital (Tymowska, interview). Medical universities have their own (usually quite powerful) associations; so do financial directors of hospitals, various categories of nurses, and public-health workers. In principle the Medical Chamber provides an overarching organization. Although membership is compulsory for doctors, however, the chambers are not necessarily representative. In Poland, the chamber has often acted like a union, organizing strikes and demonstrations. Many doctors are indifferent to or alienated from the chamber, and very few take part in its elections (Tymowska, interview).

In both countries, medical workers in general regard themselves as seriously underpaid, and they have indeed suffered substantial drops in the real value of their official salaries. Gratitude money and fees for private practice partly counterbalance dwindling real salaries but are extremely unequally distributed. Many health-care providers feel that funding is the root of the sector's problems, although awareness of the need for cost consciousness and efficiency is growing (Orosz, interview). Many also want to keep the security of public-service jobs, at the same time that they would like higher incomes and greater autonomy.

In both Hungary and Poland, local and provincial governments also have major stakes in the precise design of health-care reforms. In Poland, expenditures on health account for more than half of all expenditures at the level of the vovoidships or provinces (Kornatowski, interview). Health services are also a major function of the much smaller g'minas.[13] Even modest changes – for instance, pressure to make more use of contracting – may make vovoidship officials nervous, because they lack experience and fear that choosing one provider rather than another may provoke protests (Łuczak, interview). Subnational officials are understandably wary of proposals that increase their responsibilities without commensurate increases in authority and funding. More radical shifts in unit boundaries, or in the responsibilities and funding sources of existing units, have sweeping implications for control over jobs, money, assets, and political relationships.

The pharmaceutical sector – domestic and foreign manufacturers and distributors, and pharmacists themselves – are also obvious interested parties in health reforms. In both Hungary and Poland, excessive prescription is a serious weakness of the health-care system; coupled with rising prices, this is also a major source of increased costs. Both countries have addressed the problem partly through increased reliance on patient copayments. In turn, that has prompted concerns about the burden on the poor. Hungarian attempts to compensate through means-tested subsidies have led to widespread cheating (Orosz et al. 1998: 242–43).

Public opinion is also broadly and intensely engaged by proposed reforms in health-care arrangements. Commitment to free public service has probably been eroded in both countries by the growing use of private care and the prevailing practice of gratitude money for public providers. Surveys indicate strong public support in Poland for shifting to an insur-

---

[13] G'minas were the smallest unit for Polish local government until restructuring in late 1998.

ance system of funding, though it is difficult to judge whether the support reflects realistic expectations regarding the effects of such a shift. Other kinds of changes, however, may well prompt public outcries. For instance, when in 1995 the Hungarian government attempted to rationalize and reduce the number of hospital beds and to close some of the least efficient clinics and hospitals, there was strong popular resistance from those who had been using the targeted centers.

As with pension reforms, oversight institutions also are political players. For example, the ill-fated Hungarian attempt to cut back on hospital beds was complicated by the fact that the Constitutional Court ruled the cuts could not be carried out through a simple administrative regulation. Instead, the court required a detailed law to be presented to the Parliament, specifying how many beds were to be cut in each local jurisdiction. The predictable result was to mobilize intense local opposition (Ellena, interview).

Unassertive External Players

External forces have been much less active in promoting health than pension reforms. Many international, bilateral governmental and non-governmental agencies and groups provide technical and financial assistance to the health sector in Eastern Europe. Most of these focus on specific projects; few address broader health policies and strategies. Among these few, the World Bank has played the leading role. Even the World Bank, however, has not pursued a sharply focused sector strategy in either country (Ellena, interview; World Bank 1997). Moreover, the bank's frustration with the Hungarian government's poorly thought through reform attempts (such as the attempt to cut hospital beds) contributed to the 1996 decision to remove health-sector components from a large Public Sector Adjustment Loan.

The Missing Blueprint

Closely linked to the absence of assertive external influence is the fact that there is no dominant model for health-care delivery reforms analogous to the recent international semiconsensus regarding multipillar pension systems. Health systems vary widely among wealthy nations. Almost all confront serious problems and provoke widespread criticism from care providers and the public. Although there may be considerable agreement on broad principles and goals, and no shortage of proposals to address specific issues, in most countries there is no blueprint or even a "vision" of an improved system that commands broad consensus.

In both Hungary and Poland, we have seen that the conflict between two fairly clear broad concepts of pension reform structured debate and shaped decision making. The international semiconsensus regarding the desirability of the multipillar system not only bolstered the conviction of the proponents of the concept but also prompted direct and vigorous World Bank and other external support.

In contrast, during interviews in Hungary and Poland, half a dozen health-sector specialists remarked, spontaneously and not in response to specific questions, that there was as yet no broad vision of a better-functioning and sustainable health-care delivery system (Orosz, Csaba, Ellena, Kornatowski, Łuczak, and Tymowska, interviews). The inconclusive course of reform proposals in Poland illustrates not merely absence of agreement on a single approach, but a process that might be described as groping for approaches. Presumably the Hungarian Ministry of Finance had in mind precisely the need for a vision of health-sector reform, when it commissioned a book-length study by prominent economist János Kornai. That book, written to be accessible to the general public and published early in 1998, may indeed help to structure and advance public debate in Hungary.

The difficulties of formulating a blueprint for health-care delivery reform are rooted in the character of the sector. They flow not only from the structure of the sector, with its many levels of operation and stakeholders, but also from the complexity of health-care objectives and the difficulties of measurement and valuation. Like education, health-care delivery serves multiple goals and constituents. It is difficult to reduce the trade-offs among groups and goals to a common denominator. How shall resources be divided between improved care for children or the elderly? Principles of equity and solidarity demand that certain services and facilities be available to everyone, but how generous should that guaranteed package be? There are no adequate technical answers to these and similar questions.

Moreover, again like education and in much greater degree than pensions, health programs produce not only crucial individual benefits but also tremendously important public goods. The public-goods component implies a major role for the public sector, but the division of responsibilities among public (national and subnational) agencies, private for-profit agents, voluntary organizations, households, and individuals is highly flexible and immensely controversial (Kornai, Chapter 6, in this volume).

Given these complexities and characteristics, neoliberal economic concepts and approaches that have provided the paradigm for many of the institutional reforms in market-oriented structural adjustment may apply only partially and with substantial caveats in the health sector. And, as Kochanowicz notes, liberal analysts have given much less attention to reform of social sectors and welfare provision than to macroeconomic policies and directly productive economic sectors. The appeal of Western European social democratic models has dwindled with the growing crisis of the Western welfare state; even in strongly Catholic Poland no clear Christian Democratic approach has been articulated. But the now-dominant neoliberal intellectual current provides only partial and uncertain guidance (Kochanowicz 1997: 5).

Some Implications for the Process of Social-Sector Reforms

As more post-Communist countries move beyond initial stabilization and liberalization, social transformation issues will become increasingly central. This study uses a simple two-country, two-sector set of comparisons to explore some of the factors that ease or hamper far-reaching social-sector reforms. The contrasts between rather radical reforms in pension systems and fragmented and inconclusive change in the health sector reflect differences in intrinsic complexity, in centralized versus decentralized administration and delivery, in the variety and commitment of vested interests, in the availability of clear-cut "models" to focus proposals and debate, and in the role of external influence.

On all these dimensions, pension reform is "easier" than health-sector reform. Pension systems are much less complex administratively, nor do they generate large, powerfully organized providers' associations. In recent years a fairly clear-cut, though not uncontroversial model or vision of pension reform has helped to structure national debates. Powerful external actors, both public and private, often directly or indirectly support application of that model in specific countries. Nevertheless, in both Hungary and Poland pension reform required extensive debate, consultation, and compromise. More generally, in democracies, reforms in social sectors and especially in social services (health and education) are likely to demand extraordinary efforts to develop at least partial consensus on the broad outlines of new arrangements and to encourage coalitions willing to support specific building blocks.

The process of social-sector reforms may affect not only the sustainability of the reforms themselves but also the broader consolidation of democratic government. Put slightly differently, the manner and channels through which reforms are designed, adopted, implemented, assessed, and modified will be viewed by citizens as partial evidence of how well their political system is working.

To some extent, of course, this applies to all reforms and, indeed, to any significant change in economic policies. A government that decides most major economic and social policies behind closed doors and resorts to decrees to sidestep public debate and legislative approval forfeits the legitimacy that democratic processes can generate, even if the economic decisions themselves produce generally good results. If the pattern is long continued, citizens are likely to regard their country's democratic institutions as flawed and weak.

However, public opinion in democracies will accept top-down decision making in some matters more than others. People expect policy decisions widely viewed as arcane, requiring highly specialized knowledge, to be made by "the experts." Top-down decision making is also more acceptable to address problems viewed as urgent, where the costs of delay are obvious. Most of the public therefore regards it as appropriate that decisions regarding macroeconomic policies should be made by a small circle of high-level officials, especially in a crisis. On issues that they believe they understand in greater degree, and where there is no obvious reason for rapid action, citizens in democracies are much more likely to expect open debate and consultation. Social-sector issues in general fit this description.

At the same time, many social-sector reforms bear directly on widespread and deeply felt fears, hopes, or values. It is often noted that social-security reforms are difficult because they affect entitlements. In the post-Communist world, however, many, perhaps particularly younger people, doubt the capacity of their country's institutions and economies actually to deliver the pensions, health care, and other benefits required by law. Their doubts open space for reforms.

Although belief in entitlements may be less of an obstacle to reforms in some post-Communist countries than is often assumed, proposals for reorienting social services and transfer programs nevertheless rouse powerful emotions. The wrenching transformation of the past decade has increased opportunity, liberty, and affluence for many. But transformation has also sharply increased inequality and – perhaps more important – insecurity for much of the population. Most middle-strata people who have managed to maintain, recover, or increase their incomes must nonetheless worry about job security, declining quality of public-health and education services, and pension systems that look increasingly inadequate. Private insurance is still unfamiliar, often unavailable, and for many unaffordable.

Almost all concrete social sector reforms will generate considerable opposition and even broader skepticism, unless and until they produce clear-cut benefits. Procedural legitimacy – the widespread perception that not only the formal rules but also the spirit of open and fair debate were observed, and that all major interested groups had an opportunity to state their case – is probably a more obtainable goal than broad consensus on specific designs. It may well be that the minimum political requirements for sustainable social-sector reforms therefore coincide with what is needed to maintain or deepen confidence in the political system's capacity to heed and, at least partially, to respond to widely felt concerns. Such a double reward for attention to the *process* – and not only the design – of reform may be one of the few optimistic conclusions growing out of this most complex and daunting set of issues.

References

Bossert, Thomas, and Cesary Wlodarczyk. 2000, January. Unpredictable Politics: Policy Process of Health Reform in Poland. Unpublished manuscript.

Deacon, Bob. 1996. *Global and Regional Agencies and the Making of Post-Communist Social Policy in Eastern Europe.* Robert Schuman Centre Working Paper No. 45. San Domenico, Italy: European University Institute.

Dethier, Jean-Jacques, and Tamar Shapiro. 1998. Constitutional Rights and the Reform of Social Entitlements. In L. Bokros and J.-J. Dethier, eds., *Public Finance Reform during the Transition: The Experience of Hungary*, pp. 448–76. Washington, D.C.: World Bank.

Ferge, Zsuzsa. 1997. *The Actors of the Hungarian Pension Reform.* Paper prepared for the Fifth Central European Forum organized by the Institute of Human Studies, Vienna, October 24–25.

Gesell, Rainer, Katharina Müller, and Dirck Süß. 1998. *Social Security Reform and Privatisation in Poland: Parallel Projects or Integrated Agenda?* Frankfurt Institute for Transformation Studies (FIT), Discussion Paper No. 9. Frankfurt/Oder: European University Viadrina.

Kochanowicz, Jacek. 1997. Incomplete Demise: Reflections on the Welfare State in Poland after Communism. Unpublished manuscript.

Kołodko, Grzegorz. 1996. *Poland 2000: The New Economic Strategy.* Warsaw: Poltext Publishers.

Kopits, George. 1992. Social Security. In V. Tanzi, ed., *Fiscal Policies in Economies in Transition*, pp. 291–311. Washington, D.C.: International Monetary Fund.

Kornai, János. 1996. Paying the Bill for Goulash Communism: Hungarian Development and Macro Stabilization in a Political-Economy Perspective. *Social Research* 63: 943–1040.

1998. *Az egészségügy reformjáról* (On the reform of the health-care system). Budapest: Közgazdasági és Jogi Könyvkiadó.

Müller, Katharina. 1998. *Changing the Public–Private Mix: Central-Eastern European Pension Reforms.* Paper prepared for the workshop Transformation of Social Security: Pensions in Central-Eastern Europe, Berlin, March 27–28, sponsored by the Frankfurter Institute für Transformationsstudien, Europa-Universität Viadrina.

Orosz, Éva, Guy Ellena, and Melitta Jakab. 1998. Reforming the Health Care System: The Unfinished Agenda. In L. Bokros and J.-J. Dethier, eds., *Public Finance Reform during the Transition: The Experience of Hungary*, pp. 222–54. Washington, D.C.: World Bank.

Palacios, Robert, and Roberto Rochas. 1998. The Hungarian Pension System in Transition. In L. Bokros and J.-J. Dethier, eds., *Public Finance Reform during the Transition: The Experience of Hungary*, pp. 177–220. Washington, D.C.: World Bank.

Phare. 1997. *Pension Systems and Reforms: Britain, Hungary, Italy, Poland, Sweden.* Budapest: European Commission Phare ACE Programme Research Project P95-2139-R.

Sajó, András. 1996. How the Rule of Law Killed Hungarian Welfare Reform. *East European Constitutional Review* 5, no. 1 (Winter): 31–41.

Security. 1997. *Security through Diversity: Reform of the Pension System in Poland.* Warsaw: Office of the Government Plenipotentiary for Social Security Reform.

Slay, Ben, and Louisa Vinton. 1997. *Poland to 2005: The Challenge of Europe.* Vienna: Economist Intelligence Unit.

World Bank. 1992. *Hungary: Reform of Social Policy and Expenditures.* Washington, D.C.: World Bank.

——— 1994. *Averting the Old Age Crisis.* Oxford: Oxford University Press, for the World Bank.

——— 1997. *Poland: Country Assistance Review.* Washington, D.C.: World Bank Operations Evaluation Department.

Interviews

Hungary

Augusztinovics, Mária, Institute of Economics, Hungarian Academy of Sciences. October 27, 1997.

Bauer, Tamás, Professor, Johann Wolfgang Goethe University, Frankfurt. Member of Parliament. November 19, 1997.

Bokros, Lajos, World Bank, Washington, D.C.; former Minister of Finance. November 11, 1997.

Bruszt, László, Professor, Department of Political Science, Central European University, and Fellow, Collegium Budapest. October 15, 1997.

Csaba, Iván, Professor, Department of Political Science, Central European University. November 18, 1997.

Dethier, Jean-Jacques, World Bank, Washington, D.C. September 18, 1997.

Ellena, Guy, World Bank Regional Office, Budapest. October 7, 1997.

Ferge, Zsuzsa, Professor, Department of Sociology, Eötvös Loránd University. December 1, 1997.

Gál, Róbert, TÁRKI (Social Research Informatics Center). October 29, 1997.

Gere, Adam, Investment banker, Boston. First director of the Hungarian Ministry of Finance pension reform group. October 18, 1997.

Greskovits, Béla, Professor, Department of Political Science, Central European University, and Fellow, Collegium Budapest. October 20 and December 1, 1997.

Győrfi, István, General Director, Financial Postgraduate Training and Publishing Co., Ltd., and former staff director of the interdepartmental task force for pension reform. November 9 and December 10, 1997.

Jakabs, Melitta, Harvard School of Public Health, and former health policy staff assistant, World Bank Regional Mission, Budapest. November 12, 1997.

Kornai, János, Permanent Fellow, Collegium Budapest, and Professor, Department of Economics, Harvard University. October 9, November 3, December 9, 1997.

Ladó, Mária, Director, Institute for Labor Research, Ministry of Labor. November 5, 1997.

Long, Millard, Financial Sector Advisor, and former Resident Representative, World Bank Regional Office, Budapest. May 21 and November 25, 1996; October 1 and November 1, 1997.

Major, Mária, Deputy Secretary of State for Economy, Ministry of Welfare. December 3, 1997.

Matits, Ágnes, Pension fund advisor, William M. Mercer Kft., Budapest. March 25, 1998.

Mihályi, Péter, Deputy State Secretary, Ministry of Finance. November 5, 1997.

Orosz, Éva, Ministry of Welfare, World Bank Project Management Unit. December 3, 1997.

Preker, Alex, World Bank, Washington, D.C. November 10, 1997.

Róbert, Péter, Head of Department, TÁRKI (Social Research Informatics Center). October 29, 1997.

Rocha, Roberto, Principal Economist, World Bank Regional Office, Budapest. October 17 and December 3, 1997.

Sándor, Judit, Professor, Department of Political Science, Central European University. October 30, 1997.

Spat, Judit. Pension reform specialist, World Bank Regional Office, Budapest. March 26, 1998.

Tóth, István György, Director, TÁRKI (Social Research Informatics Center). October 29, 1997.

Ungár, Klára, Member of Parliament. December 12, 1997.

Poland

Chłon, Agnieszka, Senior Research Officer, Office of the Government Plenipotentiary for Social Security Reform. November 25, 1997.

Góra, Marek, Director, Office of the Government Plenipotentiary for Social Security Reform. May 15, 1997.

Hagemejer, Krzysztof, Social Security Specialist, International Labour Office, Central and Eastern European Team, Budapest. December 8, 1997.

Hausner, Jerzy, Chairman of the Board, Research Centre for Public Economy and Administration, Cracow University of Economics, and former

Plenipotentiary for Social Security Reform. November 28, 1997; March 24, 1998.

Kochanowicz, Jacek, Professor and Associate Dean, Department of Economics, University of Warsaw. Several conversations, week of November 24–29, 1997.

Kolarska, Lena, Director, Institute for Policy Studies. November 25, 1997.

Kornatowski, Michał, Secretary of State (Deputy Minister), Ministry of Health. November 27, 1997.

Koronkiewicz, Andrzej, National Center for Health System Management. November 24, 1997.

Kostkiewicz, Zygmunt, President, Insurance Company "Polisa." November 27, 1997.

Kuszewski, Krzysztof, National Center for Health System Management, and former Deputy Minister of Health and Social Welfare. November 24, 1997.

Łuczak, Jacek, Doctor. Dean of Department of Economics and Organization of Health, School of Insurance and Administration. November 26, 1997.

Myjak, Jarosław, First Vice-President, Commercial Union. November 25, 1997.

Rutkowski, Michal, President, "STU" Insurance Co. and President of the Board of the Insurance and Assurance Association. November 27, 1997.

Surdej, Aleksander, Assistant Professor, Cracow University of Economics. November 28, 1997.

Topińska, Irina, Professor, Department of Economics, Warsaw University, and Office of the Government Plenipotentiary for Social Security Reform. Several conversations, week of November 24–29, 1997.

Tymowska, Katarzyna, Professor, Department of Economics, University of Warsaw. November 26, 1997.

Appendix

Compiled by Cecilia Hornok.

Table A.1. *Growth in Real GDP in Eastern Europe, the Baltics, and the CIS*

	Percent Change in Real GDP							Estimated Level of Real GDP in 1997 (1989 = 100)	Projected Level of Real GDP in 1998 (1989 = 100)
	1992	1993	1994	1995	1996	1997	1998		
Albania	-7.2	9.6	9.4	8.9	9.1	-7.0	10.0	80	88
Bulgaria	-7.3	-1.5	1.8	2.1	-10.9	-6.9	4.0	63	66
Croatia	-11.7	-8.0	5.9	6.8	6.0	6.5	4.8	76	80
Czech Republic	-3.3	0.6	3.2	6.4	3.9	1.0	-0.5	98	98
Estonia	-14.2	-9.0	-2.0	4.3	4.0	11.4	5.0	73	77
FYR Macedonia	-21.1	-9.1	-1.8	-1.2	0.8	1.5	5.0	56	59
Hungary	-3.1	-0.6	2.9	1.5	1.3	4.4	4.6	90	95
Latvia	-34.9	-14.9	0.6	-0.8	3.3	6.5	4.0	56	58
Lithuania	-21.3	-16.2	-9.8	3.3	4.7	5.7	3.0	61	63
Poland	2.6	3.8	5.2	7.0	6.1	6.9	5.2	112	118
Romania	-8.7	1.5	3.9	7.1	4.1	-6.6	-5.2	82	78
Slovak Republic	-6.5	-3.7	4.9	6.9	6.6	6.5	5.0	95	100
Slovenia	-5.5	2.8	5.3	4.1	3.1	3.8	4.0	99	103
Eastern Europe and the Baltic States[a]	-3.8	0.4	3.9	5.5	4.0	3.6	3.1	96	99
Armenia	-52.6	-14.8	5.4	6.9	5.8	3.1	6.0	38	40
Azerbaijan	-22.6	-23.1	-19.7	-11.8	1.3	5.8	6.7	40	42
Belarus	-9.6	-7.6	-12.6	-10.4	2.8	10.4	5.0	71	75
Georgia	-44.8	-25.4	-11.4	2.4	10.5	11.0	9.0	32	35
Kazakhstan	-2.9	-9.2	-12.6	-8.2	0.5	2.0	1.0	63	63
Kyrgyzstan	-19.0	-16.0	-20.0	-5.4	7.1	6.5	4.0	57	60
Moldova	-29.1	-1.2	-31.2	-3.0	-8.0	1.3	-2.0	35	34

(continued)

Table A.1 (continued)

	Percent Change in Real GDP							Estimated Level of Real GDP in 1997 (1989 = 100)	Projected Level of Real GDP in 1998 (1989 = 100)
	1992	1993	1994	1995	1996	1997	1998		
Russia	-14.5	-8.7	-12.7	-4.1	-3.5	0.8	-5.0	58	55
Tajikistan	-29.0	-11.0	-18.9	-12.5	-4.4	1.7	3.4	40	41
Turkmenistan	-5.3	-10.0	-18.8	-8.2	-8.0	-26.0	5.0	42	44
Ukraine	-13.7	-14.2	-23.0	-12.2	-10.0	-3.2	0.0	37	37
Uzbekistan	-11.1	-2.3	-4.2	-0.9	1.6	2.4	2.0	87	88
Commonwealth of Independent States[b]	-14.2	-8.9	-13.1	-4.6	-3.4	0.9	-3.6	57	55
Eastern Europe, the Baltics, and the CIS	-9.5	-4.7	-5.4	-0.1	-0.2	2.0	-1.0	73	72

Notes: Data for 1990–96 represent the most recent official estimates of outturns as reflected in publications from the national authorities, the IMF, the World Bank, the OECD, PlanEcon, and the Institute of International Finance. Data for 1997 are preliminary actuals mostly official government estimates. Data for 1998 represent EBRD projections. Estimates of growth for Bosnia-Herzegovina are available only since 1995 and therefore are not included in this summary table.

[a] Estimates for real GDP represent weighted averages for Albania, Bulgaria, Croatia, the Czech Republic, Estonia, FYR Macedonia, Hungary, Latvia, Lithuania, Poland, Romania, the Slovak Republic, and Slovenia. The weights used were EBRD estimates of nominal dollar-GDP lagged by one year.

[b] Here taken to include all countries of the former Soviet Union except Estonia, Latvia, and Lithuania. Estimates of real GDP represent weighted averages. The weights used were EBRD estimates of nominal dollar-GDP lagged by one year.

Source: Economics of Transition 6, no. 2 (1998): 544.

Appendix

Table A.2. *Inflation in Eastern Europe, the Baltics, and the CIS (change in year-end retail/consumer price level in percentage)*

	1992	1993	1994	1995	1996	1997 Est.	1998 Proj.
Albania	236.6	30.9	15.8	6.0	17.4	42.1	10.0
Bulgaria	79.4	63.8	121.9	32.9	310.8	578.5	10.0
Croatia	938.2	1,149.0	−3.0	3.8	3.4	3.8	5.7
Czech Republic	12.7	18.2	9.7	7.9	8.6	10.0	9.0
Estonia	953.5	35.6	42.0	29.0	15.0	12.0	8.0
FYR Macedonia	1,925.2	229.6	55.4	9.0	−0.6	2.6	5.0
Hungary	21.6	21.1	21.2	28.3	19.8	18.4	13.5
Latvia	959.0	35.0	26.0	23.1	13.1	7.0	4.6
Lithuania	1,161.1	188.8	45.0	35.5	13.1	8.5	4.2
Poland	44.3	37.6	29.4	21.6	18.5	13.2	10.0
Romania	199.2	295.5	61.7	27.8	56.9	151.4	45.0
Slovak Republic	9.1	25.1	11.7	7.2	5.4	6.4	7.2
Slovenia	92.9	22.8	19.5	9.0	9.0	8.8	7.0
Eastern Europe and the Baltic States							
Median	199.2	35.6	26.0	21.6	13.1	10.0	8.0
Mean	510.2	165.6	35.1	18.5	37.7	66.4	10.7
Armenia	n.a.	10,896.0	1,885.0	31.9	5.8	21.8	6.5
Azerbaijan	1,395.0	1,293.8	1,788.0	84.5	6.5	0.4	3.9
Belarus	1,159.0	1,996.0	1,960.0	244.0	39.0	63.0	60.0
Georgia	1,176.9	7,487.9	6,474.4	57.4	14.3	7.1	5.0
Kazakhstan	2,984.1	2,169.0	1,160.0	60.4	28.6	11.3	10.0
Kyrgyzstan	1,259.0	1,363.0	95.7	31.9	35.0	14.7	12.0
Moldova	2,198.0	837.0	116.0	23.8	15.1	11.2	12.0
Russia	2,506.1	840.0	204.4	128.6	21.8	10.9	89.0
Tajikistan	1,364.0	7,344.0	1.1	2,133.0	40.5	163.6	10.1
Turkmenistan	644.0	9,750.0	1,328.0	1,262.0	446.0	21.5	28.0
Ukraine	2,730.0	10,155.0	401.0	182.0	39.7	10.1	22.0
Uzbekistan	910.0	885.0	1,281.0	117.0	64.0	50.0	33.0
Commonwealth of Independent States							
Median	1,364.0	2,082.5	1,220.5	100.8	31.8	13.0	12.0
Mean	1,666.0	4,584.7	1,391.2	363.0	63.0	32.1	32.6

Notes: Data for 1992–93 represent the most recent official estimates of outturns as reflected in publications from the national authorities, the IMF, the World Bank, the OECD, PlanEcon, and the Institute of International Finance. Data for 1997 are preliminary actuals mostly official government estimates. Data for 1998 represent EBRD projections. Figures for Albania for 1997 are based on the information from parts of the country where data collection was possible. The median is the middle value after all inflation rates have been arranged in order of size.

Source: Economics of Transition 6, no. 2 (1998): 545.

271

Table A.3. *General Government Balances in Eastern Europe, the Baltics, and the CIS*

	Balance as Percentage of GDP							Percent Change 1996–97	Percent Change 1997–98
	1992	1993	1994	1995	1996	1997 Est.	1998 Proj.		
Albania	-20.3	-14.4	-12.4	-10.3	-12.1	-12.7	-13.9	-0.6	-1.2
Bulgaria	-5.2	-10.9	-5.8	-5.6	-10.4	-2.1	-2.0	8.3	0.1
Croatia	-3.9	-0.8	1.6	-0.9	-0.4	-1.3	-0.5	-0.9	0.8
Czech Republic	-3.1	0.5	-1.2	-1.8	-1.2	-2.1	-2.4	-0.9	-0.3
Estonia	-0.3	-0.7	1.3	-1.3	-1.5	2.2	2.5	3.7	0.3
FYR Macedonia	-9.6	-13.8	-2.9	-1.2	-0.5	-0.4	-0.8	0.1	-0.4
Hungary	-6.8	-5.5	-8.4	-6.7	-3.5	-4.6	-4.9	-1.1	-0.3
Latvia	-0.8	0.6	-4.0	-3.3	-1.4	1.3	-1.9	2.7	-3.2
Lithuania	0.5	-3.3	-5.5	-4.5	-4.5	-1.8	-3.6	2.7	-1.8
Poland	-6.7	-3.1	-3.1	-2.8	-3.3	-3.1	-3.1	0.2	0.0
Romania	-4.6	-0.4	-1.9	-2.6	-3.9	-4.5	-5.5	-0.6	-1.0
Slovak Republic	n.a.	-7.0	-1.3	0.2	-1.9	-3.1	-2.7	-1.2	0.4
Slovenia	0.2	0.3	-0.2	0.0	0.3	-1.1	-1.0	-1.4	0.1
Eastern Europe and the Baltic States[a]	-5.1	-4.5	-3.4	-3.1	-3.4	-2.6	-3.1	0.8	-0.5

Armenia	-13.9	-54.7	-10.5	-11.0	-9.3	-6.3	-5.8	3.0	0.5
Azerbaijan	n.a.	-15.3	-12.1	-4.9	-2.8	-1.7	-3.6	1.1	-1.9
Belarus	0.0	-1.9	-2.5	-1.9	-1.6	-2.1	-3.0	-0.5	-0.9
Georgia	-25.4	-26.2	-7.4	-4.5	-4.4	-3.8	-2.5	0.6	1.3
Kazakhstan	-7.3	-1.4	-7.2	-2.5	-3.1	-3.7	-5.5	-0.6	-1.8
Kyrgyzstan	n.a.	n.a.	n.a.	-17.0	-9.0	-9.4	-8.1	-0.4	1.3
Moldova	-26.2	-7.4	-8.7	-5.7	-6.7	-7.5	-8.0	-0.8	-0.5
Russia	-4.1	-4.2	-9.0	-5.7	-8.3	-7.4	-9.0	0.9	-1.6
Tajikistan	-28.4	-23.6	-10.2	-11.2	-5.8	-3.3	-3.3	2.5	0.0
Turkmenistan	13.2	-0.5	-1.4	-1.6	-0.2	0.0	-4.0	0.2	-4.0
Ukraine	-25.4	-16.2	-9.1	-7.1	-3.2	-5.6	-3.0	-2.4	2.6
Uzbekistan	-18.4	-10.4	-6.1	-4.1	-7.3	-2.3	-3.0	5.0	-0.7
Commonwealth of Independent States[a]	-13.6	-14.7	-7.7	-6.4	-5.1	-4.4	-4.9	0.7	-0.5

Notes: Data for 1990–96 represent the most recent official estimates of outturns as reflected in publications from the national authorities, the IMF, the World Bank, the OECD, PlanEcon, and the Institute of International Finance. Data for 1997 are preliminary actuals mostly official government estimates. Data for 1998 represent EBRD projections. Figure for Albania for 1997 is based on the information from parts of the country where data collection was possible.

[a] Unweighted average for the region.

Source: *Economics of Transition* 6, no. 2 (1998): 546.

273

Table A.4. Current-Account Balances of Eastern Europe, the Baltic Countries, and European Members of the CIS, 1994–97

	Balance in Millions of Dollars					Percentage of GDP				
	1994	1995	1996	1996	Jan.–Sept. 1997[a]	1994	1995	1996	1996	Jan.–Sept. 1997[a]
Eastern Europe[b]	—	-1,389	-7,387	-13,466	—	—	-0.4	-3.1	-4.0	—
Former presentation[c]	-4,203	-9,143	-8,521	-20,619	—	-1.6	-2.8	-5.4	—	—
Albania	-43	-15	-85	-100	61	-2.4	-0.6	-4.3	-3.8	2.3
Bosnia and Herzegovina	-189	-134	—	—	—	—	—	—	—	—
Bulgaria[d]	-25	-26	-34	-50	—	-0.3	-0.2	-0.5	-0.5	—
Croatia	103	-1,711	-745	-1,129[a]	-1,239	0.7	-9.5	-5.3	-6.1	-6.6
Czech Republic	-50	-1,362	-3,083	-4,476[e]	-6,500— -7,500[f]	-0.1	-2.9	-8.0	-8.7	-1.1— -12.8[f]
Hungary[d]	3,911	-2,480	-1,104	-1,678	-1,500— -2,500[f]	-9.4	-5.7	-3.3	-3.8	-1.8— -3.0[f]
Poland[c d]	—	5,455	-311	-1,352	-3,900— -7,800[f]	—	4.6	-0.3	-1.0	-2.6— -5.5[f]
Former presentation	-944	-2,299	-5,828	-8,505	—	-1.0	-1.9	-6.1	—	—
Romania	-428	-1,639	-713	-2,336[e]	-1,375	-1.4	-4.6	-2.7	-6.6	-4.5
Slovakia	712	646	-1,032	-1,900[e]	-2,000[f]	5.2	3.7	-7.2	-10.0	-10.5[f]
Slovenia	540	-36	68	46	-35	3.8	-0.2	0.5	0.3	-0.2
FYR Macedonia	-158	-222	-348	-491	—	-5.7	-6.2	-13.2	-14.0	—

Baltic States	-67	-827	-908	—	-0.7	-5.9	-7.2	—	—
Estonia	-178	-185	-223	—	-7.7	-5.1	-7.0	—	—
Latvia	201	-27	-273	—	5.5	-0.6	-7.1	—	—
Lithuania	-90	-614	-412	-481	-2.1	-10.3	-7.4	—	-5.5
CIS									
Belarus	-506	-567	-752	—	-10.3	-5.5	-7.6	—	—
Republic of Moldova	-82	-115	-134	-180	-5.8	-6.8	-11.2	—	-11.3
Russian Federation	11,378	9,306	10,243	—	4.1	2.6	3.1	—	—
Non-CIS	8,205	9,410	11,090	—	—	—	—	—	—
Ukraine	-1,161	-1,152	-553	—	-3.1	-3.2	-1.7	—	—

[a] Official forecasts.
[b] Includes revised data for Poland. Eastern Europe aggregate excludes Bosnia and Herzegovina.
[c] Revised data for Poland.
[d] Convertible currencies; Hungary until 1995.
[e] Preliminary.
[f] Independent forecasts.

Source: The United Nations is the author of the original material. From *The Survey of Europe in 1996–1997* (New York: United Nations, 1997), p. 149, table 3.6.1.

Table A.5. *Official Estimates of the Private Sector's Contribution to GDP in Selected Transition Countries, 1991–96 (percent)*

	1991	1992	1993	1994	1995	1996
Bulgaria	27	38	41	42	48	—
Czech Republic	17	28	45	56	66	75[a]
Hungary	30	47	55	60	65	75
Poland	42	47	52	53	58	—
Romania	24	26	32	39	45	52
Slovakia[b]	—	22	26	58	65	77[a]
Yugoslavia	—	—	—	33	—	—
Latvia	—	—	—	55	—	—
Lithuania	16	37	57	62	65	—
Kyrgyzstan	26	28	39	43	—	—
Republic of Moldova	—	—	—	—	—	—
Russian Federation	—	14	21	62	70	—

[a] January–September.
[b] Employment including cooperative sector and entrepreneurs.
Source: The United Nations is the author of the original material. From *The Survey of Europe in 1996–1997* (New York: United Nations, 1997), p. 92, table 3.2.4.

Table A.6. *Share of the Unofficial Economy in GDP, 1989–95, Selected Transition Economies (percent)*

	1989	1990	1991	1992	1993	1994	1995
Azerbaijan	12.0	21.9	22.7	39.2	51.2	58.0	60.6
Belarus	12.0	15.4	16.6	13.2	11.0	18.9	19.3
Bulgaria	22.8	25.1	23.9	25.0	29.9	29.1	36.2
Czech Republic	6.0	6.7	12.9	16.9	16.9	17.6	11.3
Estonia	12.0	19.9	26.2	25.4	24.1	25.1	11.8
Georgia	12.0	24.9	36.0	52.3	61.0	63.5	62.6
Hungary	27.0	28.0	32.9	30.6	28.5	27.7	29.0
Kazakhstan	12.0	17.0	19.7	24.9	27.2	34.1	34.3
Latvia	12.0	12.8	19.0	34.3	31.0	34.2	35.3
Lithuania	12.0	11.3	21.8	39.2	31.7	28.7	21.6
Moldova	12.0	18.1	27.1	37.3	34.0	39.7	35.7
Poland	15.7	196.0	23.5	19.7	18.5	15.2	12.6
Romania	22.3	13.7	15.7	18.0	16.4	17.4	19.1
Slovak Republic	6.0	7.7	15.1	17.6	16.2	14.6	5.8
Russia	12.0	14.7	23.5	32.8	36.7	40.3	41.6
Ukraine	12.0	16.3	25.6	33.6	38.0	45.7	48.9
Uzbekistan	12.0	11.4	7.8	11.7	10.1	9.5	6.5

Notes: The share of the unofficial economy is defined over total GDP – that is, correcting official GDP for estimates of the change in the unofficial economy derived from data on electricity consumption. The 1989 data come from two survey studies conducted in the late 1980s.

Source: EBRD Transition Report, 1997 (London: EBRD, 1997), p. 74.

Table A.7. *Progress and Methods of Privatization of Medium-Sized and Large Enterprises*

	EBRD Large-Scale Privatization Transition Indicator Score	Sale to Outside Owners	Voucher Privatization			MEBO[a]	Other[b]
			Equal Access	With Significant Concessions to Insiders			
Albania	2	Primary	—	—		—	—
Bulgaria	3	Primary	Secondary	—		Primary	—
Croatia	3	—	—	—		Primary	—
Czech Republic	4	Secondary	Primary	—		Primary	—
FYR Macedonia	3	—	—	—		Primary	Secondary
Hungary	4	Primary	—	—		—	—
Poland	3+	Tertiary	Secondary	—		Primary	—
Romania	3–	Secondary	—	—		Primary	—
Slovak Republic	4	—	Secondary	—		Primary	—
Slovenia	3+	Secondary	—	—		Primary	—
Estonia	4	Primary	—	—		Secondary	—
Latvia	3	Secondary	Primary	—		—	—
Lithuania	3	—	Primary	—		Secondary	—

(*continued*)

277

Table A.7 (continued)

| | EBRD Large-Scale Privatization Transition Indicator Score | Voucher Privatization | | | | |
		Sale to Outside Owners	Equal Access	With Significant Concessions to Insiders	MEBO[a]	Other[b]
Armenia	3	—	Primary	Secondary	—	—
Georgia	3+	—	—	Primary	Secondary	—
Kazakhstan	3	Secondary	Primary	—	—	—
Kyrgyzstan	3	—	Primary	—	—	—
Moldova	3	Secondary	—	Primary	—	—
Russian Federation	3+	Secondary	—	Primary	Tertiary	—
Tajikistan	2	—	—	—	Primary	—
Ukraine	2	—	Secondary	—	Primary	—
Uzbekistan	3	—	—	—	Primary	Secondary

Notes: Progress in privatization of medium-sized and large enterprises is measured by the EBRD's transition indicators. A score of 2 indicates that up to 25% of state-owned enterprise assets have been privatized, a score of 3 that up to 50% of these assets have been privatized, and a score of 4 that more than 50% have been privatized. A + or − indicates a borderline score. Primary, secondary, and tertiary denote the first, second, and third most important privatization methods in a particular country, according to their contribution to privatization of state-owned enterprise assets.

[a] Management employee buyout.

[b] Includes asset sales through insolvency proceedings and a mass privatization program based on preferential credits.

Source: EBRD Transition Report, 1997 (London: EBRD, 1997), p. 90, table 5.7.

Index

279